The Agonistic City?

About the author

Dr Li Pernegger recently completed a postdoctoral fellowship at the Architecture and Planning School, University of the Witwatersrand (funded through its School of Governance's Life in the City Programme). She has also been an official in city and national governments in South Africa and the United Kingdom, with over 25 years of project, programme and strategic management experience in complex built environment and socio-economic initiatives. Her hands-on experiences in the state and academia give her rare insights into urban development and governance processes at national and municipal levels.

As the former Head of the National Treasury's Neighbourhood Development Programme, Li managed over R10 billion ($1.5 billion) in 100 grants awarded to 57 municipalities across South Africa. Prior to that, Li was the Programme Manager for Economic Area Regeneration for the City of Johannesburg. She focused on areas in decline, at risk, or not fulfilling their economic potential.

Li also undertook strategic consulting work for core and non-core business development for governments and the private sector after getting her Executive MBA at Birmingham University, United Kingdom. She was the Town Centre Manager for Dudley, funded by local government and the private sector, and was also in charge of driving regeneration visions for other struggling UK town centres. Earlier, she was the Manager of Economic Empowerment for Johannesburg, focusing on the informal business sector, and a practising architect.

The Agonistic City?

State-Society Strife in Johannesburg

Li Pernegger

ZED

LONDON · NEW YORK · OXFORD · NEW DELHI · SYDNEY

Zed Books
Bloomsbury Publishing Plc
50 Bedford Square, London, WC1B 3DP, UK
1385 Broadway, New York, NY 10018, USA
29 Earlsfort Terrace, Dublin 2, Ireland

BLOOMSBURY and Zed Books are
trademarks of Bloomsbury Publishing Plc

First published in 2020
This paperback edition published in 2022

Index by Jenny de Wet
Cover image © THEGIFT777/iStock

A catalogue record for this book is available from the British Library.

ISBN: HB: 978-1-7869-9909-2
PB: 978-1-7869-9910-8
ePDF: 978-1-7869-9908-5
ePUB: 978-1-7869-9905-4

Series: Politics and Society in Urban Africa

Typeset in Plantin by River Editorial Ltd, Devon, UK

To find out more about our authors and books visit
www.bloomsbury.com and sign up for our newsletters.

Contents

Maps

Unless otherwise stated, maps were prepared by Miriam Maina using QGIS (QGIS 2020) with data from various sources (AfriGIS 2014; Centre for the Analysis of South African Social Policy 2009; GeoTerraImage 2015, Municipal Demarcation Board 2015) and official statistics from Statistics South Africa (Quantec 2014).

Note that all currency conversions were derived from historical rand per US dollar exchange rates (South African Reserve Bank 2019).

Abbreviations

ANC	African National Congress
APF	Anti-Privatisation Forum
COJ	City of Johannesburg
EWN	EyeWitness News
GJMC	Greater Johannesburg Metropolitan Council
GJTMC	Greater Johannesburg Transitional Metropolitan Council
GPG	Gauteng Provincial Government
JAG	Johannesburg Advocacy Group
JMPD	Johannesburg Metropolitan Police Department
MLC	Metropolitan Local Council
MTC	Metropolitan Trading Company
RSA	Republic of South Africa
SMLC	Southern Metropolitan Local Council
TPA	Transvaal Provincial Administration

Acknowledgements

Although much of writing is done alone, it was less lonely than I expected. Thanks go to Philip Harrison especially; *The Agonistic City?* would not have existed without his guidance and belief in its value. Thanks too for the help of others: to Margot Rubin for constructive critiques; to Claire Bénit-Gbaffou, Glyn Williams, Carl Death and Sharon Lewis for engaging in debates around this research; and to Peter Griffiths for narrative development support. Thanks to the editorial team at Zed Books for seeing potential in my early scribblings. Behind every author is a family: thanks to Keith for keeping the home fires burning, and to Jo, Su, Gisela and Willi who also inspired me in different ways.

I have drawn on my journey as an urban development and city governance practitioner in local and national governments in South Africa and the United Kingdom, often bumping up against antagonistic protest and dilemmas impossible to resolve in lasting ways. In turns obsessed, exhilarated, confounded, stressed and provoked by the many practical and strategic issues of governance in informal trading, area-based development, economic development and city governance, these experiences led me first to a doctoral thesis, and then to explore the topic further in *The Agonistic City?* I thought I could create some meaning out of some of the perplexing puzzles of governance, but I found it raised many more questions than answers. This book is not a personal memoir; it belongs to all within the state who generously shared their stories. Any errors in the retelling are mine, as are the opinions and conclusions.

The South African Research Chairs Initiative in Spatial Analysis and City Planning, the Wits School of Governance and the National Research Foundation provided funding and other resources for this research.

I
Strife and the state

Urban uprising

The rise in protests and scale of activism in recent years is seemingly unprecedented. While the uprisings associated with the Arab Spring targeted autocratic leaders, many others have happened in contexts of democratic rule. These include the actions of the Occupy Movement in Western Europe and North America starting in 2011, large-scale protests in Brazil in 2013 and again in 2015 and 2016, the Umbrella Movement in Hong Kong in 2014, and the Yellow Vests Movement in France in 2018. The service delivery protests in South Africa, which are now almost endemic, have also happened in the context of a liberal democracy, albeit one that is recently established.

Before the 1990s, most scholarly texts on dissensus (the polar opposite to what a liberal democracy based on consensus hopes to achieve) focused on the role of protest in confronting authoritarian rule, including in colonial Africa, military-ruled Latin America and state-socialist Eastern Europe. This literature is large and varied and addresses political, psychological and sociological dimensions of the conflicts, largely outside democratic contexts (Diani and McAdam 2003; Hagopian 1974; Smelser 1962; Tanter and Midlarsky 1967). The targeting of democracies by protestors in the wake of the 2008 global financial crisis presents a new challenge to academic scholarship, raising questions of why people go to the streets when the options of democratic process are available, even if these processes have become increasingly blunt tools to address protesters' frustrations. An emergent scholarship suggests that recent protests signal discontent with rising social inequality but also with an apparent failure of the democratic system to address this inequality (Byrne 2012; della Porta and Mattoni 2014). Indeed, citizens' trust in the democratic state may be at a near all-time low; in a survey of 87 countries, 80 per cent of protests between 2006 and 2013 targeted the state in some way (Ortiz et al. 2013). Many protests voice discontent with the performance of democratically elected government rather than with the system itself, but there is a growing risk that this dissatisfaction may turn into a battle against the institutions of democracy (Byrne 2012; Gaon 2010; Heller and Evans 2011; Little 2008; Marinova 2011; Moreno 2011). While democracies are familiar with challenge and conflict, the nature and vehemence of recent protests is perplexing for many governments. Liberal democracy includes rules of engagement through which conflict is channelled and norms of consensus-seeking that work to moderate or resolve dissensus. However, much of the conflict in recent times has challenged the social contract underpinning liberal democracy and bewildered authorities have handled these conflicts poorly. Only rarely have governments drawn on conflict in productive ways, thereby benefiting from the wider creative input of residents in tackling difficult problems.

There is a further feature of contemporary protest that warrants mention: most recent protests have been urban in character, with scenes of popular anger unfolding in cities under varying shades of democratic governance as diverse as Paris, São Paulo, Singapore, Tokyo, London, Rome, Jakarta, La Paz, Singapore, Juba, Hong Kong and Johannesburg. The protests are often led not by the most spatially (or socially) marginalised groups living in rural areas, but by urban students and youth whose aspirations are frustrated by societal inequalities. The local-level state has become the new ground zero for resident dissatisfaction, and studies of conflict need to engage more centrally with the local interface between state and society.

Agonism in democratic conflict management

If we are concerned with defending the historical gains of democracy, we must find a different way to think about conflict's prominence in democracy, perhaps even find a positive approach to conflict. This is potentially offered in the notion of agonism, most famously and most recently associated with the work of the Belgian political theorist Chantal Mouffe.

Mouffe's (2000) *agonism*, namely the conflict between adversaries, which mutually and respectfully recognise the legitimacy of each other's view, is seen as a positive force for change that potentially produces outcomes beneficial to ordinary citizens. In agonism's constructive embrace of conflict, Mouffe (2000) places contestation, rather than only cooperation, at the heart of democratic governance. She defends democracy by expanding the idea of democracy beyond liberal notions of engagement to include conflicts that do not conform in easy ways to agreed rules and procedures. In this sense, the activists of the Occupy Movement or service delivery protests are involved in democratic action, just as the political parties contesting an election are. A democratic state that embraces agonism (an *agonistic state* for short) accepts that conflict, including protests outside procedurally prescribed frameworks, is a potentially creative and constructive force for continued democratic advancement. An agonistic state keeps the space open for expressions of dissensus rather than trying to sidestep conflict through formal consensus-seeking mechanisms.

Agonism requires us to think differently about dissensus within contexts of democratic governance. However, translating agonism into actual governance practices is complex and risky. There is arguably a fine line between dissensus that deepens democracy, expanding the space for practices that challenge social inequities and inequalities, and dissensus that erodes democracy by deepening societal division. Even Mouffe has battled with this, shifting position from a *hard agonism* in which consensus-seeking means the closure of democratic space to a *softer agonism* that accepts the need for some points of consensual closure even while sustaining the space for future dissensus. This repositioning has made her version of democracy similar to an aggregative democratic one, where policy is implemented based on the highest number of supporters (Crowder 2006; Yamamoto 2017).

We must remember that the idea of agonism has emerged largely within the apparently stable democratic contexts of Western Europe, and not in places such as postcolonial Africa and the post-dictatorships of Latin America where many institutions of democracy are newer and more fragile, and where physical violence in state–society conflict seems closer to the surface than in longer-established democracies. Theoretical work is useful in drawing out the meanings and principles of agonism, but much of the understanding of the practical possibilities will come from identifying agonism in practice in a variety of contexts, including those in established liberal democracies and where democratic transitions have been more recent. My research explores the practical possibilities of applying the concepts of agonism to the state's governance practices in cases of state–society strife. This includes identifying the ways in which agonism appears in practice, based on the understanding of agonism as situated, fluid and emergent routines (Mintzberg and Waters 1985; Ricks and Charlesworth 2003).

The risk in using a concept such as agonism is that varied and hybrid governance practices with different origins and purposes will be deductively collected under a single term. To avoid this, providing complex, detailed, well-contextualised and nuanced accounts of evolving practices at a local level is necessary. While seeking out practices that may inform a discussion on agonism, some of these practices might not be deliberately agonistic, or might be only partly agonistic, or might be agonistic only temporarily, but they do speak to the limits and possibilities of an agonistic state.

Another risk is using the shorthand of 'the state', perhaps too loosely in this book, to denote the state, including all its different administrative and political parts. Big debates and extensive scholarship unpacking 'the state' abound. It may be tempting to reduce the state to a single cohesive, unitary concept, but in reality it is multifaceted and complex. The state finds it difficult to adopt any practice consistently across all its parts. Rather, power and governance are negotiated engagement by engagement, agreement by agreement, within the state, within society, and between society and the state. So, while this book outlines the challenges of applying agonistic principles to the state's governance practices, I consider the practices of one part of the state, the local city level of the state, in Johannesburg. Ultimately, I try to draw these threads together for the benefit of the wider state.

To identify possible practices of agonism, we have to first establish where strife exists and how the state responds to it. State–society strife has many forms, taking place on city streets, in the courts and in the media. It also takes place in the boardrooms and corridors of the city bureaucracy, away from the attention of their more noisy and visible counterparts. Grievances might be specific to each context, but each city's protestors share a common desire with protestors worldwide in either calling for a more responsive state or, more radically, in questioning the underlying assumptions of the democratic state. The post-2008 global financial crisis scholarship is still emerging, and many events are too recent for adequate perspective. There is clearly a greater need for study of the complex relationship between protests, state response and the resultant changes (della Porta 2013; Jenkins and Klandermans 1995; Laws and Forester 2015). This relationship varies and is often extremely complex, requiring a fine-grained, contextually nuanced narrative to fully appreciate it. Johannesburg's democratic transformation is such a story. Despite South Africa's remarkably peaceful transition to democratic rule (Southall 2001), the phenomenon of street protests about tangible and intangible aspects of the state's service delivery has proliferated since the city's first democratic local elections in 1995. This is partly positive because it highlights a fundamental democratic freedom: the right to use streets for public protest. The local-level state, however, responded in many ways to these and other protests, including agonistically and antagonistically, sometimes even simultaneously, highlighting the constraints to, and complexities of, agonistic governance practices. Despite this, agonism presents possibilities for practical application in cases of state–citizen conflict management.

This book is the first to marry the narrative of protest with the response of the state, and to test for instances of agonism in practice.

It provides a new perspective on highly visible street protests and other less recognised forms of strife, contributing to global debates about the meaning and value of conflict in democratic governance. In investigating the possibilities of applying agonism to the state's governance practices in future state–society strife, I investigate recent cases of state–society conflict, considering the perspective of those working within the state, at the local level, in Johannesburg.

As a former government official for many years in local and national governments, I felt that issues about state–society conflict in democratic service delivery were frequently sidelined, unresolved and corrosive, with an immoveable public perception that the state responded – if it did at all – antagonistically to conflict. Even inside government, knowing the many actions taken by the state, the lack of resolution, perpetual state–society strife and negativity about the state's response to conflict troubled me, as a young architect in the Johannesburg city administration and also as a senior manager in the National Treasury engaged in development issues with municipalities across the country. Writing this book helped me to interrogate a possibly misplaced expectation that my colleagues and I should have resolved these issues rather than being in perpetual conflict. I wanted to counter the (mis)perception that the state responds either antagonistically to service delivery protests or not at all. I also wanted to see to what extent the state embraces conflict (or not) in its governance practices.

Perhaps Mouffeian agonism can encourage us not to expect the state to resolve these issues of conflict. At best, the state can keep the space open for ongoing deliberation, dialogue and dissensus around unresolved issues. We should expect these issues, then, to be never-ending ones.

Johannesburg

Within the context of Africa, South Africa ranks highly as a middle-income country with viable institutions of democracy and is governed by a local-level state with reasonable bureaucratic capacity. There are, however, extreme inequalities and high levels of criminality and violence across the country and a history of racial authoritarianism and a bitter political struggle for equality. Johannesburg, as its lead city, is a case with its own idiosyncrasies: an 'ordinary city' in the sense spoken of by Jennifer Robinson (2012), for example, but also a world city, with global ambitions. The city offers a lens through which to view the larger issues of protest by exploring state–society relationships, service delivery, and the implications of conflict for governance practices.

Such struggles are not unique to Africa and the Global South (Ellis and van Kessel 2009), having also preoccupied scholars elsewhere. Protest issues might be global ones (as in Death 2011) or highly localised (Ngwane et al. 2017). Be it in Africa or elsewhere, protestors protest mainly about the effects of globalisation and lack of access to land, housing, services and economic resources (Ellis and van Kessel 2009; Lawhon et al. 2018; Mayer et al. 2016), and declining quality of democracies (Mattes 2019).

Scholars have tended to emphasise the society part of state–society strife in unravelling the many interpretations of the meaning of protests in South Africa (Beinart and Dawson 2010; Bekker and Fourchard 2013), Africa (Koonings and Kruijt 2009a, 2009b), and the Global South (de Satgé and Watson 2018). Even those that consider the state part of state–society strife tend to look at society's perspective (Corbridge et al. 2005). As it is the local-level state, in South Africa and in many other countries, that chiefly realises democracy's objectives, I chose to focus on this part of the state's governance practices, linking them to the debate on agonism in democracy. One of the local-level state's prime governance tools for managing conflict and consensus is planning, though riddled with 'conflicting rationalities', as pointed out by Watson (2003). These conflictual processes in planning are extraordinarily complex and dynamic in Europe (Gualini 2015), but perhaps even more so in Africa and the Global South where the state is regarded as more fragmented than cohesive (Anciano and Piper 2018; de Satgé and Watson 2018; Haferburg and Huchzermeyer 2014; Koonings and Kruijt 2009a, 2009b).

Turning to post-apartheid Johannesburg, scholars have already tracked processes of urban governance and planning-political contestation (see, for example, Anciano and Piper 2018; Beall et al. 2002; Bénit-Gbaffou 2015; Burawoy and von Holdt 2012; Harrison et al. 2014; Murray 2011; Robinson 1996, 2006). Building on this body of work, I use Johannesburg to view the democratic state's response to conflict. Johannesburg's experience is not unique. Service delivery protestors in South Africa tended to target the local-level state – regardless of whether an issue fell within its jurisdiction – apparently because this is the most accessible level of government. By overcoming the scarcity of empirical research into post-apartheid city-level service delivery strife related to planning, the built environment and local governance, this book explores whether an approach built around the notion of agonism can change the state's approach to governance.

I focus specifically on the understandings, perceptions and actions of appointed and elected officials of city government in Johannesburg in managing strife. This does not provide a complete account of agonistic processes, which are inherently relational and involve at least two parties. However, the explicit focus on state actors, both officials and politicians, in processes of agonistic engagements, especially in planning matters, provided direction for the detailed study. This case focuses on texts and data citing the first post-apartheid democratic local government from 1996 up to 2015 but also incorporates some earlier material to understand the foundations of democratic city governance in South Africa.

My first unit of measurement for this research was the individual protest itself. Details of protests, reasons, locations, scale, duration, violence and actors were found by searching SA Media, an online press clipping service run by Sabinet, South Africa information providers, for Johannesburg service delivery protests between 1996 and 2015. Results were enriched with data from other sources such as 2007–2012 national human settlements data (Matshego 2012), Johannesburg's 2010 and 2011 petitions registers (Kute 2012b), Johannesburg Metropolitan Police Department's (JMPD) notifications of intention to gather between 2011 and 2013 collected by Jane Duncan (2014a), and 2003–2012 protest data collated by the Centre for Civil Society (2014). My second unit of measurement was the local-level state's response to each protest. These data were much harder to secure. I augmented protest data with personal archival material, academic accounts of protest, other reports, and additional Internet searches per protest, especially online media such as EyeWitness News (EWN), news24 and others. This information was often incomplete, so I also drew on over 30 interviews with respondents, chosen for their work at strategic levels and representation of a cross-section of race and gender within the city administration, or affiliates. These interviews provided data on the state's explicit and implicit responses to the different conflicts at different times. I compiled the data into a series of chronologies, dovetailed with a timeline of changes to the city administration across the four mayoral periods, forming the basis of this book.

These Johannesburg-specific findings provide opportunities for practitioners within state structures, in South Africa, Africa and globally, to make comparisons and gain practical insights into how the state's agonistic management of conflict might support democratic objectives. However, states in other contexts will need to be mindful of their specific democratic circumstances.

A brief outline

In the chapters that follow, you will find out about the patterns and themes of Johannesburg's post-apartheid service delivery protests targeting the local-level state over two decades, an overview of the dynamics of protest in the city alongside a detailed account of three dissimilar protest case studies (for Johannesburg's location and study areas, see Map 1.1), and the local-level state's responses to those protests. You will recognise agonism's capacity to encourage more productive outcomes and conflict management practices in your city. You will see whether agonistic principles were in evidence in the local-level state's responses to conflict, and you can gauge agonism's practical possibilities for the state's future engagements in processes of conflict.

Citizen dissatisfaction (and resident dissatisfaction, given the high proportion of foreign-born contributors to cities around the world) is on the rise globally, and trust in democracy and the state has decreased, frequently manifesting as protest action, with profoundly urban dimensions. The nature and scale of this state–society strife sits at odds with democracy's ideal for cooperation, with the state seeing this conflict as negative, and as a threat or even a sign of the failure of the state and of governance. These struggles are not unique to Africa, but scholars have tended to focus on the society part of state–society strife. Agonism, centring contestation rather than cooperation in democratic governance, seems to provide an alternative tool with which to approach conflict management, despite its limited translation into practice. The key question, then, is around understanding the practical possibilities of applying concepts of agonism to the state's governance practices in state–society strife. This question is answered through the analysis of the post-apartheid city administration's complex responses to three cases of long-running conflict.

Chapter 2 proposes that agonism's placement of conflict at the centre of democracy provides an alternate approach to urban conflict management. I present agonism's innovative aspects: its potential as an agent of positive change; the state's role in transforming antagonism to agonism; and the need to keep the space of conflict open. I also present agonism's limitations: its opposition to the need for some consensus; its discounting of the potential of antagonism to realise change; and its risk of fetishising conflict. Further, I show that despite vigorous theorising around agonism as a concept, emergent explorations of how agonism is translated into practice remain modest. I tie these contributions into a framework to visualise the implications of agonism in practice; this is necessary to enable the deeper study of Johannesburg's conflict management practices. Debates informing South Africa's potential for agonistic conflict management conclude this chapter.

Chapter 3 reveals the complexity, extent and temporality of conflict in Johannesburg. It plots over 450 low-income and middle-class protests on a periodised timeline, exploring the similar and dissimilar tactics used by these two groups to achieve their objectives. What emerges is a clearer

Map 1.1 – Johannesburg's location, spatial-economic structure and study areas

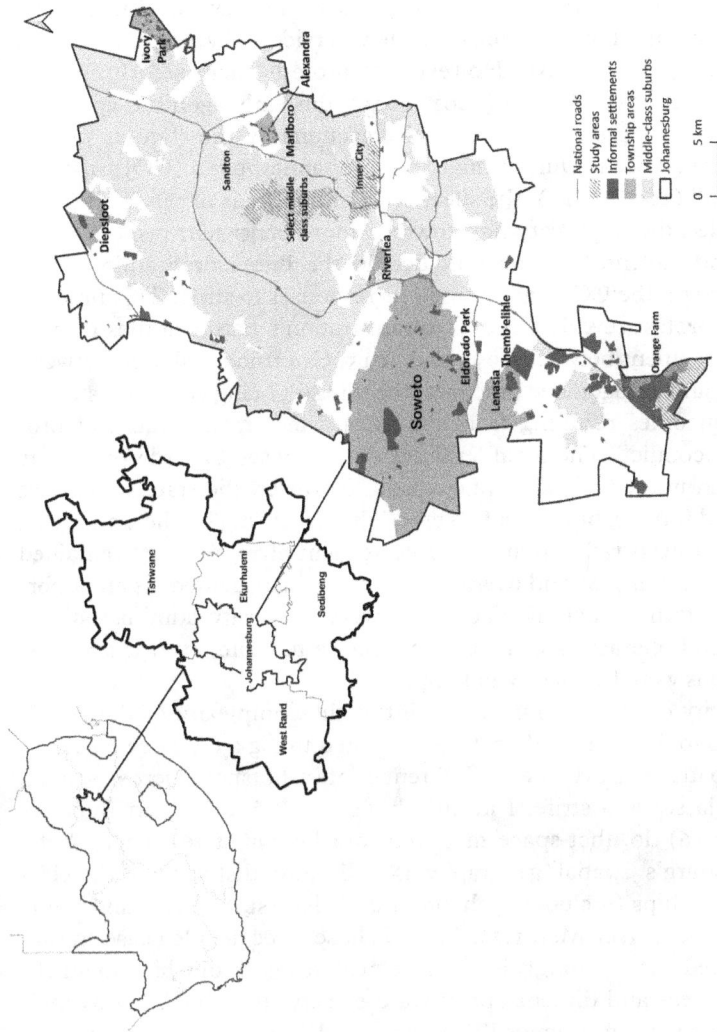

Legend:
- National roads
- Study areas
- Informal settlements
- Township areas
- Middle-class suburbs
- Johannesburg

0 5 km

Labels on map: Ivory Park, Diepsloot, Sandton, Marlboro, Alexandra, Inner City, Select middle class suburbs, Riverlea, Soweto, Eldorado Park, Lenasia, Themb'elihle, Orange Farm, Tshwane, Ekurhuleni, Johannesburg, Sedibeng, West Rand

Note: Johannesburg's position within the Gauteng province and South Africa; the spatial-economic divide between middle-class suburbs, townships and informal settlements; hatched areas indicate the location of the three study areas.

Source: Author's formulation

picture of protest trends and underlying themes and the city administration's changing responses from the more agonistic to increasingly antagonistic ones. Before apartheid ended, political protests subsumed service delivery protests targeting the national government. However, the transition period (1996–2000), beginning with Johannesburg's first democratic local government elections, saw the new local-level state interacting with the then relatively few service delivery protestors in somewhat agonistic ways. However, as protests increased during the consolidation of the unicity (2001–2005), this early agonistic approach shifted towards growing antagonistic reactions by the state as protest themes concretised. During the City of Johannesburg's (COJ) maturation period (2006–2010), the sheer scale of hundreds of service delivery protests led the administration towards more consistent responses. As more, and violent, protests unfolded in the bureaucratisation period (2011–2015), the COJ standardised its responses to strife. This timeline of rising protest reveals the city administration's particularities of conflict management between 1996 and 2015. Governance shifted between agonistic and antagonistic practices, the mindset being anti-protest, with varied outcomes resulting from the inconsistent management of processes of conflict. The local-level state's responses towards protestors were often immediate and antagonistic. However, the state sometimes responded further, but at a later stage. Then, focusing on the underlying issues of protests rather than the protests themselves, the state remained largely conflict-averse and overlooked conflict management as an opportunity for transformation. Clearly, however, the city administration's policies and operations changed in response to strife, even if agonistic interactions were frequently not apparent.

This city overview could only hint at the complexity of the state's responses to the variety of protests. I wanted to dig a little deeper to see if these patterns held true in different protest hotspots, across spaces, stories, classes and strife. I intuitively felt, as Björkdahl and Buckley-Zistel (2016) do, that space mattered somehow in state–society strife. Johannesburg's spatial geography is split into distinct middle-class areas, townships (including Johannesburg's largest, Soweto) and informal settlements (see Map 1.1). Thus, I chose three detailed case studies of sustained and seemingly intractable protests, each of which highlight different areas and dimensions of state–society strife and the possibilities for agonism in practice. The angry and frustrated groups in each story use different strategies to force the state to respond. Informal settlement residents create the impression of a violent and ungovernable city, informal traders render a prime rates-earning area unviable, and the middle class stirs up the media and threatens to withhold service and rates payments. The state had to respond to each group to mini-mise eroding its political, reputational and financial credibility to remain sustainable enough to provide the items that city residents need.

Starting in Johannesburg's Deep South, Chapter 4 details the water wars in the low-income area of Orange Farm where the constraints to agonistic practices are clear. This chapter touches on the then informal settlement's origins and the seeds of discontent sown pre-1996 within the context of emerging urbanisation policy for such settlements. We see the first water services protests emerge between 1996 and 2000. The local government was hardly responsive, though it was impacted by restructurings and the 1997 financial crisis, as well as its view of Orange Farm as a financial and governance liability. The COJ became antago-nistic towards the Orange Farm Water Crisis Committee's blocking of its water-saving measures, including the installation of prepaid water meters, between 2001 and 2005. Later, between 2006 and 2010, the COJ became more responsive to the issues underlying the protests but was still antagonistic in dealing with other escalating protests about basic services, housing, a local councillor's insensitive purchase of a lux-ury vehicle, and poor-quality projects. The COJ was more responsive and proactively implemented service delivery measures, especially after 2008. Between 2011 and 2015, the local-level state adopted a business-unusual approach to protests and provided basic services despite sig-nificant financial limitations and ambivalence towards Orange Farm's seeming permanent informality. Here, I uncover agonism's limits in dealing with the temporal aspects of protest; the state's responses to protests were different in the short term to its longer-term ones. Also, the literature on agonism disregards the impact of contextual factors on the potential for agonistic state–society engagement. Coherent responses to varied and complex protests were almost impossible. Even when practices were not agonistic, they were nonetheless democratic as in the local government's growing acknowledgement of the underlying concerns of protestors in Orange Farm, engagements to resolve them, and making concessions.

Moving to Johannesburg's geographic and historic centre, Chapter 5 deals with the case of informal trading in the Inner City. I touch on the sector's phenomenal growth from 1988 as race and other laws were repealed, and the resultant tensions. Informal traders protested against the local government's push to support prioritised Inner City regeneration by relocating them from streets into markets and carry-ing out by-law enforcement, and against foreign traders, between 1996 and 2000, which met with the city administration's responsive and partly agonistic practices. Next, local government became increasingly antagonistic between 2001 and 2005 at trading's perceived anarchy. Between 2006 and 2010, local government's zero tolerance approach to the irritant of trading saw it carry out concerted enforcement campaigns. In the 2011–2015 period, traders protested about the right to trade when the COJ implemented *Operation Clean Sweep*, leading to a Constitutional Court challenge. This chapter observes the complexities of implementing agonistic principles in governance practices. The city administration initially demonstrated an agonistic stance, adopting some agonistic practices. However, over time, it became increasingly antagonistic. Responses to protesting traders took place at three levels. Responses to incidents of protests were typically immediate and forcible, especially if protests were violent. However, the city administration was more likely to respond with a mix of agonistic and participative measures, although inconsistently, to the issue driving the contention, or to its underlying cause. Despite this, any agonistic practices were usually overshadowed by the city administration's repressive approach to protest incidents and the significant constraints it faced in governing the informal trading sector.

Finishing off in Johannesburg's well-serviced northern suburbs, Chapter 6 highlights the processes of conflict between middle-class protestors and the city administration over billing. This conflictual engagement unfolded from 1996 to 2000 as the new local government's 'one city, one tax base' approach to redress apartheid's ills was implemented, leading to a rates boycott and the state's resultant antagonistic response to these malcontents. The local government's efforts to centralise billing between 2001 and 2005 resulted in mistakes in dealing with the growing billing crisis. Its main response was to create channels for complaints, but it remained mostly in denial of protests. Next, the local government's solution to the billing crisis between 2006 and 2010, the *Phakama* programme, created glitches, which led to erroneous cut-offs and the middle class's renewed outrage at the COJ's hostility about not acknowledging billing issues. The local government responded defensively between 2011 and 2015 at media claims of never-ending queues and the alleged billing battle, citing sabotage of its billing system. More errors led to its first qualified audit. It then introduced transformation measures in billing management, followed by ever-more billing inconsistencies and more protests. After a second qualified audit, it admitted it had no scheme but was aiming to improve customer service. This chapter highlights how the state's responses (even ones that are not agonistic) to protest can bring about outcomes that match protestors' expectations more closely, but in turn created new reasons for dissatisfaction. However, any responsiveness to dissensus by the local-level state was not acknowledged much in the media, subsumed as it was by opposition politics, which also mediated this state–society strife. That, and racism, further complicated the potential for agonistic governance.

Chapter 7 presents findings on the possibilities of applying agonistic principles to the state's governance practices, relevant for any state institution responding to strife. However, these findings are complex, with the state inconsistent and conflict-averse in its handling of strife. Agonism's main possibility lies in its potential to improve the nature of the conflictual state–society interaction to find mutually acceptable new solutions to challenges. However, the evidence shows that the state's agonistic practices are limited and uneven. Short-term responses to protest events are usually antagonistic. But in the longer term, a greater extent of receptiveness – agonistic or not – to protestors' demands is clear in the local-level state's concessions and changes made in response to protest action. There is, however, a bias towards formal protest channels. Outcomes of processes of state–society strife include institutional modifications, policy and programmatic shifts, and operational changes. Many constraints to agonistic governance practices are also identified, not least of all that the state is less holistic in reality than it appears at face value. These understandings highlight the local government's (sometimes unknowing) partial recognition of the centrality of conflict and the adoption of an 'ethos of agonism' (Wingenbach 2011) in some governance practices.

2
Agonism in public practice

Why agonism?

Before 1989, less than 13 per cent of the world's countries were democracies; today, 63 per cent are fully or partly democratised (Freedom House 2005, 2018). However, disappointment is rising at the unmet promise of the democratic state, not only in South African cities, but globally (Heller and Evans 2011; Scott 1998), to tackle inequality, exclusion, poverty, the absence of trust and ineffective governance (Diamond 2008). Others, though, such as Tilly and Tarrow (2015), claim this 'contentious politics' is the way dissenters change government policy, by working within the system, even if aggressively through public protest, rather than overthrowing it. Although conceptions of liberal democracy are many, the prevailing one consists of commitments in varying degrees to representation, political equality, protection of rights, deliberation and participation. Typically, the liberal democracy is cooperation-based and consensus-seeking, trying to ensure individuals will agree to accept the group's decision even if they do not all necessarily agree with it (Prothro and Grigg 1960).

Can we embrace these conflicts in democracy? Chantal Mouffe's (2000) notion of *agonism* situates conflict centrally in state–society interaction rather than on the sidelines. Mouffe offers the agonistic model of democracy as an alternative to consensus-seeking modes, one that accepts the necessity and inevitability of conflict but directs conflicts towards deepening and enriching the pluralist democracy. Rather than looking to legitimate democratic decision-making that may only provide a temporary relief from strife, Mouffe turns to the means necessary to sustain active engagements, even contests and conflicts, over differing positions. Power and politics are located at the heart of democracy, rather than at its fringes; the role of the state is to ensure spaces for conflict remain open. Importantly, Mouffe (2000) differentiates an antagonism that is destructive and not interested in maintaining democracy from an agonism that progressively opens up democratic space and deepens democracy. In antagonism, the struggle takes place with 'an enemy to be destroyed' (Mouffe 2000, p. 102). But in agonism, the struggle is between 'legitimate enemies' or 'adversaries' or 'opponents' that recognise the right of 'the other' to hold different positions and ideas, which might, and should, clash. However, the intent is not to destroy 'the other' (Mouffe 2000). Agonism is not about reaching a final position, even if partial closure of the conflict does result, but rather about keeping the democratic space open for future contestation.

Mouffe's position is, however, far more complex than the brief description above. Mouffe herself has changed her stance over time, becoming less radical (Laclau and Mouffe 1985; Mouffe 2000). Positions (as with state–society strife) are often ambiguous; Knops (2007), for example, is insistent that Mouffe's argument is quite consistent with deliberative democracy, where conflict can be deliberated away, thus preserving democracy. Mouffe herself acknowledges that a consensus or degree of closure may be necessary at times to ensure social stability. Certainly, one can argue around the degrees of openness and closure, or conflict and consensus, or formal process and challenges to formal process, which should be promoted in a pluralist democracy. However, the key point is that agonism embraces the conflicts of democracy rather than being threatened by them.

This chapter locates the origins, position and understanding of Mouffeian agonism relative to classic writers' wider investigations into dissensus in liberal and radical democracies, as well as other more contemporary commentaries on intersecting concepts, such as the democratic state's roles in conflict, the state–society relationship, consensus, and antagonism and violent conflict. Put simply, if one considers the typical conflict–cooperation spectrum in a liberal democracy, consensus is punctured by moments of dissensus. However, in a radical democracy, dissensus is punctured by moments of consensus. I juxtapose the main characteristics of liberal and radical democratic thinking for illustrative purposes. However, in reality, the divisions between the notions are not so stark; rather, they are intertwined and exist in differing degrees. I distinguish between them, perhaps too simplistically, to highlight the logics underpinning engagement in processes of conflict in democracies. In the liberal democracy, society aims for gradual changes, thus deepening governance practices. In the radical democracy, society aims to break away from the existing conditions to radically transform society.

Mouffe's agonism sits much closer to radical democracy's antagonistic conflict, which makes no attempt to reach consensus, than it does to liberal democracy's cooperation and consensus-seeking actions, with elections as the most important decision-making moments. While this may cause alarm to practitioners, given the rise of conflict in cities across the world, agonism does provide innovative responses to this.

Innovations of agonism

Mouffeian agonism brings at least four innovations to democratic thought of import to the state when engaging with conflict, in considering liberal and radical democratic conceptions of conflict. The first and most fundamental innovation, relative to the dominance of liberal democracy, is agonism's tenet that conflict is central to the democratic state, not cooperation. Dissensus in democratic states is not a new concept. But in most Western democracies, fashioned over hundreds of years on the classical liberal thinking of Locke (2009 [1690]), Smith (1981 [1776]) and Mill (1863), dissensus is seen as a problem, pushed to the sidelines, to be overcome through cooperation-based approaches (Schaap 2006). Although the notion of democracy has multiple interpretations – as an ideal, a form of government, and a mode or process of governance (Gutmann 2007; Pinkney 1993; Staeheli 2010; Tilly 2007) – most portray liberal democracy as a system of government with political power underpinned by principles of cooperation, representivity, participation, aggregation, collaboration, deliberation, majority decision-making, consensus, equality, respect for the pluralism of diverse pressure groups, and an orientation towards the rational and procedural (Cunningham 2002). In these conceptions, despite the freedoms of speech and association, and the right to hold different views, unmanaged dissensus or dissensus outside the rules of engagement is tolerated but largely unwelcome and discomforting for those working within the state. Most liberal democracies desire the maintenance of stability and so tend to constrain conflict (Wingenbach 2011).

Before Mouffe developed her notion of agonism, she was far more radical in her view of the position of conflict in democracy. In partnership with Ernesto Laclau, Mouffe's take on radical democracy in their publication *Hegemony and Socialist Strategy* placed antagonism at the heart of democracy (Laclau and Mouffe 1985). Influenced by the writings of Marx (1897) and Gramsci (1919), their publication describes radical democrats that disrupt democracy by overthrowing the dominant hegemony by insurgent and violent means.

However, 15 years later, Mouffe (2000), in her pivotal text *The Democratic Paradox*, offers agonism as a more moderate view of conflict, but still placing conflict at the very heart of democracy. However, she has now given agonistic conflict a special status. This kind of conflict is different from antagonistic conflict and plays an important role in democracy and governance. Her agonism is a form of conflict between adversaries, based on the theoretical notion that this conflict is a vital and necessary facet of democracy. It is a positive, rather than destructive, force for change. In agonism, opponents recognise and respect the legitimacy of each other's view. This is different to antagonism, where the opponents are deadly (rather than friendly) enemies that ignore each other's views and the form of conflict is open and extreme.

Second, agonistic conflict is an agent of positive change. It can potentially bring about creative transformation in democratic states, rather than liberal democracy's controlled and limiting conflict, or radical democracy's potentially destructive conflict. In the agonistic democracy, Mouffe's (2000) innovation lies in identifying agonistic conflict as a positive force, acting as the bridge between the passionate conflict of radical democracy and the rational and restrained conflict of liberal democracy. Agonistic conflict is radical in its aspiration to drive change for the better but is embraced within a framework that recognises the rights of others to hold different views, thereby creating and maintaining the space for conflict. Moreover, argues Mouffe (2000), the process of agonistic strife, and one's ultimate respectful recognition of the adversary, changes one's behaviour and one's being in a *gestalt* sense; this greater sense of deep awareness of the complexity of the overall conflict, the adversaries and the context, makes room for deep transformation. Seeing such conflict as normal and necessary in attaining the ideals of democracy has become increasingly popular (Bénit-Gbaffou 2015; Brown 2015; Merrifield 2013).

However, agonism is not the only path towards change. In the liberal democracy, conflict, if it follows the rules, can drive change, but change could also result from non-conflict-based engagements (Weber 1946 [1919], 1978) or regulated outcomes-based strife (Locke 2009 [1690]; Mill 1863; Smith 1981 [1776]). But while the liberal democratic state is (theoretically) tolerant of conflict, it tends to limit itself to rational engagement in the 'public sphere' (Habermas 1991 [1962]) and to suppress open conflict (Weber 1946 [1919], 1978). The state is the mechanism to achieve collective goals and drive change in striving for social justice; the state fixes the problem, undermining the scope for society's involvement. The state's ability to fix the problem is also significantly constrained by its enormously complex structure and its context (Tilly 2007).

In the radical democracy, though, the antagonistic Marxist class-based struggle aims to bring about radical socio-economic change by overthrowing the existing dominant order with no attempt at reaching consensus. Only this large-scale conflict can bring about real freedom because the state, as the tool of the dominant class seeking to maintain the class system (Gramsci 1919; Laclau and Mouffe 1985), tends to suppress or mediate conflict, even forcibly. Here, the state is the problem (Marx 1897). However, the state can pre-empt or suppress dissenters' desire to protest by playing on their aspirations to be like the dominant elite group by popularising its ideas and beliefs (Gramsci 1919). So, while agonism is a path to change, and may be radical, it requires a degree of accommodation across positions rather than over-throwing one with another.

Third, another of Mouffe's innovations is that the democratic state must be the one to transform antagonism to agonism. Agonistic conflict depends on the nature of the state–society relationship, which is a critical determinant in the shaping and outcomes of the processes of conflict. As the state is the distributor of resources and benefits, it is frequently both a target and a source of dissensus (Jenkins and Klandermans 1995), and it is only the democratic institution that can change the nature of the conflict and make it potentially positive. The issues underpinning conflict mean that society frequently protests against the state as it is the most significant institution of democracy. The agonistic state generally takes the lead in processes of conflict by providing options to society to facilitate the creation of their identities through iterative interactions (Mouffe 2014). Here, the state, implies Mouffe, must transform antagonism into agonism by channelling protest so dissenters can raise contentious issues. This agonistic interaction is predicated on the construction of 'the other' as a 'friendly' enemy or a 'legitimate enemy', rather than a deadly 'enemy to be destroyed' (Mouffe 2000, pp. 129, 13 and 102 respectively). The 'friendly' enemy is one whose ideas can be disagreed with but whose right to have those ideas is non-negotiable; further, adversaries share the common ground of liberal democratic values of equality and freedom, although we may disagree with 'the other' on the meaning and implementation of those values (Mouffe 2000).

However, in the liberal democracy, there are as many conceptions of the relationship between the state and society and the degree of their overlapping interests as there are contending interests. As governments can never be fully representative, despite fair election processes, as ultimate resolvers of political conflict, the state–society relationship extends to the intervals between elections. During these intervals, the liberal democracy manages conflict mainly through deliberation, participation, compromise and cooperation to reach agreement through rational and technical arguments, with citizens' voices being heard through, for instance, voting, ballots and referendums (Fung 2003), and also through alliances, shared interests, compensations and other means. This constantly shifting state–society relationship ranges between conflictual and collaborative, and is informed by: the balance of the adversarial–collaborative, antagonistic–agonistic and liberalist–deliberative dynamics between them; the location of power; the ability to affect change; the control of the functions of governance; and impacts of timing, context, issues considered, historical influences and whose perception of the conflict is in play (Chambers and Kopstein 2008).

In the radical democracy, though, the state is biased in its actions towards the dominant elite in society; is in antagonistic opposition against most of society; and is powerful, oppressive, coercive, a bully and a 'parasite' (Marx 1897), although the power of protest itself by the subjugated working class tends to be underestimated (Domhoff 2005). In Laclau and Mouffe's (1985) conception, this power is diffused amongst the competing groups in society.

Fourth, consensus is never final. This precept, another of Mouffe's (2000, 2013) innovations, presents the meaning of consensus within the cycle of conflict as something that is perpetually open-ended. This is different to the conceptions of consensus in radical and liberal democracies. Mouffe (2000) argues that the space where different groups meet to deliberate policy can never be free of power due to the pluralism of groups, each with their own sets of needs and values, hampering a resolution based solely on technical logic. This space can only ever be truly free of power in all its forms in a perfect democracy, which does not exist. Thus, Mouffe contends that reaching consensus is neither possible nor desirable. Agonism keeps democracy healthy, with agreements – partial, temporary or incremental – tending to be brief stops in a sea of conflict.

However, in the liberal democracy, the underlying assumption within much of the literature of the 2000s is that consensus, or at least agreement, might always be possible, if only enough and the right sorts of deliberation and participation measures are undertaken. Yet despite its consensus-seeking orientation, others acknowledge that while voices may be theoretically equal, weaker voices are often not heard in the public sphere where political and other decisions are debated and made (such as Walzer 2004). These agreements reached are generally seen as binding and contractual, even on those who were unable to participate.

The radical democrat's view, though, is that the purpose of conflict is to overthrow the current oppressive system; hence, consensus represents the interests of the dominant class (Marx 1897). The inclusion of everyone is conceptually impossible (Laclau and Mouffe 1985), meaning no consensus can ever be possible.

Although agonistic democracy may share some common dimensions with radical and liberal democracies about conflict, the balance between these dimensions – namely the orientation towards the centrality of dissensus, the role of conflict in driving change, the democratic institution's role in the transformation of antagonism to agonism, and the impossibility of consensus – is new. These innovations have potentially significant implications for how democratic states practise conflict management and urban governance. However, there are also four limitations to agonism, which are important for the state and its actors to consider.

Limitations of agonism

First, Mouffe (2000) acknowledges, as conflict cannot be never-ending, the need for some consensus to ensure stability, provided this consensus does not foreclose conflict. This means that it can only ever be, at best, a 'conflictual consensus' (Mouffe 1999, p. 756) – incomplete, limited or a temporary breather from constant conflict (Mouffe 2000). Wingenbach (2011) suggests it is neither possible nor recommended for a democracy to exist in a perpetual state of crisis, and continual non-consensus might even be dangerous. Mouffe, however, remains vague on the exact dimensions of consensus, argues Erman (2009). Indeed, within Mouffe's work, the distinction between *agreement, compromise* and *consensus* in terms of agonistic processes is quite unclear. Reaching consensus means that a decision-making step in the state–society conflictual relationship is required. Writers thus struggle to position agonism's open-ended consensus relative to the prevailing consensus-seeking liberal democratic processes. Some believe agonism works best with only the participatory, representative and deliberative aspects of liberal democracy (Knops 2007; Westphal 2018; Wingenbach 2011). Others see them as remaining fundamentally independent (Tambakaki 2009), although they might overlap at the decision-making stage (Gürsözlü 2009). Beaumont and Loopmans (2008) claim that neither the dissensus-based agonistic democracy nor other cooperation-based democracies are sufficient on their own to deal with conflict. Lastly, Mäntysalo (2011) presents agonism as a logical progression in the evolution of democratic thought and arguably as an improvement on aggregative and deliberative democracies.

Second, inherent in Mouffe's writings is the disregard of antagonism as a driver of change. Significant critique is levelled at agonism's inadequacy at dealing with antagonism and the implicit belief that one can always find common ground between opponents and convert antagonism to agonism (Mouffe 2000; Pløger 2004; Schaap 2006; Wingenbach 2011). But even *antagonism* itself has multiple meanings in the literature, with the distinction between antagonism and agonism hard to differentiate at times. Antagonism can take the form of protests that are an 'appeal to the authorities to behave differently' (Byrne 2012, p. 114), or a matter of one's social and political perspectives can influence the reading of antagonism as agonism (Pløger 2004). Some claim that proponents of agonism are naive about the potential limitless destructiveness of antagonism (Schaap 2006). The democratic state could thus be endangered if antagonism is not placated or suppressed; indeed, democratic institutions themselves can perpetuate antagonism if they do not invest in agonistic practices (Mihai 2014) or if they embed antagonism into policy by ignoring conflict (Lundberg et al. 2018). In the Mouffeian conversion of antagonism to agonism, the assumptions are that the agonistic institution always has enough capacity and ability to convert all antagonism into genuine respect between adversaries, some democratic principles are shared between adversaries, and the conflict does not run the risk of irreversibly damaging the constancy of democracy (Wingenbach 2011). The agonistic institution is also assumed to have sufficient level-headedness and 'reciprocity' to exchange privileges for mutual benefit (Schaap 2006, p. 261), and a willingness to engage with its adversaries (Houwen 2010). Breen (2009), further, is sceptical about agonism's idealism, which makes it naive about issues of power and unlimited and violent antagonism.

Third, the risk of fetishising conflict is that the inordinate fixation on conflict comes at the expense of addressing underlying unmet needs. The preclusion of interaction that could enable consensus is therefore a shortcoming of agonism (Morrell 2014). However, conflict, especially when antagonistic and violent, is extremely difficult to downplay. Indeed, Mouffeian agonism simplifies conflict, overlooking its multiple forms and the real likelihood of being unable to tame all types of conflicts, some of which are intractable (Roskamm 2015). Fundamental to this book, then, are the expressions of dissensus that the state typically encounters. Frequently, these protests are cast as 'challenges to authority embodied by collective actors in public settings' (Ratliff and Hall 2014, p. 274). Protests are wide-ranging. They include those that happen on streets or behind closed doors. They can manifest as marches, boycotts, sit-ins, stayaways, petitions, memoranda, media lobbies and many more. Protests can range from peaceful to violent, with both protestors and the state exercising aggression, despite openly antagonistic protest generally considered as outside the rules of liberal democracy (Keane 2004; Paret 2015). However, the meaning of violence is ambiguous and contested in the literature (Walby 2013) and warrants further explanation. *Violence* in protest means actual physical harm carried out by protestors against a person (Collins 2008; Eisner 2009) or property. Violence can include emotional harm (Wikström and Treiber 2009), intimidation, physical assault, attacks on foreigners, vigilantism, murder, vandalism, arson, throwing stones as projectiles, looting, and destruction (Paret 2015). The state regards violent protest as generally undesirable (Eisner 2009; Lancaster 2018). The use of violence contributes to the sense that violent protest is an illegitimate form of dissensus. Further, violence can be extended to include the threat of harm to person and property rather than only actual violence (Paret 2015; Ratliff and Hall 2014). Here, actions are emotionally and symbolically charged with fear, fury and hostility, and full of 'bluster and bluff' (Collins 2008, p. 21), although not intrinsically anti-democratic (von Holdt 2013), and sometimes even justified (Zinn 2002). Violent actions might include, although this is not always so clear-cut: verbal and physical challenges such as yelling; insulting; digging up and barricading of roads with burning tyres; throwing of objects and brandishing of sticks, clubs and other weapons; and other confrontational gestures accompanying marches, pickets or generally peaceful protests. Indeed, the use of physical violence by protestors is less common than one imagines (Collins 2008; Ratliff and Hall 2014), given the media's exploitation of actual and threatened violent protest for its shock value, even when it is the state that has perpetrated the violence (Morwe 2010).

Fourth, the single greatest shortfall in the notion of agonism is the limited literature translating agonism into practice and recording of actual governance practices. Since Mouffe (2000) promoted the notion of agonism, its initially slow application has increased but is still restricted to descriptive-analytical assessments of a handful of planning and governance-related cases originating mainly in Australia, the United States, South Africa, Finland, Denmark, Germany and the United Kingdom. Although applied agonism is relatively undeveloped with ambiguous findings, these normative, descriptive-analytical cases do provide some lessons about agonistic conflict management for its institutionalisation. However, as seen in the ambiguities surrounding the notion of agonism itself, these are hardly clear-cut guidelines for the implementation of agonistic governance. State actors and especially planners, intrigued about an agonistic approach to manage conflict, will be frustrated by scholars' focus on agonism's conceptual aspects (Schaap 2006), with only minimal guidance and insights offered into the application, adaptation and institutionalisation of agonism into governance practices. The detailed exploration that follows, in later chapters, of agonism in

Johannesburg's responses to a wide range of protest action is therefore critical in responding to this shortfall and identifying agonism's potential to transform governance practices.

Applying agonism to practices of governance

While it is true that long before the introduction of agonism, states have responded to conflict with varying degrees of success, the approach of state practitioners towards dissensus has also shifted significantly in recent years. Since the 1970s, the role of planners and planning, a critical component of governance by the state, has shifted from an elitist, conflict-averse approach to one more open to conflict's potential for change (Grabow and Heskin 1973). Then, planners in the liberal democratic context were regarded as rational, analytical, collaborative, regulatory, resourceful, diplomatic and administrative, and as providers of information, mediators, negotiators and facilitators. Planners assumed any problem resolution was based on collaboration with technocratic solutions (Forester 1987), and consensus achievable through methodical and logical debate (Healey 1996). From about the 1990s, however, the role of the planner has become less well defined. Planners increasingly have to tackle greater complexity, inequalities and conflict (Sandercock 2000), with planning gaining prominence as a political, not just technical and administrative, activity in the strengthening of democracy (Allmendinger and Haughton 2010). Expectations of planners and other state actors is high: in conflict, they can always do more (Forester 2009). In liberal democracies, consensus-seeking planning is ineffective at dealing with different world views, extreme urban conflicts and competing interests (Stiftel and Watson 2005). On the one hand, Friedmann (1987) believes that the planner must be impartial, separate from the community and the state, but adept at reflection and imagining options within the context of a state willing to redistribute resources. On the other hand, Sandercock (1998), foreshadowing agonistic principles, advocates that planners must adopt a more 'radical' approach to dealing with conflict, imparting skills to the protesting community and working in allegiance with it rather than with the state, even to the point of crossing over to the community and facilitating community-instigated solutions. She identifies risks, though, of 'radical' planning, such as the 'romanticisation' of the planner's role, the prioritisation of interests of one group at the expense of the larger society, and adoption of possible 'repressive' actions by both the community and the state.

However, she also alerts planners to their potentially transformative role in attaining social justice by challenging power and exclusion.

Now planning is seen as an ever-evolving, cross-cutting and politicised discipline, with planners influencing and shaping governance (Pløger 2006), but largely informed by the dominant context of liberal democratic ideology (Gunder 2010). Planners and other state actors deal daily with conflict in ways that are typically consensus-seeking (Forester 1987). However, planning can also be a way to suppress antagonism, though one that is bound to fail (Roskamm 2015). Despite agonism's proponents arguing it is more than a mere experiment (Lowndes and Paxton 2018), its implementation and institutionalisation by the state remains under-specified and under-tested. This is not surprising given that the intersection between conflict and its impact on state governance has only recently been recognised as an area demanding study (see Death 2011; Forester 2009; Gualini 2015; Haferburg and Huchzermeyer 2014; Kuhlmann and Bouckaert 2016; Laws and Forester 2015; O'Connor 2014).

As scholars increasingly recognise the potential of conflict to drive positive transformations (Forester 2009; Lederach 2014), more attention is being paid to how agonism can be specifically and generally applied in governance practices. Mouffe (2013) proposes that institutions of the state can demonstrate a broad commitment to agonistic principles, but for her the state institution needs to take its cues from protestors. Here, the protestors' activism signals the wish for a change by alerting the institution to an issue that may need to be addressed, possibly by antagonistic and violent means if they feel their voices are not heard. Her agonistic institution supports the centrality of dissensus in the democratic state, considers conflict as a potential agent of change, aspires to attain developmental and democratic aims by improving its current practices and changing them where necessary, and displays a deep respect for its adversaries. Likewise, Lowndes and Paxton (2018) argue a broadly agonistic approach is possible by avoiding bureaucratisation of the institution and its practices to allow agonistic interactions to spring up from the institution's imperfections. Wingenbach (2011), too, contends that the institution's agonistic capabilities can be grown by proactively concentrating on opportunities to improve 'soft elements' such as citizens' expectations, customs and culture, and 'hard elements' such as statutes and policies.

But what might detailed principles and examples of agonistic governance practices by the state look like in reality? Even Mouffe (2013) evidently finds agonistic practices hard to recognise. Bäcklund and Mäntysalo (2010) also identify this gap between the theory and practice of agonism and contend that if agonism's impact on institutions and planning practices is not understood, then the notion of agonism can hardly be translated into practice. However, there is an emerging literature on both the broad agonistic approach and detailed practices in models or governance that provides some insights. I have synthesised hints and tips for agonistic practices from these diverse cases in a framework to operationalise agonism in practice in my research. These practices, worth exploring further, come from diverse studies ranging across planning (Bäcklund and Mäntysalo 2010; Bond 2011; Hillier 2002), participation and deliberation (Dryzek 2005; Hillier 2002; Silver et al. 2010; Westphal 2018), institutional politics (Wingenbach 2011), public administration (Fortis 2014), urban design (Munthe-Kaas 2015), urban politics and governance (Pieterse 2008), abortion policy (Goi 2005), healthcare (Weale 2016), and military leadership (Fraher and Grint 2018).

My framework considers five overlapping and interlinked main lines of inquiry into state–society conflict, drawing on the interpretation, testing and synthesis of the aforementioned texts combined with other pertinent texts (namely Fung 2003; Glover 2012; Gunder 2003; Healey 2009; Mäntysalo et al. 2011; McManus 2008; Murtagh and Ellis 2011; Pernegger 2014, 2016; Pløger 2004; Sager 2013; Schaap 2006; Tambakaki 2014). In this way, agonism serves both as a lens through which to explore the state's approach to conflict and assess whether its approach reflects an agonistic agenda or not, and as an analytical tool for research. My framework outlines principles of detailed agonistic practices matched with examples of practices along an agonistic–antagonistic spectrum of possible governance practices.

The first of the five lines of inquiry of the framework is into the nature of the state's qualification of the conflict in general, but also of the protest event itself. Here, principles of detailed agonistic practices by the state above all include adopting a broad spirit of agonism, acknowledging the centrality of conflict, and accepting the impossibility of its eradication. Practices also include showing an openness to conflict; treating conflict as an opportunity to encourage innovation, change, human creativity, and empowerment, as well as raising awareness about the complexities of public policy extending beyond its mere technical aspects; and tolerance for being shaken out of complacency. Further, practices encompass seeing conflict as part of a political process that allows adversaries to have a new chance to win between formal elections, and not censuring or denigrating protest or protestors. Somehow the agonistic state simultaneously in the conflictual interaction maintains a balance between encouraging innovation and preserving stability. Examples of practices at the agonistic end of the spectrum of governance practices are evident in a state that accepts and acknowledges conflict, treats it as an opportunity for positive change, takes it seriously, and views it as a normal part of everyday governance. Examples at the antagonistic end of the spectrum include describing protest and protestors in negative or derogatory ways; dismissing, ignoring or being unsympathetic to dissenters' claims; seeing protest as a crisis; and responding to protest with undue force.

The second line of inquiry is into the nature of the state's portrayal of dissenters. Here, principles of detailed agonistic practices by the state embrace the expression of a deep agonistic respect towards dissenters, and the treatment of conflict as an opportunity to build current and future constructive state–society relationships. Other principles are the recognition of protestors as possible instigators of local solutions, the appreciation of raised issues as potentially highly emotive, and the acknowledgement of dissenters as being currently and previously unheard by the state. Another principle, which may be challenging to adopt, is the consideration of needs but with a focus on values, although Dryzek (2005) argues that agonism focuses too much on the value systems of contesting parties rather than on the contested need, with the effect that deadlock cannot ever be overcome. Governance practices at the agonistic end of the spectrum of state practices include examples such as regarding dissenters as Mouffeian (2000) 'adversaries' rather than 'deadly' enemies; treating them with respect, as citizens and residents, as belonging and as worthy; and considering them as partners. More examples include seeing dissenters' claims as legitimate and using spoken and written language carefully, not indiscriminately, both internally within the state and publicly. Examples of antagonistic practices of the state include treating dissenters as mere customers rather than as citizens or residents, not belonging, illegal, outsiders, deadly foes, criminals and undesirable; as frustrating, a nuisance, absurd and irrational; or as violent, threatening, harmful and to be afraid of.

The third line of inquiry is into aspects of the state's response to the dissenters' claim at different levels (not merely to the initial protest event, but also to the effects of the issue under contention, and to its root cause). Here, principles of detailed agonistic practices incorporate the state's provision of channels and spaces for contestation, and the recognition of the validity and legitimacy of any claim, whether formally or informally made. Other principles include the genuine consideration of the claim and appropriate responses at all levels, the prioritisation of responses at senior political and management levels, the synthesis of the differing aspects of any contested issue, the willingness to do more, and the empowerment of protestors. Agonistic practices of the state include adopting an agonistic approach, prioritising the role of conflict in governance, and acknowledging, recognising and legitimising dissenters, even perhaps empathising or cooperating with them. The agonistic state manages conflict proactively, recognises informal approaches, has the door open to dissenters, is both citizen- and customer-centric, and is willing to engage. This state also encourages debate, reframes the issue with an eye to addressing the claim, builds bridges, experiments, empowers citizens, and responds to the dissensus by making changes or granting concessions. However, examples of antagonistic governance practices include being unresponsive, defensive and resistant to change, and reframing the claim to deny or narrow it. Antagonistic practices also encompass the denial, dismissal, disparagement, placation, suppression, appropriation, criminalisation and refusal of dissenters and their claims, and being reactive, antagonistic, aggressive, controlling, threatening, hostile, accusatory, repressive and violent.

The fourth line of inquiry is into the nature of the state's response to issues of dynamics of power (mainly but not only related to engagements in processes of conflict). Here, receiving much critical attention from scholars, the agonistic state upholds the principles of agonistic practices, including emphasising the processes of open-ended contestation itself, rather than on decision-making processes. Further, the agonistic state supports the levelling of the playing field by proactively uncovering, acknowledging, tackling and moderating uneven systems of power to minimise exclusion, and providing measures to deal with power imbalances that are often purpose-made for each controversial context. It also explicitly provides or facilitates robust, shared spaces and channels for agonistic debate, the politicisation of issues, the playing out and not taming of conflict, hearing objections and facilitating participation. It keeps the place of power empty and separates the sphere of interaction from the state institution. It acknowledges and addresses the requirements for the appropriate effort, resources and actions, often a great deal, to facilitate the agonistic engagement in the conflict between the organisation and the dissenters. This requires providing process leadership by individuals imbued with an orientation towards agonistic approaches, empathy, ethics, resilience, reflexivity and sensitivity. Further, in agonistic conflictual interactions, the state co-creates with adversaries the agenda for the debate; identifies common ground between the state and dissenters such as shared values and democratic ideals; facilitates a collective sense of citizenship with a shared identity, beliefs and outlook; and draws on passion and not only logical-rational reasoning. Examples of practices at the agonistic end of the spectrum of governance practices are evident in a state that recognises adversaries' legitimacy, considers claims, and overtly opens up processes of participation. Although possibly counter-intuitive, agonistic practice would be the inclusion of members in public dialogue selected on a conflict basis to ensure fairness towards those that are normally excluded. Agonistic practices could also include the provision of resources or support to weaker adversaries. Agonistic interaction would be based on the issue under contention, with the agonistic state mediating the conflict, following up on issues, and creating the appropriate mechanisms for agonistic dialogue. Examples of governance practices at the antagonistic end of the spectrum, however, would typically include reinforcing exclusion and entrenching deep divides, locking out adversaries, adopting placatory measures and refusing to engage about the issue under contention, acting divisively, and undertaking minimal or no engagement with dissenters.

The last line of inquiry, into the form of the agreement reached, and the outcome if no agreement was reached, seems to be the most perplexing aspect of operationalising agonism for scholars, with agonistic interaction in processes of conflict the dominant theme. Here, the agonistic state endorses the principle of the management of conflicts rather than their resolution, and tends not to be consensus-seeking. Rather, it finds new ways to improve governance, striving for perfection but recognising perfection is impossible (presumably while balancing positive outcomes and minimising negative ones, avoiding the creation of an institutional vacuum, and not damaging state–society relationships). However, to be practical, agonistic governance combined with other traditional approaches might facilitate decision-making in the case of wicked problems. Here, the agonistic state is likely to favour the creation of locally developed solutions for better and more sustainable urban development as the more appropriate response, especially in the postcolonial post-apartheid South African context. The agonistic state recognises that in any decision-making process, the usually unheard voices are to be included as a prerequisite for consensus. The agonistic state, then, acknowledges and reminds itself that when any decision is made, it is incremental, iterative, piecemeal, partial, impermanent and short-lived, and it incorporates this decision into its practices. The agonistic state, even when no consensus is possible, recognises that agonistic practices can provide benefits for governance and conflictual state–society interactions. These benefits include surfacing citizens' competing concepts about possible solutions, thus aiding the deliberate improvement of urban development, urban governance and the local democracy. Other benefits can be the bringing together of antagonistic opponents and exposure of their underlying beliefs to each other, which can lead to mutual recognition of each other's viewpoints and possible shifts in attitudes, with positive and material consequences. Further, agonistic practices might provide new understandings into the values of the organisation, widen orientation towards incorporating more stakeholders, deepen the sense of local community, and raise broader policy issues and reset priorities. Examples at the agonistic end of the spectrum of governance practices include the state's tendency to manage conflict rather than resolve it, openness towards changing its behaviour or being, and demonstration of an implicit accord with dissenters evident in its actions. Agonistic practices comprise putting procedures in place that permit participants' decision-making, empowerment and self-expression; allow for joint decision-making; co-create initiatives with adversaries; agree to joint initiatives; and advocate for reciprocity of actions. Other practices include agreeing partially, modifying the state's processes, undertaking complete or incomplete changes, and adopting incremental solutions. Examples of governance practices at the antagonistic end of the spectrum include reaching no agreement, escalating conflict, demonstrating no reciprocity, and reneging on decisions made.

None of these lines of inquiry into the state's agonistic governance can be conducted without considering the opportunities for and impediments against such governance. The combination of institutional history, the specific actors and the historical state–society relationship may even make agonistic engagement impossible, argue Bäcklund and Mäntysalo (2010) in their case study on five Finnish cities. Hence, the research behind this book identified, as far as was practical and possible, the constraints that impeded agonistic practices and the positive aspects that facilitated agonistic practices. These could include the cultivation of a positive orientation to conflict and to change, the provision of resources of all kinds for the management of conflict, and the exposure of underlying beliefs, ideologies and physical concerns, say, about violence. Also identified are other parallel issues impacting on the conflict, such as the presence of intra-organisational tensions and cohesion; the understanding of management and organisational culture, attitudes and abilities, bases of mistrust, the historic relationship and any goodwill impacting on the relationship; and the identification of alternative ways in dealing with the issue under contention, operational challenges and opportunities, the inclusion of other role-players, and their agendas and resources.

Making analysis even more complicated is that sometimes these identified agonistic practices look like those encountered in other democratic models. Indeed, some scholars even seem uncomfortable at using agonism on its own in practice. For instance, Hillier's (2002) model of conflictual interaction ranges between consensus-based and agonistic democratic models, and includes strategies for adversaries to reach 'consensus' or 'compromise' through 'negotiation', 'bargaining' or 'lobbying' (Hillier 2002, pp. 124 and 127). Dryzek (2005) cites success in certain countries when the deliberative style of interaction is injected with Mouffeian agonistic passion to overcome the anaesthetising effect of rationality and to handle profound arguments. This differs from Bäcklund and Mäntysalo's (2010) argument that agonism is a progression from the different participation approaches of consensus-seeking democracies. Silver et al. (2010) conclude, in case studies of urban activism in Belfast, Berlin, Philadelphia, São Paulo and Durban, that effective participation combines consensus-driven and agonistic practices. However, the balance between these two approaches shifts according to the stage of the policymaking cycle, with agonistic practices being more appropriate at the start-up stage and consensus-seeking ones at the decision-making and implementation stages. Sophie Bond (2011) also conceptualises a mixed model for urban governance and planning practice underpinned by both collaborative democratic theory and agonism, with her framework setting the principles for engagement but leaving space for their interpretation as engagements unfold. Certainly, governance approaches to conflict in contexts of differing democratic models could be scrutinised more. What is also not clear is what mix of, and how many, detailed practices constitute agonistic practice? And can the state undertake agonistic practices if it has not adopted a broad agonistic approach? Perhaps, even if it is seemingly impossible for any state to entirely adopt agonistic principles and actions, an orientation towards agonism may result in benefits that other approaches have not yielded so far.

Conflict management in South Africa

Four debates inform the South African state's potential for the agonistic management of service delivery strife: the meaning of service delivery protests for the state; the extent to which protest counts yield broad trends in protest; the basis of the state–society relationship; and the state's apparent shift towards being conflict-averse.

First, what do service delivery protests mean for governance? The next few paragraphs point to the complexity of this phenomenon for the state. The right to protest in South Africa is a constitutional right. Exercising this right is a well-established routine in the country. The protests about service delivery targeting local government that form the focus of this book are among many, many others that take place every day. In fact, strike action and labour-related protests reflecting workers' discontent with employers about salaries and working practices far outnumbered service delivery protests (Grant 2014). Other notable large-scale and localised protests include anti-globalisation protests, targeting the International Monetary Fund, the World Bank, and related financial and banking institutions since the late 1990s, as part of a global resistance against capitalism. This anti-globalisation sentiment has found its way into service delivery protests in South Africa, especially against the payment for basic services. Other notable protests include those in March 2010 by the informal mass transit sector and at other times against the state's continued efforts to formalise this sector; *Occupy South Africa* in 2011; resistance to the new road tolling scheme by the Gauteng province in 2012 and 2013; the seemingly spontaneous *#RhodesMustFall* and *#FeesMustFall* protests at universities in March and October 2015; and politically motivated protests throughout the post-apartheid period, but especially after Jacob Zuma became the president in May 2009.

The post-apartheid phenomenon of service delivery protests fits into this wider backdrop of protests. Service delivery protests are commonly thought of as only the highly visible protests that take place in streets and public spaces targeting local government. However, service delivery protests are broader, covering any sort of protest about the delivery of services. *Service delivery* means the local-level state's provision of any tangible essential or other service as well as the service itself to the public, which cuts across poor and wealthy areas. The variety of services includes the supply of water and electricity, refuse removal, street cleaning, public transport, infrastructure, health services, housing, parks, management and development of informal traders, social amenities, billing, and paid parking. Service delivery also includes the organisations and institutions of the state, as well as its resources, personnel and relevant processes that deliver these services. Protestors tend to be dissatisfied about the local government's projects, programmes and operations, the lack thereof, or their pace and quality (Jain 2010; Ngwane 2010). However, sometimes protestors also seek financial or political advantage over the service delivery systems (Alexander 2010; Booysen 2007; Matlala and Bénit-Gbaffou 2012; Oldfield and Stokke 2004; Olver 2017; von Holdt et al. 2011).

In addition to these tangible aspects of service delivery, the term 'service delivery' also contains intangible aspects about expectations and our ideas of what democracy is. Service delivery contains an embedded promise to the majority of citizens of transforming society as a way to redress apartheid's injuries and negative effects on social justice (Mc Lennan 2009). One might even incorporate other development ideals such as the 'right not to be poor' (Skogly 2002). The post-apartheid state made explicit and implicit promises, thereby creating expectations in citizens' minds of what service delivery entails. Thus, promises of simple and complex services and public goods are often conflated with rights, growth, redistribution and development as contained in the *Freedom Charter*, the *Bill of Rights for a New South Africa*, the *Constitution of the Republic of South Africa* (RSA), national and local government policy and legislation, and manifestos of the ruling party. Further, service delivery protest is shorthand for any struggle that tries to shape our ideas of what democracy and the democratic state looks like. By including this intangible aspect inherent in service delivery, the role of the state is extended to more than just a deliverer of services, in South Africa and globally (Cohen and Arato 1994; Comaroff and Comaroff 2004; Friedman 2001; Jessop 1990; Kasfir 1998; Keane 2003; von Holdt et al. 2011). These intangibles also drive service delivery protests, as in those that contain objections to the state's inherent capitalist policy principles, such as the principle of payment for services (Naidoo 2007; Pernegger 2016). Scholars can thus claim these protests signify the failure not only of service delivery, but also of the state and democracy (Agüero et al. 2007; Harber 2009; RSA 2008). However, other scholars argue these protests call the state's attention to particular issues, sanctioning the state's role even while censuring its responses (Alexander 2010; Booysen 2007; von Holdt et al. 2011).

Service delivery protests also cut across races and economic classes. Scholars on service delivery protests, such as Alexander (2010), present these protests as undertaken exclusively by low-income communities on the streets of South Africa. However, the middle class also carries out protests (see Chapter 6). Lastly, while street protests are (relatively) easy to identify and count, a plethora of other sometimes less-visible forms of service delivery strife in South Africa remain under-researched, such as petitioning, boycotting, meetings, media coverage and other subversive tactics.

This multidimensionality of service delivery strife means the agonistic state's job of responding is an enormously complicated one that must address the tangible aspects of service delivery, which is the focus of this research, as well as the intangible ones. The implications of Mouffe's (2000) notion means the agonistic state must marshal many different types of resources and skills in order to respond effectively to strife's push-pull forces, while displaying deep respect for protestors, and channelling this conflict in a productive manner.

Clearly, responses to street protest incidents are needed, as immediately as possible. This is a daunting challenge, even when protests are not violent. Violent protests make it even more overwhelming, with violence meaning different things to scholars on South African service delivery protests. Sometimes violence might be threatened but is rarely followed through (Karamoko 2011). Sometimes protests become violent because of forcible policing but this is not always clear-cut (Earle 2011; Hough 2008; Karamoko 2011; Paret 2015; von Holdt et al. 2011; Winton 2004). Alexander et al. (2018) call protests disruptive when roads are blocked by, say, burning tyres, and violent when lives and properties are endangered. In my research, as the state's responses to protest incidents would likely be different if protestors threatened violence to those where it did not encounter violence, I classified them as violent. No matter the definition, however, what is clear is that protestors turn to violence as a last resort against the state's unresponsiveness (Booysen 2007; Duncan 2014b; von Holdt et al. 2011), and violent protests are on the increase (Alexander et al. 2018). When the state responds to violent protest with force, it diminishes the chance for agonistic engagement. Indeed, I found the state was less likely to adopt agonistic practices to individual protest incidents than it did to the underlying issues. Further, even if one assumes the state understood perfectly the scope of the underlying issues, it still had to deal, when responding, with its own organisational transition processes, maladministration, corruption, weak leadership, low institutional capacity, imperfect data, fiscal and skills resource shortages, and inappropriate decision-making processes.

Second, surely the number and frequency of protests indicates broad trends in citizens' dissensus and possibly local governments' health? However, even the most basic information about service delivery protests is contested, namely counting protests. Data collection methodologies, motives, and definitions of service delivery protest vary enormously across the different data sets gleaned from police reports or the media (Alexander et al. 2015, 2018; Lancaster 2016; Multi-Level Government Initiative 2012; Pernegger 2016). Numbers of protests are hard to pin down. Across South Africa between 2005 and 2015, 1,078 service delivery protests took place according to Municipal IQ (2018), a data intelligence company tracking protests against local government. However, Alexander et al. (2018) report significantly more, 2,796 protests, over the same period. Commentators generally regard protest data as unreliable and inconsistent (Alexander 2010; Alexander et al. 2015; Jain 2010; Karamoko 2011; Lancaster 2016; Ngwane 2012; Nyar and Wray 2012). However, broad trends are discernible.

For instance, most service delivery protests since soon after the 1994 national elections were initially peaceful public marches or assemblies (Municipal IQ 2009, 2010). However, between 2004 and 2016, about three-quarters were likely to be disorderly or violent, and all protests increased until around 2015 when protest numbers flattened off (Alexander et al. 2018). Distinct peaks of protests occurred across most data sets. Protest accounts are incomplete: half of all protests are likely to receive no media coverage at all (Wilcox 2013). Even when protests are covered, the media tends not to cover protestors' goals or protest outcomes (Morwe 2010). Previous efforts by protestors to have concerns addressed before they protested are also likely to remain unreported (Duncan 2014b). Few identify broad trends that may have relevance for their future management, other than Lancaster's (2018) recommendation that protests should be studied for just this purpose. Area-specific dynamics are also hardly addressed in these counts. Data seem to carry an underlying assumption that the state does not respond at all to protests (Duncan 2016). While the unreliability and incompleteness of protest data clearly has a knock-on effect on the state's ability to respond appropriately, least of all agonistically, my research shows that it certainly does respond to protest incidents as well as to the underlying issues.

Third, what is the basis of South African post-apartheid local government's engagement with society? New wall-to-wall local governments were created to deliver services to all South Africans, many of whom had not encountered legitimate local governance before. Local government, at the interface with society, features prominently in setting social development and human rights expectations through service delivery. The design of the new local government was influenced by two international trends with competing objectives: the developmental state and New Public Management.

The 1980s and 1990s concept of the state, which is proactive and interventionist rather than hands-off in its economic development (Woo-Cumings 1999), was taken up by the ruling party, the African National Congress (ANC), partly in response to South Africa's near doubling of unemployment between 1994 and 1998 (RSA 2008). Here, the new developmental local government was to address not only economic development issues, but also apartheid's legacy (Khosa 2002; Parnell and Pieterse 1999), and was to treat all South Africans as active citizens rather than as customers (RSA 1998).

However, the concept of developmental local government was diluted by New Public Management, on the rise since the 1970s, which was a collection of public administration policies to improve, professionalise, refine and downscale bureaucracies and stimulate management improvements, adopt more business-minded principles and distribute decision-making to local structures. New Public Management placed more importance on technical rationality than on state–society relationship-building (Cameron 2015; Chipkin 2013; Flyvbjerg 1998; Hay et al. 2006; Hood 1991; Watson 2003).

However, New Public Management appealed to the South African state, which had to tackle the mammoth task of providing proper infrastructure and services to many who had never had them before. The state felt it had little option but to proceed in a highly technocratic, systematised and managerial manner to meet this challenge. To fund this work, and increasingly treating the citizen as customer, the state pursued cost-recovery imperatives despite widespread minimal affordability for services (Everatt 2008; McDonald and John 2002; Smith 2004). Ultimately, transformative governance and planning was more challenging in reality than in theory (Harrison 2013). Real transformation of the South African state has yet to be realised: some believe the state has experienced a 'transition without transformation' (Picard 2005, p. 176), and others that this transition is still incomplete (von Schnitzler 2015).

The tension between these two concepts of development and fiscal sustainability meant the state–society relationship increasingly, but not exclusively, centred on the provision of service infrastructure projects and the principle of payment for services (Pillay et al. 2006). Although local government may have created institutional channels of participation (Bénit-Gbaffou 2008), this tension meant genuine and agonistic state–society engagement was likely to be limited.

Lastly, what is the state's position on conflict? In 1996, the state seemed to have an agonistic approach to conflict, centred in the experimental new institution of the *Truth and Reconciliation Commission* hearings that tried to confront apartheid's injustices to promote healing. The commission channelled antagonism into agonistic engagement, thus opening new possibilities for the future, although it was also criticised for closing down dissent. However, since then, although the state has increased participatory measures, conflict appears to have little prospect in realising democratic ideals (Anciano and Piper 2018; Haferburg and Huchzermeyer 2014; Koonings and Kruijt 2009b). Indeed, the state seems to have increasingly rebuffed dissensus, possibly seeing it as a threat to its legitimacy, as it quelled service delivery protests with force. Even when the state does acknowledge and centre conflict, it seemed to treat it as unwanted. The democratic state's stance today seems, on the face of it, to have become largely conflict-averse. However, a closer interrogation of the state's responses to protest at different levels, in Johannesburg's case, shows a far more complex picture of the state's position on conflict.

The notion of agonism is complex and offers arguably intellectual and practical resources for understanding the complexity of dissensus in democratic governance in new ways, and for deepening the state's conflict management practices at broad and detailed levels, despite its limited translation in reality. In South Africa's service delivery strife, agonistic conflict management is impacted by key debates. These imply it is the state's task to gather and use the skills it needs to manage, but not necessarily resolve, this conflict. As is true of most democracies worldwide, the customer-centric relationship between the South African state and its citizens leaves most citizens feeling they have only limited ways to interact with the state, thus constraining the state's prospects for agonistic governance. The Johannesburg case, outlined in the next chapter, presents service delivery strife as it intersects with the city administration's responses. Three case studies of individual intractable conflicts follow. These stories highlight the necessity for an organisation to have a broad approach as well as implementing a number of detailed agonistic practices to be able to claim it is agonistic, even if only partly so. While instances of intentional agonism were limited, the city administration did benefit from creative solutions when it engaged residents agonistically. Greater research of agonism in practice may clarify its innovative potential, which could be particularly relevant for cities struggling to sustain their financial obligations and devise appropriate policy solutions in cases of strife.

3
Johannesburg's conflict and governance timeline

Linking strife and Johannesburg's organisational development

The first municipality of Johannesburg, initially a mining camp, was declared in 1897, a decade after gold was discovered. It governed a mere 13 square kilometres, the extent of its current-day Inner City alone, and served around 100,000 people. Today, the city administration governs 1,645 square kilometres and serves over 4.9 million people through its departments, agencies and seven administrative regions (A to G) (see Map 3.1). The city, although no longer reliant on gold mining, is the single biggest contributor to South Africa's economy. As the greatest urban agglomeration in the country, this metropolis is a critical force in the South African, African and global contexts. Many important changes have happened in Johannesburg since its mining days, but arguably those in the post-democratic period have even greater significance for governance and state–citizen conflictual interactions. The metropolis remains still highly unequal spatially and economically, with deep divisions between the concentrations of the poor in low-income townships and informal settlements, and their wealthier middle-class suburban counterparts (see Map 1.1).

The timeline of city strife as it intersects with the post-apartheid shifts in governance opens with a snapshot of pre-democratic service delivery protests in Johannesburg. It then details the ANC-dominated local governance of the city since the first democratic local government elections in late 1995. This is periodised in five-year spans correlating with the four main shifts in the city administration's organisational evolution under the ANC and the mayoral terms of office ending in 2015, shortly before the 2016 local government elections, which led to the coalition city government led by the main opposition party, the Democratic Alliance. In applying the lens of agonism, outlined in the previous chapter, as far as is practical, this chapter explores the local-level state's qualification of conflicts over each five-year period: its portrayal of dissenters; its response to the dissenters' claims; the nature of its responses to issues of dynamics of power; and the forms of agreements reached.[1]

Insights are provided, focusing on the role of the local-level state, into the multiple and shifting forms of strife in each period: from street-based protests, by mainly low-income communities – forming two-thirds of all city households and earning incomes below R76,800 ($11,546) per annum (Quantec 2014), increasing in variety, number and violence over the periods, to other less direct forms of confrontation, by wealthier middle-class groups, with the top 2.4 per cent of city households earning R1.23 million ($0.16 million) per annum, 16 times more than their poor counterparts (Quantec 2014). This chapter concludes with observations about the changing particularities of protest and the shifts over time in the main trends in the city administration's capacity for agonistic engagement in these episodes of conflict.

Apartheid political protests (pre-1996)

Johannesburg is no stranger to protest. Indeed, a remarkable and rich history of conflict characterises Johannesburg's birth and growth and is well documented in the literature, starting with possibly the first protest in Johannesburg in 1897: white males protested against unemployment and demanded the national state's intervention in the form of a public works programme (Van Onselen 1982). Other notable protests thereafter related to processes of British imperialism, the formation of the Boer Republic, and labour action, including various strikes by miners, railwaymen and tramway workers in the 1910s and 1920s; the black squatter movement of the 1940s; the mineworkers' strike of 1946; and the defiance campaigns of the 1950s and 1960s. Most readers will be familiar with the anti-apartheid political protests of the 1960s to 1990s. Johannesburg's transition to democracy included strikes, stayaways, marches, boycotts, campaigns, rallies and bombings, and the South African state's violent rebuttal of the Sharpeville demonstration in 1960. The city also attested to the Black Consciousness Movement of the 1960s and 1970s; the Soweto student uprising of 1976; and subsequent school and other boycotts, labour strikes and rise of anti-apartheid actions.

Bar few exceptions, though, as in the Alexandra bus boycotts of the 1940s and the 1950s (Bonner and Nieftagodien 2008), protests were politically motivated and targeted the national government. Far fewer protests about local services were reported during the apartheid period, but those set the scope and tone for later service delivery protests. For instance, in the 1970s and 1980s, boycotts against rent and tariff increases and protests about housing and land shortages targeted the then Black Local Authorities and provincial and national governments. As early as 1985, black and coloured communities were upset about chronic service delivery shortages endemic to Johannesburg's deeply polarised settlement patterns (Beall et al. 2002). Here, overflowing sewerage, lack of refuse removal, disease, the inadequate quality and quantity of community facilities (including schools), overcrowding, and lack of housing were widespread in *townships* (Wilson and Ramphele 1989). Townships are low-income dormitory areas created before and during apartheid to house black, Indian and coloured communities and segregated from white areas, underdeveloped to this day. They are still labelled as townships, despite sometimes containing small pockets of middle-class groups, with residents experiencing enormous resentment and frustration at their ongoing deprivation and helplessness.

Macro-political changes, such as the abolition of the pass laws in 1986, thereby allowing blacks to access the city, the unbanning of the ANC and other political organisations, and the release of President Nelson Rolihlahla Mandela and other activists in 1990, raised the hopes of frustrated communities. Likewise, early city-level changes, such as the desegregation of public swimming baths and recreation centres in 1989 by the Johannesburg City Council (*New York Times* 1989), were a portent of the many political and administrative shifts to come.

Unlike today, municipalities in 1990 were answerable and subordinate to the other spheres of government. As part of the move to ultimately decentralise governance to independent spheres of government at local, provincial and national levels, this all began to shift in Johannesburg when the Central Witwatersrand Metropolitan Chamber was formed in 1991. This was in line with the terms of the state–society negotiated agreement of the 1990 Soweto Accord to end the rents and service charges boycotts in the townships. The Metropolitan Chamber's main members, the Soweto Civic Association, the Johannesburg City Council, the provincial government (the Transvaal Provincial Administration, and in 1993 its restructured follow-on organisation), and the Greater Johannesburg Local Negotiating Forum, drove the redesign of future independent city governance across the main metropolitan conurbations of Johannesburg, Pretoria, Germiston and surrounding urban areas (Turok 1993). It initiated a new non-racial governance agenda in Johannesburg, introducing localised policies to overcome pervasive urban problems caused by the lack of basic services and extreme housing shortages, especially in areas previously defined as black-only, and stabilised pre-election interim city administrative functions and budgets (Turok 1993). In a sense, the

Metropolitan Chamber and the later Forum can be seen as creating an agonistic space as it forced together different interests across racial lines for the first time in local governance (Mabin 1994; Sekele 2000; Turok 1993). One of the first agreements negotiated by the Metropolitan Chamber in 1992 was to expand Johannesburg's administrative footprint to what we know as the boundaries of the city today, incorporating 13 separate black, coloured, Indian and white municipal administrations. These overlapped with the magisterial districts of Johannesburg, Randburg, Roodepoort, Sandton, Alexandra, Lenasia and Soweto (COJ 2001a). This transition towards the realisation of democratic local government was sped up by ongoing international political pressure, the violent and deadly clash between the ANC and the Inkatha Freedom Party at Shell House (the ANC's former headquarters) shortly before the country's first democratic national elections in April 1994, and the subsequent inauguration of Nelson Mandela as the country's first democratically elected president.

The conflictual but seemingly agonistic engagement and arbitration about the form of administrative structures to govern Johannesburg between the Greater Johannesburg Local Negotiating Forum's members resulted in an agreement in November 1994 to promulgate seven autonomous Transitional Metropolitan Sub-Structures (MSSs) with boundaries corresponding to the civic associations' functional areas, plus a central Greater Johannesburg Transitional Metropolitan Council (GJTMC) (Tomlinson 1999b).

Hence, in December 1994, and concurrent with similar legislated makeovers at national and provincial levels of government, the then provincial government amalgamated these 13 former municipal administrations into the GJTMC and seven Transitional MSSs to govern the greater Johannesburg area. Further, the state's *Reconstruction and Development Plan* (RSA 1994) made explicit and implicit promises to the previously disenfranchised and poor people of South Africa to deliver services, infrastructure, housing, access to jobs and a share in the wealth of the country. However, it soon became evident that operational and organisational shortfalls of the new local government structures, among other challenges, made it unlikely that these promises could be realised (Cameron 1995). Thus, not even nine months later, in September 1995, another interim stage of the transitioning of Johannesburg's local government resulted in the trimming down of the seven MSSs into an arguably more sustainable city administration of four independent, decentralised Northern, Southern, Eastern and Western MSSs and a new core transitional GJTMC (Tomlinson 1999b). The city's footprint was further expanded to include Orange Farm to the south and other informal settlement areas to the north. This provisional governance arrangement readied the way for Johannesburg's first democratic local government elections in November 1995 under its first black mayor, Councillor Isaac Mogase, at a time when local government had not enjoyed much political credibility with previously disadvantaged citizens until then (COJ 2011w).

In the lead-up to these first democratic local government elections, political protests overshadowed the only three service delivery protests targeting local government that could be identified. Protests about service delivery may not necessarily have been that dissimilar thematically to those post-democracy, but the dividing line of the first democratic elections marked the start of the new relationship between citizens in previously disadvantaged areas with a newly representative and legitimate local government (Ballard 2005). The state's shift to prioritising local governance further heightened expectations for service delivery. Citizen frustrations began to be progressively directed at local government, initialising the increasing and progressively violent service delivery protests over the years to come. Protests were concentrated in low-income areas as the city administration was persistently unable to overcome apartheid's legacy of extreme economic and spatial inequality in Johannesburg, evident in Map 3.1. Even then, in 1995, the GJTMC encountered resistance from informal trading associations, a detailed account of which is provided in Chapter 5. The GJTMC tried to manage informal traders in response to the rapid escalation in their numbers, especially in the Inner City, when the national government loosened restrictive business legislation (RSA 1993b). Despite the city administration's agonistic interactions, the associations used the tactic of mass street marches to force the GJTMC to consult only with them, and not the individual traders in project areas, about its proposed market developments and operational management (Muthialu 2012).

Agonism in the transition period (1996–2000)

In driving the democratic post-1996 developmental agenda, the now renamed Greater Johannesburg Metropolitan Council (GJMC) and the four Metropolitan Local Councils (MLCs) grappled with transitioning the divergent former administrations into a cohesive city administration. They were preoccupied with restructuring and growing institutional capacity to implement their new policies, which included driving cost-recovery imperatives. Although this period saw relatively few street-based service delivery protests (21 observed between 1996 and 2000), many of the main themes of the protests, against issues of basic services raised – housing delivery, anti-privatisation and informal trading – were to continue for decades to come. Goodwill from the smooth political transition from apartheid to democracy ensured some state responses, when it did respond to protest, were agonistic, but not all.

Map 3.1 – Protests across Johannesburg, 1996–2015

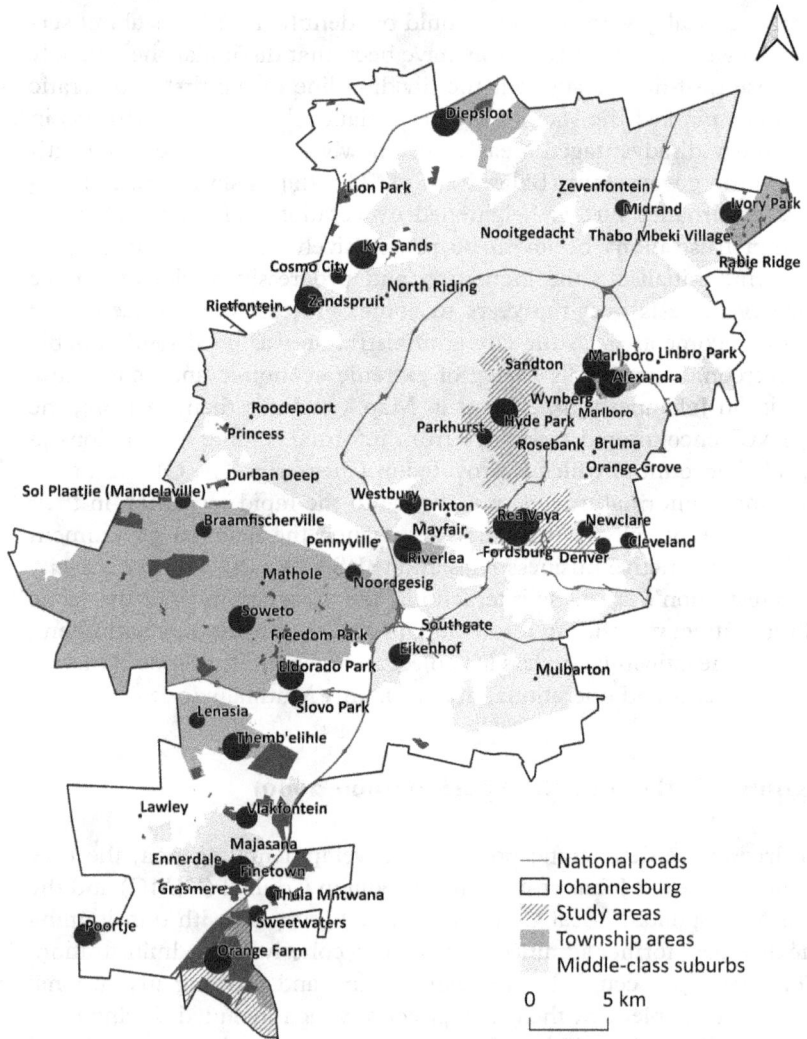

Note: Black dots mark the origins of protests – the larger the dot, the greater the number of protests.

Source: Author's formulation (data derived from Pernegger 2016)

Already in mid-1996, the GJMC was feeling a financial squeeze. The *Masakhane* (Let's Build Together) campaign launched by President Mandela the year before, urging citizens to pay for rates and services, was not working, as municipal debt continued to mount. Certainly, the need for financial resources to fund infrastructure development must have contributed to the city administration's pragmatic and hard-line attitude towards the Sandton rates boycotters. Some businesses and residents (then largely white) objected through the courts to the GJMC desire for 'one city, one tax base', a rallying slogan adopted by townships during apartheid (Pillay et al. 2006). The 'one city, one tax base' concept was a proposal to redistribute property rates between the wealthier middle-class suburbs, generally the former white areas in the northern parts of the city with more developed infrastructure, to the low-income areas with infrastructure deficits (Pillay et al. 2006). This boycott, and also its handling by the city administration, critical for the future billing crisis, likely soured the relationship between the city administration and the middle class (see Chapter 6).

Also, in 1996, the earliest anti-privatisation resistance by low-income communities against the city administration was evident. A group of women marched to the Office of the Mayor and undressed to mark their extreme disrespect for the city administration's mandatory pre-paid water meter installations in Orange Farm (Coalition Against Water Privatisation et al. 2004). Prepaid meters were regarded by the city administration as a mechanism to both provide minimum free water to low-income households and to curb water losses (Mazibuko vs City of Johannesburg et al. 2009). However, the 'water wars' (Bond, 2004a), fought by low-income communities, was essentially against the commodification of the provision of water services and for the access to water as a basic human right (Naidoo 2010) (see Chapter 4). Echoing the earlier Soweto rents boycotts of the 1980s, coloured townships protested in the streets against the Southern Metropolitan Local Council's (SMLC) application of a flat-rate charge for services in February 1997. This protest was so aggressive that Jessie Duarte, the Member of the Executive Council for Safety and Security in the Gauteng Provincial Government (GPG), used the police and the army to subdue protestors, censuring them for their perverseness and recklessness (ANC Daily News Briefing 2006a). Various, likely agonistic, meetings followed between protestors, the SMLC's mayor and other politicians, and the provincial Local Government and Development Planning department, resulting in the city administration's agreement to do write-offs of arrears due to unpaid service charges (ANC Daily News Briefing 2006b). Also, in February, and fuelling the resistance of the poor against the South African state's cost-recovery efforts and evictions from illegally occupied land or buildings, poor residents lobbied in one of many worldwide anti-globalisation protests against what they saw as the undemocratic policies of the World Bank and the International Monetary Fund (Shah 2011).

City centre streets were beset by a number of recurrent protests by picketing informal traders in August and October 1997 against the GJMC's implementation of new markets in support of Inner City regeneration plans. Their anger was also directed at non-South African black traders, in the form of physical assaults and anti-foreigner rhetoric (Peberdy and Crush 1998), foreshadowing those across South Africa a decade later in 2008, and required the police and army to intervene to protect foreigners' lives as well as overcome looting and property damage. The COJ's response to these attacks was limited to the agonistic development of a partial solution with the traders, namely for jointly agreed criteria for market allocations, which effectively favoured local traders.

By 1997, the GJMC's financial crisis was becoming woefully obvious. It had been unable to pay its creditors for months (COJ 2001a) due to 'relaxed revenue management, difficulties with the new valuation roll, the high level of spending of funds it did not have, and increasing capital expenditure demands' (COJ 2006e, p. 26). In October, one of the GPG's directives insisting on corrective actions by the city administration stipulated the formation of the Transformation Lekgotla, a ten-councillor committee empowered to drive immediate reforms to sort out the financial crisis (COJ 2001a). This financial crisis seemingly marked the city administration's shift from its implementation of the developmental local government framework to focusing more on the citizen as customer and greater fiscal prudence, and seemingly becoming less inclined towards an agonistic strife with citizens.

The GPG proclaimed the first set of by-laws to manage informal trading for Johannesburg in July 1998 and the GJMC began enforcing the by-laws, for the first time in a decade (Province of Gauteng 2004). In the Johannesburg context, although some retail survivalist and typically black traders operated in formally designated and managed trading spaces on and off the streets, most operated informally in the streets, with all widely referred to as 'informal traders'. Predictably, in September 1998, Inner City informal traders protested, violently. This time, protestors joined forces with UMSA, the Unemployed Masses of South Africa, mixing an anti-enforcement motive with anti-foreigner sentiments and a concern for unemployment, and were forcibly quashed by the state (Peberdy and Talibe 1997). Other protesting groups were also left dissatisfied by the state's unresponsiveness. However, in a victory for the 'one city, one tax base' approach, the Sandton rates boycott came to an abrupt halt in October 1998 when the Constitutional Court ruled that the GJMC's actions had been lawful (Fedsure Life Assurance Ltd and Others vs Greater Johannesburg Transitional Metropolitan Council and Others 1998c).

Heeding concerns about the extent of poverty in Johannesburg, by the end of 1998 the city administration had started implementing its *Indigency Management Policy*, providing subsidies to poor households for the first ten kilolitres of water used (Mazibuko vs City of Johannesburg et al. 2009). However, this policy was criticised for its limited success due to operational challenges with its implementation (Naidoo 2010). Further, the May Day protest in Seattle in 1999, the largest march of its time against capitalism and globalisation, continued to encourage the anti-capitalist movement in South Africa.

In January 1999, the first city manager, Khetso Gordhan, arguably encouraged an agonistic management culture, albeit internal to the city administration. He created much-needed, high-spirited rounds of 'frank and informal discussion' (COJ 2001a, p. 51). He sought inputs from even the more junior managers and project staff, as well as senior managers' buy-in for the plan of political and administrative corrective measures needed to address the causes and effects of the financial crisis, *iGoli 2002* (GJMC 1999d) – *iGoli* meaning 'Place of Gold' – and for the transformation of the city administration into a more performance-driven organisation (COJ 2002b). However, civil society was less than enthusiastic with *iGoli 2002*'s ideological aspects, especially its outsourcing of key service delivery functions, even though the city administration was to be the owner of the service provision entities. For instance, the GJMC set up the Metropolitan Trading Company (MTC) in April 1999 to develop and manage markets for informal traders and taxi ranks (GJMC 1999d). In a similar vein, grassroots protestors in South Africa and elsewhere objected to capitalism and globalisation in the worldwide June 18 campaign. Thabo Mbeki, taking over from Nelson Mandela as president in June 1999 until 2008, ushered in a technocratic governance ethos (Glaser 2010) and a propensity for task-based approaches, which intensified the disconnect between the local-level state and citizens, making agonistic engagement difficult.

In September 1999, informal traders marched against their eviction from Braamfontein, a precinct within the Inner City, demanding the GJMC's recognition of their status as legitimate businesses (Motala 2002). Although the GJMC adopted a conciliatory tone, traders were soon to become increasingly agitated as the GJMC's decision to transform its 16 formerly uncoordinated law enforcement agencies into an integrated JMPD on 1 November 1999 came into effect. The new JMPD incorporated informal trading by-law enforcement

(Abrahamse 2012). Further, deeply dissatisfied Orange Farm protestors blockaded the nearby main highway, an important arterial route
in the south of the city, objecting again to what they called the city
administration's move to privatisation. Likewise, also in 1999, the
Soweto Electricity Crisis Committee formed in objection to electricity cut-offs and prepaid electricity meters in Soweto (Wafer 2005).
In July and November 2000, there were even more anti-privatisation
protests, this time in opposition to *iGoli 2002* (City Press 2000).

These actions did not stop *iGoli 2002*'s recommended integration
of the former GJMC and the MLCs into the unicity, the metropolitan
municipality of the COJ, in October 2000, including additional areas to
the north-east and north from the former adjacent Modderfontein and
Midrand municipalities. The choice of an executive mayor, one with
decision-making authority and not merely the ceremonial role of former
mayors, soon after the local government elections on 5 December 2000
was a significant step in improving governance as it placed accountability for service delivery firmly within the political domain. Johannesburg's
first executive mayor, Councillor Amos Masondo, steered the COJ
through its next consolidation phase, with one of its first actions to
re-centralise the MLCs' separate financial systems (COJ 2006e), a difficult task that ultimately contributed to incorrect billing.

By 1999, it was clear that the city administration had to implement
further measures to ensure financial sustainability; it could not be 'business as usual', as declared in the 1999 *iGoli 2002* cost-driven rescue
plan (GJMC 1999d). More so, however, the GJMC's emphasis on
the technical, rather than participatory, aspects of the plan and infrastructure development meant it was less likely to engage agonistically
as it was unwilling 'to host conflicts over differing interests that are at
stake' (Bond 1998, p. 67) as it concentrated on service delivery's technical challenges. Indeed, the city administration appeared to gradually
deepen its hostility towards protestors in the period to come.

Growing antagonism in the consolidation period (2001–2005)

The COJ became increasingly sensitised to the issue of protests, which
more than trebled in number between 2001 and 2005, with 71 protests identified relative to the previous five-year period. In tandem, the
institutions of the municipality were consolidated into the single but
complex unicity structure made up of departments of the core administration; a number of stand-alone but municipal-owned entities dealing

with sectoral service delivery such as water supply, electricity supply, traffic policing, informal trading development, and roads management; and 11 Offices of the Regions with limited local-level functions.

In March 2001, and riling many in middle-class suburbs, the COJ initialised its new centralised billing system and issued many thousands of incorrect bills in the process. This error proved to be not a one-off mistake, sparking the billing crisis that was to enrage middle-class ratepayers over the next decade (see Chapter 6). Cause for complaint, too, among the car-loving middle class, were faulty traffic lights in the city's northern suburbs and associated traffic congestion. The issues were severe enough to warrant attention in the COJ's planning documents, the *Integrated Development Plan* of 2003–2004 and its updated 2005–2006 version, leading ultimately to the COJ's adoption of a private sector-funded traffic management pointsmen initiative branded by South African insurance firm OUTsurance in 2005.

The COJ was extraordinarily task-focused in this period and made strides in service delivery across Johannesburg to tackle the substantial services backlog in townships and informal settlements, as well as the simultaneous growing demand for services. Know that the city's population increased by 30 per cent in the decade since the first democratic local government came into power, from 2,861,077 in 1996 to 3,719,788 in 2005 (Quantec 2018). Despite the still many shortfalls in the provision of basic services, the COJ's tarring of 314 kilometres of roads in Soweto between 2003 and 2005 was one particularly noteworthy achievement (COJ 2004e). But citizens' expectations, especially in Soweto and other poor areas, still ran high, and the volume (and violence) of street protests in this period accelerated rapidly, crystallising into four distinct service delivery protest themes.

First, the COJ's push for cost recovery of services rendered to serviced areas, and the ongoing lack of availability of especially water and electricity services in the newer informal settlement areas, but also in other low-income areas, fuelled many protests during this period, mainly in Soweto, Orange Farm, Themb'elihle, Alexandra and Eldorado Park (see Map 3.1). This set of street and other forms of protests was certainly influenced by recurrent global annual May Day protests, as in those against the Doha Development Round in 2001, symbolising South Africa's struggle of the working class against capitalism and apartheid (Shah 2011). Notably, the Soweto Electricity Crisis Committee led a particularly long-lived and concentrated battle over a decade using many channels to voice its objections, from court action to 'mobbing' Mayor Masondo's home in the Kensington 87 incident in April 2002, where protestors were shot at by the mayor's bodyguard and arrested by the police (ioL News 2002a; news24 2003). Low-income communities rebelled against the COJ's allegedly capitalism-friendly long-term vision, *Joburg 2030* (COJ 2002c), launched in February 2002, seen as responsible for entrenching poverty (Naidoo 2010). Also unpopular and leading to marches accompanied by threats of violence in Alexandra, the Inner City and Sandton was the COJ's hosting of the World Summit on Sustainable Development in August 2002, seen as promoting globalisation (Death 2010). Likewise, resisting the 'commodification of water' (Dawson 2010a, p. 381), a mass meeting in Orange Farm in 2002 led to the establishment of the Orange Farm Water Crisis Committee, who, together with the Anti-Privatisation Forum (APF), were to fight the water wars for over a decade against the COJ's water-saving, cost-saving and cost-recovery endeavours. The COJ's inconsistent responses to the protestors likely arose from its fragmentation despite organisational consolidation efforts. For instance, it called for objections to its proposed tariff increases in April 2002 and offer of 'relief measures' (COJ 2002e), while Mayor Masondo's referred, in his first midterm address, to members of the Soweto Electricity Crisis Committee as 'odd individuals' with 'strange views' that 'habitually oppose' the COJ's initiatives (COJ 2003d).

Second, the survivalist traders, mainly on pavements in the Inner City, staged recurrent protests against the COJ's policy of evictions for non-payment of rentals by its MTC, responsible for managing public markets. Protests included a march by the Inner City informal traders led by the Informal Business Forum from Yeoville, in the eastern part of the Inner City (see Map 5.1 and Chapter 4), in September 2002 (ioL News 2002d).

Third, seemingly impromptu street protests in the Inner City and informal settlements, located at the city's periphery or within defunct industrial areas, signified the poor's growing frustration at the lack of land and housing. For instance, an anti-eviction campaign in December 2002 and the Workers Library and Khanya College anti-eviction protest in July 2004 stemmed from Inner City improvement efforts, and other protests in informal settlements such as Diepsloot, Zevenfontein, Marlboro, Wynberg and Kliptown (in Soweto) (see Map 3.1) were related to lack of housing and other development of these areas. Street protests grew more organised under the umbrella of the global Landless People's Movement, various housing and land campaigners active in Johannesburg since 2001 (Greenberg 2004). In January 2003, the Landless People's Movement and the residents of the small former Eikenhof informal settlement (to the east of Soweto) protested their eviction by the COJ, which had earmarked the area for development as a cemetery. This protest resulted in the COJ's antagonistic response, using the controversial Red Ants, private sector security guards appointed by the COJ, dressed in distinctive red overalls, to reportedly fire on protestors and make arrests (Libération Afrique 2003). The Landless People's Movement protested aggressively on the day of national elections, 14 April 2004, resulting in 57 protestors being allegedly 'jailed and tortured' (APF 2005b). However, the COJ seemed to largely sidestep the underlying causes of these protests, namely the lack of appropriate housing policy, for many years (Pernegger 2020).

Fourth, middle-class protests about issues such as billing and traffic congestion also became prominent. Although hardly ever staged in the streets, these protests nonetheless took multiple forms and became increasingly protracted and well supported by the middle class, especially in the media, over this period.

An apparent lull in Johannesburg's service delivery street protests in 2005 – after their peak in 2004, with nearly half or 31 of the 71 protests in this period taking place in 2004 alone – may have been due to Mayor Masondo's promises of projects and budgets to improve informal settlement conditions in his *State of the City Address* (COJ 2005a). But perhaps it was the 2004 protests that contributed to the shift in the COJ's use of its almost solely task-based approach for the delivery of services to include more explicit, relationship-oriented elements. Certainly, the COJ's other systematic measures acknowledging the need to 'deepen democracy at a local level by building strong government institutions that are people oriented and sustainable' (COJ 2004e) may have reduced the number of protests. Here, the COJ introduced potentially more relationship-based formal and possibly agonistic participation channels seen as helpful in channelling protest, such as the new call centre, Joburg Connect, and people's centres in each of its Regions in 2001. The COJ also established the petitions management system in 2001 within the Petitions Unit, and its political oversight counterfoil of the Petitions and Public Participation Committee. Clearly, the petitions mechanism was the COJ's preferred protest channel as it took up 15 per cent of the mayor's first midterm address (COJ 2003c), and the COJ showcased the petitions system as an organisational strength in its first international bond offering in April 2004 (COJ 2004a). However, despite the petitions mechanism's potential to contribute to improved governance and community participation, it took off slowly as an alternative channel for street protestors. Over the period, it received about 100 petitions at the start, increasing to about 150 petitions per year, with approximately half of these calling for traffic-calming measures in specific middle-class suburbs and low-income townships (COJ 2003b).

Also, in 2001, as another way to connect with citizens more meaningfully, the COJ prepared guidelines for ward committees, consultative groups made up of members of community groups chaired by ward councillors, and started annual mayoral roadshows. Likewise, in 2003, the COJ embarked on an annual *Integrated Development Plan* outreach. The COJ's measures had variable outcomes due to their complexities, the influences of many factors and the COJ's minimal control over some of the elements that directly impact citizens (Mohamed 2010). Possibly as a concession to street protestors and in response to the underlying causes of protests in low-income areas, the COJ introduced its *Social Package* in 2004, offering free water and electricity, subsidised sanitation and refuse removal, and writing off of arrears incurred by indigent households (COJ 2005b). The COJ also announced an *Indigent Arrears Write-Off* scheme in 2005 to alleviate poverty in low-income households, but the APF criticised the COJ for being misguided and not tackling the human rights issues underlying the protests (APF 2005c).

Consistent responses in the maturation period (2006–2010)

Soon after the local government elections in March 2006, the COJ matured its governance model for improved integration of operations in line with the demands of its new *Growth and Development Strategy 2006* (COJ 2006b), seen as a more holistic strategy than *Joburg 2030*. The COJ separated executive and legislative functions, and consolidated its former 11 Offices of the Regions into seven, coordinated by the Planning Department, as well as tasking them with a more explicit urban management and community interaction role (COJ 2011v).

The particularly cold winter of 2007 in Johannesburg and the first post-apartheid recession in South Africa, ushering in the COJ's maturation period of 2006–2010, likely contributed to escalating street protests by low-income groups, with 174 increasingly violent protests identified during this period, more than double relative to the preceding five-year period. Protestors against the commodification of water and electricity joined forces for a few months in 2006 with the Landless People's Movement to protest the lack of housing and basic services in Orange Farm and Soweto, but also in informal settlements in the industrial areas of Marlboro and Wynberg. These protests largely evaporated after the Soweto Electricity Crisis Committee lodged its case against prepaid water meters in court. Thereafter, most of the protests in this period tended to be about the lack of basic services, housing and land. Traders protested throughout this period, mainly against the JMPD's enforcement of the informal trading by-laws, peaking in July 2007 and March 2010, and against exclusion from the 2010 FIFA World Cup event in South Africa in late 2010.

The middle class, meanwhile, continued to protest about billing issues. But it also protested about the proposed *By-Laws Relating to Dogs and Cats* in early 2006, traffic congestion, the alignment of the *Rea Vaya* (We Are Going) bus rapid transit system (for the provision of affordable mass public transport to combat pollution and congestion) through their suburbs of Saxonwold and Rosebank (see Map 6.1), potholes, and on-street paid-parking measures to deal with parking congestion.

The 2007 peak in frequently violent service delivery street protests in Freedom Park, Marlboro, Alexandra, Denver, Vlakfontein, Mandelaville, Phiri, Themb'elihle, Kliptown and Orange Farm, as well as in almost every other informal settlement across Johannesburg, compelled the COJ to develop a *Proposed Protocol for Dealing with Community Protests*. This protocol reinforced political accountability for the management of community tensions and proposed standard responses to manage citizen relationships during protest incidents according to the level of threat to properties and lives (COJ 2007g).

However, the most notable blaze of protest took place against foreigners in May 2008. These anti-foreigner attacks, often mingled with service delivery concerns, sparked initially in the eastern township of Alexandra and spread across townships and informal settlements in South Africa, resulting in over 60 deaths (Kirshner 2014). The state's ineffectual responses reportedly exacerbated these attacks (Misago et al. 2009): political leaders and the different spheres of government offered up 'contradictory responses ... did nothing ... [or] ... in other areas ... acted swiftly to stop violence' (Everatt 2011, p. 29). However, the COJ, with its Migrants' Help Desk in operation since 2006, promptly denounced the attacks (COJ 2008b) and apologised to foreigners (COJ 2009c). The COJ helped foreigners by setting up a joint operations centre with other parts of the state (COJ 2008d), formed partnerships with human rights and refugee support groups (COJ 2008b), and convened a meeting between Mayor Masondo, the Minister of Housing and 500 community representatives (*Mail & Guardian* 2008). Post-conflict, the COJ reintegrated displaced foreigners (COJ 2008n) and set up a Johannesburg Migration Advisory Committee (COJ 2009c).

Providing increased support to poor households according to their level of deprivation, Mayor Masondo briefed the press in June 2009 about the COJ's *Expanded Social Package* (ESP) or *Siyasizana* (*We Are*

Helping Each Other), available also to informal settlement residents and to non-account holders (COJ 2008j). Notwithstanding *Siyasizane*, more protests about poverty and inferior housing in Diepsloot, Ivory Park and Kliptown erupted, with the associated violence prompting a national minister to condemn violent protestors on 22 July 2009 for using 'illegal means to achieve their objective' (BBC News 2009). This destabilisation of low-income communities might also have been attributed to the disruptive effects of leadership changes at political and administrative levels. As Christine Walters, a councillor for the ANC and member of the Mayoral Committee holding a variety of portfolios in city politics since 1994, put it, 'you had a disturbance in the political environment'. She said she had a sense that until then, 'the ANC with the alliance [had] always managed the space' and that the former cohesiveness of the political party, civil society and communities had largely disintegrated (Walters 2012).

Politicians, the ruling party, the government and the administration blamed themselves and each other from 2009 for the street protests as if each entity of the state were entirely separate elements of the system of governance. Examples of the disintegration within, and the confusion between, the party, state and administrative roles played by political leaders were demonstrated in the national government's criticism of the ineffectiveness and irresponsibility of local government (news24 2009). President Zuma also insisted that the state get tough on government managers (South African Government News Agency 2010), as if to distance politicians from poorly performing officials, yet avoiding the reality that a significant number of senior officials were political appointees.

The COJ's functioning, including its Petitions Unit and the Petitions and Public Participation Committee, continued to mature steadily during this period. Petitions increased to about 250 per year by the end of the period. The concept of petitioning as a channel to protest, initially seen as a middle-class protest mechanism, gained currency in low-income areas. The COJ's petitions register shows that between July 2010 and June 2011, 44 per cent of all petitions had come from citizens of Region D, particularly in Soweto. Peter Kute, the assistant director of the Petitions Unit, stated that a further third of petitions linked directly to the same causes that underpinned street protests arising in other low-income areas. Complex and costly issues such as large-scale problems of housing shortages, evictions and poor living conditions were raised, as were other equally important issues affecting service delivery such as corruption. The Petitions Unit achieved some successes in the adoption of a 'walk with them' approach, according to Kute, the COJ working side by side with protesting petitioners to resolve the issues raised (Kute 2012a). But in practice, the COJ's potential turnaround time for some of the knottier problems could be as long as seven years, as in the housing demands made by petitioners from Kya Sands, just one of Johannesburg's informal settlements, due to the COJ's budgetary and capacity constraints. Simpler challenges, often related to traffic management issues, yielded more success, as with the angry Meadowlands petitioners; the COJ installed traffic-calming measures outside a local school to reduce the risk of more children being killed by speeding motorists (Kute 2012a).

The COJ proved that it could change its operations arising from its interactions with protestors. City officials learned hard lessons from conflictual interactions with taxi operators during the first two-year phase of implementation of the *Rea Vaya* BRT system (Wood 2014). Lisa Seftel, the COJ's Executive Director of Transportation, explained that the COJ developed, negotiated and agreed with affected participants a sophisticated codified conflict management system. Previous city–stakeholder conflict was translated into agonistic codes, with both parties supportive of the broad goals of the BRT system but not necessarily in agreement about the details of its implementation. Further, the department also put capacity in place to deal proactively with any new antagonistic aspects of conflict that this systematised approach could not deal with by appointing a Deputy Director of Safety for the project (Anonymous 2012c). But such systematisation was by no means standard across the COJ's operations. For instance, in its efforts to facilitate the regeneration of the Inner City and close down overcrowded and under-serviced buildings, it created temporary accommodation in an old building known as the MOTH Hall for residents evicted from buildings targeted for redevelopment. However, it was unable to manage this facility, ultimately contributing to the very situation that it sought to address (Pernegger 2020).

But some state–citizen engagements could not be aligned with agonistic principles. A planned *Regional Spatial Development Framework* workshop for Orange Farm in 2010, attended by 500–600 eager stakeholders, was overcome by antagonistic violence threatened by a small but highly militant group. A senior planner in the COJ's Development Planning and Urban Management Department responsible for planning in Regions D, E and G reported city officials had no option but to close the meeting after a colleague defused the situation. Ultimately, the plan was prepared by officials and approved by the council despite having had minimal input from Orange Farm residents (Strijdom 2012). The incident shows that the conversion of antagonistic engagement between the state and its citizens into an agonistic one is not always possible.

Further, despite the city administration's proclaimed initially open approach towards street protest, the JMPD reportedly imposed a blanket ban on all marches towards the end of this period (Duncan 2010). Nonetheless, this did not prevent some marches and at least a couple of street protests from still taking place, including a thousand-strong march to Mayor Masondo by street and market traders in May 2010 objecting to the lack of benefits accruing to the poor from the imminent FIFA World Cup event.

Consolidating responses in the bureaucratisation period (2011–2015)

The COJ's focus turned inwards in the build-up to the 2011 local government elections, observed Councillor Walters, possibly constraining its ability to exercise ingenuity in resolving conflicts. She recalled that Mayor Masondo's first term of office was characterised by 'a high level of energy, and the type of leadership that was really exemplary', but this vitality flagged during his second term; she noted that 'we started seeing people becoming tired … you started seeing the organisation having fatigue, and [it] became deeply bureaucratic' (Walters 2012). This inertia may have contributed to the COJ's reduced willingness to try out new approaches in state–society conflictual interactions. Rather, it continued to translate its previous experimental practices in dealing with protest into everyday practice, thus potentially improving its capacity to deal with protest more systematically despite ongoing evidence that citizens found these now routinised channels of protest ineffectual at addressing their concerns (Brown 2015).

By 2011, the start of this period of bureaucratisation, Johannesburg's city administration had become a multibillion-rand organisation consisting of 11 central departments, seven Offices of the Regions, 11 independent entities, 28,017 employees, and 260 councillors. Political oversight and administrative functions to attain strategic aims had become significantly more complex, multilayered and clustered (COJ 2014d). Despite Mayor Masondo's prominent claims in March 2011 about the COJ's real service delivery achievements in his outgoing *State of the City Address* (COJ 2011a), such as increasing access to water to 98 per cent and basic sanitation to 91 per cent of all households, service delivery protests about basic services, housing and land issues had become commonplace in almost every informal settlement and township from 2011 to 2013. The police's tragic shooting of Andries Tatane, a trader, during a service delivery protest in the Free State province in March 2013 sparked citizen outrage across South Africa. Tatane's death triggered far more and increasingly violent street protests in the country, nearly as many in the following two years as there were in the preceding five years (Municipal IQ 2012). Likewise, in Johannesburg, the number of protests about these same issues, as well as informal trading rights, between 2011 and 2013 alone was as high as in the entire previous five-year period. Even the middle class protested more, but mostly about billing, traffic management, potholes and paid parking.

Police used rubber bullets to disperse crowds and arrested protestors in immediate response to street protests, ever-more violent particularly after the massacre by police of striking miners in the Marikana mining town, 100 kilometres to the north-west of Johannesburg, in August 2012. City protestors sometimes stoned police and cars, torched properties and used barricades of burning tyres to block roads. The COJ, too, tended to be rather brusque, with the new executive mayor, Councillor Mpho Parks Tau, condemning 'mob violence' (COJ 2011t). As most of the protests were about housing, the Member of the Executive Council for Housing in the provincial government, Humphrey Mmemezi, responded with efforts to calm the sometimes hundreds of protestors by addressing them and holding mass hearings. Local street protests were lent increasing legitimacy by the Occupy Movement's mass mobilisation in New York in September 2011. However, the Minister of Police was swift to highlight the invidious role of the police in managing protests to be 'both nasty and nice' (DefenceWeb 2011) with well over 80 per cent of protests in South Africa reportedly violent (Chigwata et al. 2017).

At a more systematic level, the COJ adopted a 'business-unusual' approach (COJ 2011j), prioritising issues of inequality and citizen relationship management. The COJ adjusted and experimented with the institution, again making changes to improve service delivery and align the COJ's different structures with the themes and goals of *Joburg 2040 Growth and Development Strategy* (COJ 2011s). Further, the Development Planning and Urban Management directorate was split and the functions of the Offices of the Regions relocated to a new department called Citizen Relationship and Urban Management within the Office of the City Manager.

The COJ also emphasised, in mid-2012, the ideal of 'social inclusion' throughout its *Integrated Development Plan of 2012–2016*, certainly on paper, prioritising marginalised areas and aiming to ensure that Johannesburg would be 'a city where none go hungry' (COJ 2012f, p. 68). However, somewhat naively and revealing its disquiet about the ongoing service delivery protests, it also aimed in the same plan to 'eliminate protests' and see petitions decline steadily over a three-year period by 90 per cent from the 2012–2013 levels (COJ 2012f, p. 78). Nonetheless, showing the COJ's ongoing challenges with metropolitan governance, and call for more community participation in local ward committee and petitions processes, in practice the Petitions and Public Participation Committee expressed frustration that the petitions system was often undermined not just by officials, but by uncooperative ward councillors (Kute 2012a).

Again, in mid-2013, the deeply concerned COJ included the risks of street protests into its plans. In the *2013/16 Integrated Development Plan*, service delivery protests were listed as one of the COJ's top ten 'disaster hazards' (COJ 2013b, pp. 195–196). The COJ also made urgent arrangements for private security guards to protect councillors that had been attacked. The COJ's capacity to deal with protests remained a challenge, with high staff turnover rates reported especially in functions demanding a high degree of interaction with residents (COJ 2014d). In a more imaginative response to underlying spatial segregation partly driving protests in low-income communities, Mayor Tau announced the COJ's *Corridors of Freedom* initiative to reduce inequality in the city by improving spatial integration in his *State of the City Address* in May 2013 (COJ 2013f), resulting in animosity from middle-class landowners in targeted development areas (Pieterse 2014).

From the end of 2012 and throughout 2013, the One Voice for All Hawkers Association, the Workers and Socialist Party, the South African Informal Traders Forum, the African Traders Committee, and informal traders protested publicly around 14 times about police harassment, the lack of trading spaces, and infringements of their right to trade. Ultimately, the COJ's overly vigorous and disastrous enforcement and clean-up exercise in December 2013, *Operation Clean Sweep*, was challenged in the Constitutional Court, which instructed the COJ to allow traders to return to their trading sites in the Inner City.

In February 2014, the Gauteng police commissioner reported that 569 service delivery protests had taken place in the province in the previous three months alone, with one in five turning violent (*Daily Maverick* 2014). The South African Human Rights Commission's (2014) damning report to Parliament in March 2014 of the still dismal state of water and sanitation services in informal settlements, and politicians' contradictory statements about service delivery protests, did not bode well for the ANC in the upcoming May 2014 national elections. The ANC's poor election outcomes and its reduced share of provincial and city votes, down by 10 per cent on its 2009 position (*Business Day* 2014a), may have spurred the bureaucratisation and integration of existing measures across spheres of government to deal proactively with public protests and prioritise service delivery. Measures included the Gauteng Premier's Hotline and the coordination of service delivery concerns through the *Ntirhisano* (Working Together) war room (COJ 2015), a programme allowing for speedy intergovernmental trouble-shooting of service delivery problems, and the national government's emphasis on basic service delivery in its *Back to Basics* programme targeting municipalities.

The COJ increasingly formalised its processes for dealing with service delivery-related dissensus. For instance, its Visible Service Delivery Forum integrated the work of service departments, Offices of the Regions and ward councillors to address pressing issues in neighbourhoods. The COJ began to operationalise a programme of service charters and standards, develop a 'single window of coordination' for service delivery matters and focused on 'getting the basics right' (COJ 2014a, pp. 179 and 36 respectively). However, the COJ also tried to find less bureaucratic and more imaginative solutions to some problems as in its *Find & Fix* application of April 2014 used by the public to report potholes (Johannesburg Roads Agency 2015). The COJ also approved the setting up of an Ombudsman's office for citizens to approach when all other avenues about service delivery concerns had been exhausted.

Intuiting, possibly too late for the upcoming local government elections, that citizens might not necessarily repay the ANC's service delivery attainments in votes in light of their shifting expectations, as borne out by de Kadt and Lieberman's (2015) observations, Mayor Tau acknowledged the need to create a new state–society relationship. He announced the new *Jozi@Work* programme (or 'movement' as he called it) in August 2014, an economic empowerment project that tied low-income communities to public spending in targeted areas in a 'coproduction' service delivery model (COJ 2015). In May 2015, Mayor Tau emphasised again, in his *State of the City Address* (COJ 2015), that the COJ supported the 'back-to-basics' approach. He also promised that service delivery standards would be agreed with all service entities, with any failures being speedily dealt with through a coordinated central point, a hub that linked front-line departments for rapid response and also connected to the GPG's *Ntirhisano* war room (COJ 2015). However, although this period of bureaucratisation may have provided the COJ with capacity to deal with protests, it did not necessarily always yield effective outcomes. For instance, in the previously acclaimed petitions system, by July 2016, only 18 per cent (or 260) of the 1,446 petitions lodged since 2011 had been resolved (*Randburg Sun* 2016). Nonetheless, these proactive measures, Premier Makhura's proclaimed 'activist' government (GPG 2016a, p. 233) and the COJ's costly citizen relationship management (*The Star* 2014b), presumably contributed to the observed decline in the level of protests in Johannesburg in 2014 and 2015 (Chigwata et al. 2017).

Large-scale countrywide protests such as the anti-foreigner uprisings in March 2015 and the *#FeesMustFall* education-related protests in October 2015, although not directed at local government, as well as the ongoing service delivery protests in Johannesburg and South Africa, as recorded by Municipal IQ (2018), show the culture of protest endured beyond 2015. These protests possibly contributed to the ANC's loss of Johannesburg to the Democratic Alliance-led coalition council after the August 2016 elections.

Particularities of conflict management in Johannesburg

For Johannesburg's city administration to be agonistic, it needs to have a deep understanding of the richness and complexity of service delivery strife to be able to engage with protestors, irrespective of applying any agonistic principles. Responding to the many sorts of protest that unfolded between 1996 and 2015 meant the local-level state had to have sufficient capacity to deal with them, and even more capacity to do so agonistically. Unsurprisingly, the degree of agonism exercised was inconstant and not always effective, although some channels offered more prospects than others for agonistic interaction, such as the Petitions Unit's 'walk with them' strategy (Kute 2012a). Although there is a lack of detail on service delivery protest incidents, this chapter does provide some insights into the particularities of protest action in Johannesburg. Protests of all types intensified between 1996 and 2015, and bearing out national data, street protests increased in number and violence. The complexities of these protests showed an enormous variation across Johannesburg, in terms of spatial areas, specific themes and channels of protest. Protests by low-income groups may be distinct from those by the middle class, but they also share some similarities.

Most of the service delivery protests happened in low-income areas, reflective of significant service delivery challenges and the city's extreme inequality. In fact, 95 per cent of street protests observed in the data were concentrated in just six hotspots (see Map 3.1), but which are home to 57 per cent of the city's population (COJ 2008c; Quantec 2014). These hotspots were the Soweto and Alexandra townships, the settlements of Orange Farm, Diepsloot and Ivory Park, and the Inner City. These protestors used the relatively low-cost (to them) strategy of street-based protest extensively, sometimes resorting to violence. However, they also more rarely used other higher-cost channels, such as petitioning and the courts, often with the support of advocacy groups. Protestors targeted local government but also lobbied other spheres of government if they believed they might influence the outcome. The middle-class protests, although originating in the middle-class areas, were not necessarily as tied to space as low-income protests were, pointing to their different modes of protest and greater mobility choices. The middle class preferred to utilise any channel other than street protest, although rare exceptions are recorded.

The service most likely to be the subject of dissent in low-income communities was a lifeline or essential service, such as water or electricity provision, or job-related services needed in order to survive. However, the rate-paying middle class located in the wealthier northern suburbs (but increasingly in some township areas such as Soweto too) implicitly acknowledged that basic services had already been delivered to them and protested about added-value services that support a desired quality of life such as billing, road maintenance, planning or paid-parking provision. Looking to the underlying themes of protests, these were multifaceted and complex in low-income areas but single-issue-based in middle-class areas.

The scale of protest by low-income groups varied between a few people to groups of hundreds of people when staged in the streets, with the participant numbers likely to decline as higher-cost channels were turned to. However, even small street protests could have significant reach when covered by the media. Representative groups, if any, were unclear and fluctuated over time. Middle-class protestors had easier access to multiple channels of protest such as email, press and social media, including chat apps; not only was it easy to organise protests, but literally thousands found it relatively easy to protest. Role-players driving middle-class protests were easily identifiable and tended to feature consistently in the protests over time relative to their low-income counterparts. Duration-wise, protests by both the low-income and middle-class groups ranged from a few hours to several days, and recurred over weeks, months and years.

A few insights into the city administration's responses to protests are offered. The city administration responded at more than one level and through more than one part of the city administration, with each part having its own imperatives and attitudes towards protest, which resulted in inconstant and ambiguous responses. To the protest incident itself, the enforcement agencies, namely the JMPD from 2001, sometimes with the national police (except in the case of middle-income protests), the ward councillor, the Office of the Region, the Petitions Unit, the service entity and political representatives from other relevant spheres of government with local-level responsibilities directed initial responses to individual protest incidents. Then, later, the service entity, members of the Mayoral Committee, policymakers, planners, legal advisors, affected departments and other relevant spheres of government responded to the collective effects and issues underlying the contention. It is apparent the city administration experienced a constant struggle to maintain an appropriate balance between the empowerment of citizens in line with developmental local government principles and the delivery of services to customers on a cost-recovery and sustainability basis. The temporal aspect of the city administration's responses to protest, either immediately (often antagonistic) or later (more likely to be agonistic, or at least responsive), is not considered in literature on agonism in practice. Further, while there were distinct sets of protests, these did not necessarily correlate with set patterns of responses by the city administration.

The city administration seemed mostly conflict-averse, focused as it was on the enormous service delivery challenge facing the city. While street protests by low-income groups were a low-cost strategy to express objections, motives for objections could be challenging for the city administration to decipher and respond to appropriately. Further, the sheer number of protests, their intricacies, unique community and area dynamics, and timings and contexts of protests resulted in incomplete political and administrative responses unsuited to agonistic interactions. In some circumstances, the city administration may have viewed its antagonistic or forcible response as appropriate, as in when it saw no other course but to respond firmly to the Sandton rates boycott's potential damage to its financial viability and sustainable city development, or when violent protestors threatened lives and damaged property. Sometimes the protestors' antagonism needed to play out before any agonistic interaction could be considered, as in the case of protest against the city's planning outreach for the *Regional Spatial Development Framework* for Orange Farm in 2010. Fatigue and the destabilisation effect of organisational restructurings may have weakened the city administration's ability and desire to be experimental, prerequisites for agonistic interactions.

In the longer-term responses to underlying issues, many varied and incremental impacts on the city administration's policies, agenda and structure are evident. However, responses might not have always been directly attributed to any specific protest, but rather to a critical collective of protests about a specific theme or community. Responses may not have been consistent or instantaneous either. Such responses to city strife include the partial restructuring of the city administration for improved service delivery, adjustments to projects and plans, and the allocation of more resources to specific issues under contention.

Further, service delivery protests made the city administration extended and improved its range of more structured channels for protest and potentially agonistic strife, such as the petitions system and the Petitions Unit, and regular participation processes for the *Integrated Development Plan* and other project and planning exercises. However, limits to these channels were plain in their reliance on protestors and state actors having the appropriate resources to use them, and the city administration's operations being harmonised across its various sectors. Sometimes the local-level state's response to a protest provoked an unanticipated reaction from the target community, triggering more protest rather than creating any temporary understanding between protestors and the state.

Quite possibly, an agonistic interaction may not always have been in the best interest of residents as it may have been antagonistic conflict itself that provoked changes to the city administration, as in the Sandton rates boycott. Such antagonism did not always yield positive outcomes, as in the case of the COJ's court-forced relocation of Inner City evictees to a temporary facility that subsequently fell into disrepair. Sometimes, however, antagonism could impede interactive initiatives, as in the instance of the *Regional Spatial Development Framework* plan that had to be prepared by the COJ's officials in isolation from the Orange Farm community's input due to the disruption of the planned participation session by antagonistic protestors.

The timeline of the city administration's organisational evolution revealed key facets of agonistic practice. Action–reaction interactions of state–society conflict were not at all linear processes. However, the overarching organisational orientation towards conflict in the democratic city administration appears to be largely anti-conflict other than in the 1990s, despite a seeming shift and grudging acceptance of the necessity for conflict management capacity. However, the city administration overlooked conflict management as an opportunity for transformation, boding poorly for prospects of agonistic conflict management. Nonetheless, there were multiple smaller responses, within this broad shift away from potentially agonistic conflict management, towards a more conflict-averse approach. In the earlier periods, despite great institutional and policy fluidity, and possibly because of the overarching dynamic negotiations in the 1990s about the shape of the new local government structures and post-apartheid goodwill, the city administration's emphasis was geared more towards experimentation and relationship-building, yielding more agonistic interactions, although arguably not as many as one might have expected.

In later periods, though, the city administration focused more on the implementation of tasks for service delivery and arguably less on relationship-building, increasingly routinising its processes after 2008 in regard to its immediate responses to protests. This created more standardised capacity for engaging in strife but also made the city less innovative in these interactions. Less prospects for agonistic interactions were evident, other than a few examples, such as the 'walk with them' strategy at resolving petitions (Kute 2012a). As the later periods were characterised by more and increasingly violent protests than earlier periods, they needed greater attention from the city administration. But although more responses were needed, the resources to do so remained largely unchanged. Certainly, the literature on agonism does not mention the organisation's orientation towards task or relationship management as a factor in its ability to act agonistically, although Blake et al.'s (1964) work implies that a relationship-building orientation for organisations might better serve agonistic practices. Evidently, the city administration's maturation was not matched by a progressive drawing on of agonistic principles in strife, suggesting that the development of agonistic capabilities needs to be consciously created and built over time.

In closing, it is impossible to provide a wall-to-wall timeline of the responses to all strife in Johannesburg due to data limitations. However, the democratic city administration's evolving efforts at governance hint at broad shifts between agonism and antagonism in its immediate and longer-term responses to the enormous variety of continually changing themes and trends in service delivery protests by low-income and middle-class groups. It displayed its largely anti-protest mindset yet made considerable and meaningful attempts to try out, systematise and revise ways of interacting with processes of dissensus. This broad outline masks intricate micro-instances of unique and long-standing conflicts between the city administration's unsynchronised parts and its local citizens. The next three chapters provide detailed narratives that deepen our understanding of the extraordinary complexity of intractable state–society strife. These stories, on the water wars in the low-income settlement of Orange Farm, the informal trading struggles on the streets of the Inner City, and the billing backlash by middle-class residents, will fill in many gaps in this incomplete picture.

Note

1. Some of the material in this chapter was published in Pernegger (2014).

·4·
Water wars of Orange Farm

Overwhelmed by urbanisation at the periphery

Picture a city with a population of around 200,000 people – perhaps
Aberdeen in Scotland, Gleiwitz in Poland or San Bernardino in
California. Now imagine Orange Farm, an informal settlement, also
with 200,000 residents, sprawled over 30 square kilometres and situated 40 kilometres south of downtown Johannesburg. But instead of
being developed over hundreds of years, Orange Farm has, in less than
three decades, grown from an orange orchard in the 1980s and home
to a handful of farming families, to Johannesburg's largest and newest
settlement on its periphery, with the city administration only recently
accepting and beginning to invest in it as a legitimate urban area. This
story shows how the city administration responded to the 'water wars'
(Bond 2004a) waged by Orange Farm residents, as well as to other service delivery protests, between 1996 and 2015. Initially overwhelmed
by this and other similar settlements' extraordinarily rapid growth star-
ing in the late 1980s, the city administration hardly responded to the
earliest protests, becoming increasingly antagonistic until 2008 when it
became more overtly responsive to dissenters' concerns.

Orange Farm's story starts in South Africa's 1980s. Apartheid meant
the state provided no plans to accommodate black residents in cities
other than in extensions to existing townships. The resultant crisis of
black homelessness led to 'hidden' urbanisation, especially prevalent
in the southern parts of current-day Johannesburg, which had become
home to displaced farmworkers and others unable to find or afford
accommodation within the established townships in the south of the
city, such as Soweto and Lenasia (well documented by Black Sash
1989; Crankshaw 1993; Guillaume and Houssay-Holzschuch 2002;
Stevens and Rule 1999). In the disassembly of apartheid, however, the
state acknowledged the enormity of hidden urbanisation in the *White
Paper on Urbanisation* of April 1986 and sought pragmatic solutions for
an 'orderly urbanisation' by sanctioning 'controlled squatting' (RSA
1986b, pp. 19 and 20–21). Many more national and provincial proc-
lamations followed, allowing organised squatting in the Orange Farm
area. By December 1988, the state had settled the first 600 families in
the area, voluntarily and forcibly, from nearby farms and other areas in

the city (Crankshaw 1993). Only in 1993 did the state officially name the settlement Orange Farm (RSA 1993a).

Orange Farm to this day remains isolated spatially and economically from the rest of Johannesburg (see Maps 1.1 and 4.1). Orange Farm falls within the former statutory green belt of agricultural land that separated the urban conurbation of Johannesburg in apartheid times from smaller industrial towns even further south. Johannesburg's southernmost tip, or the Deep South as the local-level state dubbed it, is home to about three-quarters of the city's informal settlements, such as Themb'elihle, Vlakfontein, Hospital Hill, Finetown and Poortje, to mention a few, with Orange Farm the largest in population terms (see Map 4.1) (COJ 2001c). This sense of isolation is reinforced by the pre-existing income and racially based north–south divide already obvious in 1960s Johannesburg caused by the east–west topographical barrier of former mining land (Beall et al. 2002), and the lack of urban development and employment centres along most of the passenger rail and the main highway route between Orange Farm and the city centre. By the time of the creation of the first democratic local government in South Africa in 1996, Orange Farm's unemployment was at 50 per cent (Quantec 2014), representing one of the largest concentrations of poverty in the city. Amidst the dissolving apartheid governance structures, the local-level state was completely unprepared to address rapid urbanisation's governance requirements and the streams of people, predominantly black, settling in their thousands in Orange Farm.

Planning for black communities was initially a national government function during apartheid. Then, as international pressure against apartheid mounted, the national Constitutional Development and Planning Department devolved the function of the development of black communities in 1987 to the Transvaal Provincial Administration (TPA) (RSA 1987), including the responsibility of relocating 'squatters' to Orange Farm. The TPA was by then a loose incorporation of various former segregated and fragmented local and regional governance functions. It remained largely in disarray until its reconstitution as the new GPG after the 1994 national democratic local elections (Lodge 2005). Despite the TPA's apartheid conservatism, it was prepared to engage constructively with 'squatters' about development in April 1989 in a 'humane fashion' (South African Institute of Race Relations 1990, pp. 238–239 of 1461). The TPA could provide only limited basic services (Crankshaw and Hart 1990). However, no service delivery protests in Orange Farm were recorded, possibly as protest focused on apartheid issues throughout the late 1980s and early to mid-1990s. Further, many Orange Farm residents thought then the settlement was a dream come

Map 4.1 – Orange Farm locational features and informal housing

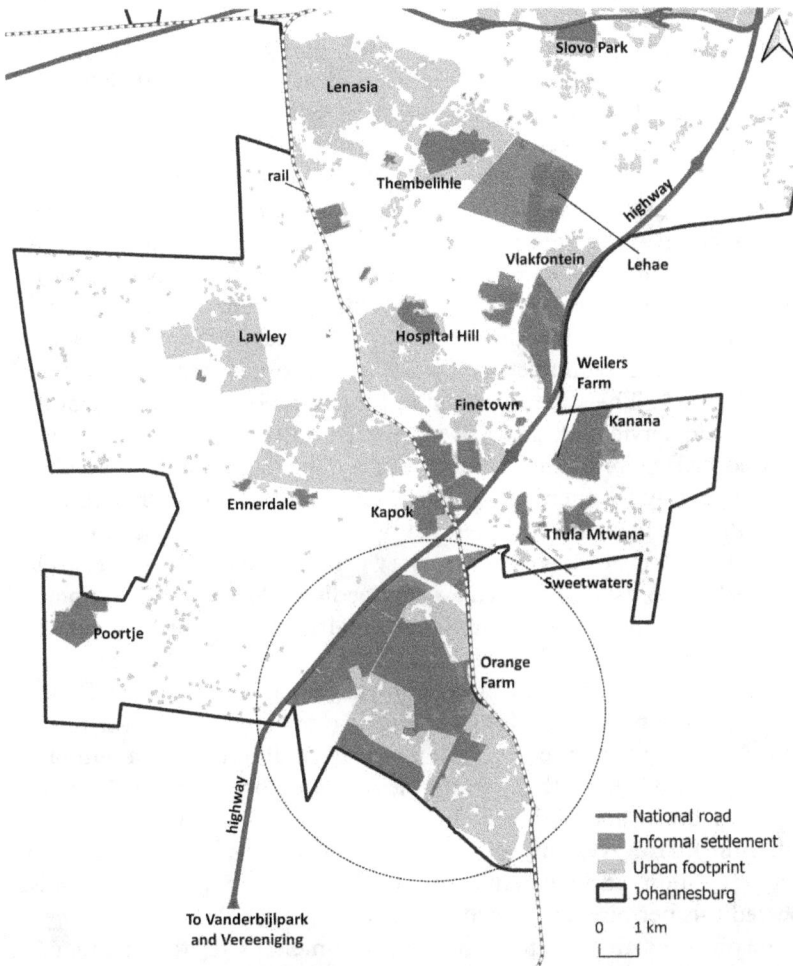

Note: The greatest extent of formal housing is between the rail line and highway in the north of the settlement and the lowest is at the southern tip.

Source: Author's formulation

true, with conditions better than elsewhere (Crankshaw and Hart 1990; Mtshelwane 1989). Orange Farm symbolised a move away from apartheid, allowing black South Africans to own homes (Hindson 1987). Here, black residents were not persecuted, but had secure tenure, more services than in other 'squatter areas', a school, a crèche, and access to public rail transport (Crankshaw and Hart 1990). Even the TPA was optimistic that Orange Farm could be one of the first 'cities of the future' (TPA 1990, p. 68).

The state's earliest governance efforts of Orange Farm between 1989 and 1995 were minimal, jumbled and overtaken by other transition processes. Initially, the TPA engaged with the local church and the residents committee only (Crankshaw and Hart 1990), although this eight-man committee allegedly did not represent the community's interests (Mtshelwane 1989). In 1990, the TPA formalised local governance arrangements for Orange Farm and promulgated regulations for its control and management (Province of Transvaal 1990). The TPA also announced it would serve as the interim local authority, making local development decisions and taking advice from the Orange Farm Informal Committee, set up according to new regulations (*The Sowetan* 1990). The state soon realised it could not provide the standard of basic services in areas of controlled squatting to match those provided elsewhere in the city and nor would their residents be able to afford to pay for them (RSA 1990). By 1992, the initially enthusiastic TPA had become overwhelmed by the 'abnormal proportions' of Orange Farm's growth; it compared its work to 'a boat which finds itself in rapids' (TPA 1992, pp. 7 and 49). Needing administrative support, the TPA appointed consultants, Municipal Management Services, in July 1993 (Naidoo 2010). The TPA also proclaimed at the same time more substantial formal governance arrangements for Orange Farm. The TPA gave permission for Orange Farm to establish its own Black Local Authority (Province of Transvaal 1993), although such authorities symbolised the controls of apartheid (Cameron 2002), with many already at the brink of financial and administrative collapse (Bennet et al. 1986). However, any concerns were swept away 18 months later when transition arrangements for new local government structures repealed this permission (Province of Gauteng 1995c).

The post-apartheid state saw local government as key to implementing its *Reconstruction and Development Programme* (RSA 1994), tabled by President Mandela in Parliament in November 1994. The new state refashioned new Metropolitan Local Councils from the various former local authorities. Orange Farm fell then briefly under the jurisdiction of the newly proclaimed Vaal Transitional Metropolitan Council and its Northern Vaal Transitional Metropolitan Sub-Structure (Province of Transvaal 1993). However, only eight months later, on 1 September 1995, Orange Farm was incorporated under the jurisdiction of the provisional and independent GJTMC and its local counterpart of the Southern Metropolitan Substructure. This arrangement was in preparation for the first local government elections for Johannesburg. On 1 November 1995, the entities of the GJMC and the SMLC came into being (Province of Gauteng 1995a, 1995b). By the end of 1995, the SMLC had taken its first steps to assembling an interim management team to take over the TPA's functions in Orange Farm, led by three local councillors, with institutional support drawn from the five former administrations active in the area and the TPA's consultants (SMLC 1995).

Despite the confusion of governance by the nearly 20 different organisations in the first seven years of Orange Farm's existence, while its population grew steeply, the 1996 official census data (Quantec 2014) showed the state had somehow provided the then 31,152 households and 124,507 people with limited services. However, the standards were inferior to elsewhere in Johannesburg. For instance, although everyone had access to water, only 18 per cent of households had a tap in the dwelling; the rest used taps in their yards (37 per cent), communal taps (41 per cent) and other forms of water provision (4 per cent). Further, although everyone had access to sanitation, only 28 per cent had flush or chemical toilets in their house; others used pit latrines (65 per cent) or other forms of sanitation (7 per cent). Although three-quarters of all households lived in shacks, the settlement's roads were ungraded, and the quality and quantity of water and sanitation services left much to be desired, this did not detract from Orange Farm's popularity. Indeed, its population continued to grow.

The *Reconstruction and Development Programme* assured citizens that water is 'an indivisible national asset belonging to all South Africans'; its aim for the supply of water was to ensure 'some for all rather than all for some' (RSA 1994, pp. 8 and 80). Affirming the user-pays approach, it also noted that the 'principle of payment for services is fundamental to the implementation of the RDP, with due cognizance given to poverty, administrative constraints and an equitable and fair default procedure' (RSA 1994, p. 19). The ANC's *Masakhane* (Let's Build Together) campaign reinforced this payment principle (ANC 1995). The programme also raised citizens' expectations by making numerous commitments to specific development and redistribution goals to overcome apartheid's legacy (Pillay et al. 2006). It stated citizens would have a say in the management of water. It was this promise by the *Reconstruction and Development Programme* that was to play a major role in the water wars over the decades to come, with a fifth of all protests originating in Orange Farm, the second most vocal community in Johannesburg after Soweto, by count of protests.

Excluding the city's edge (1996–2000)

During the city administration's transition period between 1996 and 2000, its governance practices may have included some hints of agonism, but this was not evident in Orange Farm. The SMLC and the GJMC found it virtually impossible to plan for the still steeply growing population located at its southernmost tip, the so-called poor relegated to living at the edges of cities and the 'excluded outsiders' (according to Murray 2008, p. 96). Certainly, their economic prospects were unlikely to improve, with over 60 per cent of Orange Farm's households living below the national official poverty line of R840 ($177) per household per month at the time (GJMC 1996). Competition for jobs in the city was fierce. Although unskilled workers in Johannesburg made up about 90 per cent of the service sector, the changing city economy demanded increasingly sophisticated skills and the number of jobs was declining in virtually every economic sector during this period (Beall et al. 2002). Amenities, too, were minimal in Orange Farm. For instance, the closest school was 7 kilometres away and the nearest clinic was over 10 kilometres to the north (GJMC 1996).

The reality of the enormity of the budget required to address the lack of services and homelessness hit home within months after the local government elections. The SMLC sought funds for urgent infrastructure projects in Orange Farm in May and June 1996 (SMLC 1996a, 1996c). In June 1996, the national government, concerned about the lack of resources to implement the *Reconstruction and Development Programme* and having already closed the programme's office in April 1996 (Pillay et al. 2006), began to pursue a new macroeconomic strategy, *Growth, Employment and Redistribution (GEAR)*, hoping to drive up national economic growth to fund the programme's promises (RSA 1996). The state expected absolutely everyone to pay for services; even Orange Farm was targeted for a *Masakhane* workshop in September 1996 (ANC 1997; SMLC 1996b).

The Orange Farm community, impatient with the lack of services, began to resist the state's user-pays approach. By the end of 1996, the first two water-related protests in Orange Farm had taken place. In one, a group of women marched to the Office of the Mayor, undressing to mark their defiance against the state's mandatory prepaid water meter installations in Orange Farm, part of the World Bank's suggested financial restructuring initiative for service delivery in the early 1990s (Bond 1998). These protestors were among others countrywide increasingly expressing resentment against what they saw as the encroachment of the global capitalist system on human rights. Two national ministries announced contradictory policies in May 1997: one aimed to provide free 'lifeline' water; the other endorsed cost-recovery principles (Bond 1998). Unsurprisingly, township activists protested, sometimes violently, in Gauteng and two other provinces between July and September 1997 against the local government's inflexible cost-recovery measures, including the cutting off of basic services for non-payment (Bond 1998). Meanwhile, in October 1997, the SMLC continued to struggle to supply infrastructure to meet the need for services in Orange Farm. For instance, the SMLC's search for capital funds for the construction of a critical sewer project in October 1997 (SMLC 1997a) was abruptly halted by the crisis of the city administration's imminent insolvency (Emdon 1998).

The enormity of the city administration's financial crisis shocked the new councillors (Beall et al. 2002). The crisis forced city leaders to take corrective measures by June 1998, including stopping any new projects and cutting that year's capital budget by two-thirds (Emdon 1998). Recovery prospects remained gloomy as the Sandton rates boycotters continued to withhold rates payments, further handicapping investment in the city from mid-1996 (Emdon 1998). Only when the Constitutional Court upheld the city administration's 'one city, one tax base' policy, its way to unite the geographically polarised city, in October 1998, was it then able to implement its service delivery approach. The GJMC also used the crisis as an opportunity allegedly to motivate for the radical restructuring of city institutions to be more financially stable (Beall et al. 2002). Significantly, the GJMC responded to the rising dissatisfaction of poor citizens' exclusion from the benefits of the new democracy by the end of 1998. It launched a citywide *Indigency Management Policy* to provide subsidies to poor households for the first 10 kilolitres of water provided (Mazibuko vs City of Johannesburg et al. 2009). This policy had limited success only as the GJMC encountered operational challenges during its implementation (COJ 2004d). This was due, in part, to the high degree and uncertainty of Orange Farm's continued incorporation into Johannesburg's boundaries, even as late as at the end of 1998. The city administration still debated whether Orange Farm's inclusion made any sense, until the need for certainty of governance compelled the state to finalise the boundaries, reconfirming its inclusion in the city (Emdon 1998).

It was evident to the GJMC that it had to do more to ensure financial sustainability. The plan it developed was *iGoli 2002* (GJMC 1999d), which centralised the core city management functions and corporatised the service delivery entities responsible for the provision of water, electricity, refuse collection and other services. This corporatisation aspect of the plan fanned anti-privatisation sentiment. *iGoli 2002* called for the restructuring and streamlining of city functions, meaning that, again, the administration had to cut its budgets, this time for the next three years. That meant, for instance, only R44 million ($7.29 million) in capital funds was available for the 2000/01 financial year for the entire city, in contrast with the R10 billion ($0.83 billion) peak in capital budget planned for 2015 (COJ 2015), so no investments in backlog infrastructure were possible anywhere, least of all in Orange Farm. Another key thrust of *iGoli 2002* was to identify savings. One way to achieve this was for the administration to overcome water losses, so providing appropriate water infrastructure became a critically important initiative. *iGoli 2002* also noted the importance of the concept of running the city administration as a business, labelling its relationship with residents as customers rather than as citizens.

In October 1999, the water reservoir supplying Orange Farm ran dry (SMLC 2000b). Many residents there were without water for six weeks until the SMLC, Rand Water and the adjacent Lekoa-Vaal Metropolitan Council could provide short-term water tankers, with a longer-term solution needing an estimated R187 million ($30.42 million) (SMLC 2000b). The anti-privatisation lobby resisted the announced agreement between the GJMC and a private sector water services company by the end of 1999 to work together to supply water, seeing this move as another against pro-poor service provision (Beall et al. 2002). Protestors staged a peaceful blockade of the main route into Orange Farm about the proposed installation of prepaid water meters.

Despite its financial constraints, the SMLC, sometimes with the provincial government, tried to formalise Orange Farm, making small inroads into various housing, planning, land and infrastructure challenges (COJ 2001b; SMLC 1996a, 1996d, 1997a, 1997b, 1997c, 1998a, 1998c, 1999b, 2000a). The SMLC and the GJMC also tried to boost economic development in Orange Farm. They created a small market for informal traders, prioritised discussions for integrated public transport management, and facilitated shopping centre development (GJMC 1999e; SMLC 1998b, 1999a).

However, it was clear by 2000 that Orange Farm, as indeed most parts of Johannesburg, needed far more investment in over-extended infrastructure. The financial crisis and the shortfall in infrastructure provided the GJMC and the MLCs with the impetus to merge its many parts into a single metropolitan entity in 2000 to better deliver services (Beall et al. 2002), and justified its focus on fiscal sustainability, cost-recovery and water-saving actions. Despite being legally incorporated into Johannesburg since 1995, the city administration largely omitted the Deep South and Orange Farm as part of the city, by not planning and budgeting for its development, and only gradually and grudgingly took on this responsibility in future periods. This lack of responsiveness by the city administration to Orange Farm residents' needs, although other parts of the state were delivering services to them, meant it failed to initiate or build state–society relationships. However, hints of the city administration's agonistic engagements with other groups were evident during this period (see Chapter 5).

Antagonism in the water wars (2001–2005)

As the COJ metropolitan municipality began the five-year process of institutional consolidation between 2001 and 2005, other parts of the state had already made enormous strides in providing access to water and sanitation services in Orange Farm. The state more than doubled the number of water connections; it now supplied 77 per cent (or 36,800) of all households with water to the house or yard (Quantec 2014). This delivery outstripped Orange Farm's population growth of 31 per cent to 163,250 people, and the 53 per cent growth in household numbers to 47,813 dwellings, between 1996 and 2001. Although 97 per cent of households had access to some form of sanitation, some 42 per cent now had access to flush and chemical toilets while others continued to use pit latrines and other forms of sanitation. Formal dwellings, too, now made up 60 per cent, or 28,643, of all households (Quantec 2014). Nonetheless, residents saw this progress as inadequate. Between 2001 and 2005, the newly consolidated COJ faced a fourfold increase in service delivery protests in the city compared to the previous five-year period; half were about water services alone in Orange Farm. In 2001, the new Office of Region 11, one of the COJ's 11 sub-areas of jurisdiction reporting to the core executive team in the city centre offices, was responsible for Orange Farm's hands-on daily management. Johannesburg Water, the stand-alone corporatised entity of the COJ, also started operations in January 2001 in line with the *iGoli* 2002 plan to deliver water and sanitation services. The COJ continued to seem indifferent to objections about the corporatisation of water (van Rooyen et al. 2009). The COJ was 'dismissive' of the APF's opposition to the plan and its expressed anti-capitalist sentiment; this antipathy was reportedly mutual (COJ 2001a, p. 73).

The COJ's long-range plans for informal settlements and their servicing needs were contradictory. Although it acknowledged citizens had the right of access to housing, its first strategic plan to include Orange

Farm and the Deep South in 2001, the *Spatial Development Framework* described Orange Farm as a 'liability' (COJ 2001c, p. 13), due to its unsuitable location at the city's periphery. Johannesburg's planned north–south development corridor did not even extend southwards beyond the city centre, reinforcing Orange Farm's spatial and economic isolation. Unemployment in Orange Farm ranged between the official rate of 58 per cent and the COJ's estimate of 70 per cent in 2001 (COJ 2004b; Quantec 2014), meaning that its residents were unable to pay for the minimal services they received. The COJ saw these poor communities in the Deep South as 'net spenders rather than contributors for rates' (Beall et al. 2002, pp. 78–79). As the COJ claimed informal settlements were temporary, pending their relocation, and cost recovery of services was unlikely, service levels provided should be minimal (COJ 2001a). City councillors observed the state's investment at the time was limited and poorly coordinated (Radebe 2012; Walters 2012). In February 2001, the Minister of Water Affairs and Forestry, Ronnie Kasrils, announced the provision of free water to each indigent household (RSA 2001). In response, Johannesburg Water planned to supply the 6 kilolitre free monthly allocation per household as part of a broader package of free services, which the COJ was to approve only a year later (COJ 2004d).

In June 2001, Johannesburg Water began to plan to reduce the unaccounted-for water losses that cost the COJ R323 million ($40.11 million) annually (COJ 2006e). These losses were most prevalent in Soweto, Orange Farm and in informal settlements. Johannesburg Water proposed to repair and replace damaged infrastructure and residential plumbing at its own cost. It also planned to ensure the provision of the free water allocation and to reduce future financial losses by installing prepaid meters from mid-July 2001 to low-income areas (van Rooyen et al. 2009). This decision met with much criticism from activists, namely that the state commodified water for profit at the expense of the poor rather than treating it as a human right (Fiil-Flynn and Soweto Electricity Crisis Committee 2001). Worldwide anti-globalisation sentiment ran high, as marked by protests against the World Summit on Sustainable Development in August 2002 in Johannesburg (as we saw in Chapter 3). Johannesburg Water's sharp tariff increases and increased cut-offs of services to non-paying households exacerbated tensions (McKinley 2003). The COJ piloted its first prepaid meters successfully in Orange Farm in 2002, which informed the design of its future water projects (McKinley 2003). However, activists accused the COJ of lying about the levels of participation and agreement with the community about the meters (Smith 2006). Dissenters also censured the COJ for installing prepaid meters under the guise of supplying new water systems to households that had never had water in the past, forcing poor residents into payment systems they could not afford (Naidoo 2010), and planning to use prepaid meters to enable service cut-offs for future non-paying customers (McKinley 2003).

To campaign against prepaid water meters, protestors created the Orange Farm Water Crisis Committee in 2002. Led by Bricks Makolo, the Committee staged many of the clashes in the water wars (Naidoo 2010), as well as protesting about the commodification of other services, poor quality of life, and lack of jobs (Bond 2004b). The Committee frequently joined other grassroots movements – the Soweto Electricity Crisis Committee and the APF – in these struggles (Wafer 2005). Trevor Ngwane, a former ward councillor expelled from the ANC for opposing the *iGoli 2002* plan, headed the APF, which was linked with at least 20 other activist groups, including the Soweto Electricity Crisis Committee and the Orange Farm Water Crisis Committee, all sharing similar anti-capitalist ideologies (APF 2007a). The Committee marched, held rallies, campaigned in the media and took legal action against the COJ (McKinley 2003). In response, the COJ replaced its former 1998 *Indigency Management Policy* with the *Special Cases Policy* (COJ 2004d). This made the COJ one of the first municipalities in South Africa to provide the poor with an allocation of free basic water and electricity, free sanitation and refuse removal services, and limited free health services. As part of this package, the COJ also implemented a zero assessment rate for properties valued below R20,001 ($2,708), meaning that residents in informal settlements and in some parts of townships in effect did not pay rates to the city administration (Savage et al. 2003).

However, the COJ was still adamant it would reduce unaccounted-for water losses and provide minimum free water citywide, especially to areas that had not yet had water, or metered water, before. The COJ launched its extensive and politically endorsed *Operation Gcin'Amanzi* (Save Water) in July 2003 to achieve these goals (Pillay et al. 2006). *Operation Gcin'Amanzi* initially targeted one of Soweto's suburbs, Phiri, because unaccounted-for water losses there were extraordinarily high at 68 per cent (van Rooyen et al. 2009). At that time, Sowetan households paid a monthly flat rate for unmetered water (Mazibuko vs City of Johannesburg et al. 2009), meaning some consumed far more water than they paid for, and hence they resisted *Operation Gcin'Amanzi*. Unsurprisingly, informal settlement residents also were the most dissatisfied residents in Johannesburg according to a 2003 survey by the COJ, with the gap between the importance of water and sanitation services and satisfaction levels twice that encountered in other parts of the city (COJ 2004d). However, despite the COJ recognising the extremely limited social services and infrastructure of the

Deep South area encompassing most of the city's informal settlements in its *Regional Spatial Development Framework* (COJ 2003e), it allocated only a negligible 4 per cent of its capital budget in 2003 to the whole of Region 11. To appreciate the magnitude of the investment needed in services, the upgrading of Orange Farm's gravel roads alone needed R173 million ($16.87 million), but the COJ allocated just R13.9 million ($1.36 million) to all of Orange Farm, a mere 1 per cent share of the COJ's capital budget relative to 5 per cent of the city's population (COJ 2002b, 2003e; Quantec 2014).

The structure of the water tariff announced by Johannesburg Water mid-2003 for the forthcoming year also drove dissensus in Orange Farm. The tariff purportedly prejudiced the poor with its inordinately high increase of 32 per cent for the lowest-but-one step of the rising block tariff. However, although wealthier consumers using greater amounts of water could easily have borne greater price increases, the increases for the higher consumption steps were far more modest (between −2 and 14 per cent) (Dugard 2010). Despite higher water prices and the roll-out of *Operation Gcin'Amanzi*, the resultant income was not enough to ward off the auditors' discovery that Johannesburg Water was bankrupt, in September 2003 (van Rooyen et al. 2009).

During 2003, the Orange Farm Water Crisis Committee, with the support of the APF and Ngwane, aggressively countered the COJ's *Operation Gcin'Amanzi* with its own *Operation Vulamanzi* (Open Water). The Committee blocked installations of new water meters, ripping them out or bypassing them, and illegally reconnected dissenting households directly to the water supply system (Coalition Against Water Privatisation et al. 2004). The COJ took a dim view of the APF's alleged 'bullying' of non-protesting residents to join the protests and its political tactics (van Rooyen et al. 2009, p. 64). In one instance, the COJ and Johannesburg Water felt they had no option but to obtain an interdict against the protestors (van Rooyen et al. 2009), and called on the police and the Red Ants private security firm to forcibly stop protestors' destructive actions (APF 2003). Xolile George, the Regional Director of the Office of Region 11, in the line of fire of service delivery protestors in Orange Farm and other areas in the Deep South between 2003 and 2006, acknowledged these protests were about 'political posturing' as much as they were also valid grievances that fell within 'the realm of human rights' (George 2012).

Eventually, by 2004, given that the COJ had already formalised 47 informal settlements, with the state providing thousands of houses, the COJ had to concede that 'settlements are permanent and will not face relocation in the future' (COJ 2004e, p. 7 of 17). However, Mayor Masondo was quick to point out in his *2004 State of the City Address* that resources were constrained (COJ 2004e). For instance, the COJ could promise improvements to only less than a tenth of households in informal areas in Johannesburg between 2004 and 2006. But for the first time, the COJ publicly earmarked Orange Farm among others for development.

The COJ again tried to popularise the installation of prepaid meters in fractious townships and informal settlements by writing off long-standing services arrears through its *Indigent Arrears Write-off* scheme in 2005. This was a concession by the COJ in acknowledgement of the protests, rather than evidence of any consensus negotiated with protestors. However, water activists believed the COJ's write-off policy was misguided as it did not tackle the human rights aspect of water services. Nonetheless, the APF conceded that the COJ's action had been more transparent than its former efforts (APF 2005c). The APF's demand for a pro-poor tariff structure was partly satisfied as the step after the free water allocation of the rising block tariff increased but at a cost lower relative to that of the higher steps. Thus, for the first time, greater tariffs applied to the larger water users, which could afford to pay the increased rates, effectively subsidising smaller water users. This progressive pricing is a policy that continues to this day (Anciano 2012; APF 2005a, 2005c).

Although the COJ adopted a more agonistic approach in this period towards protest channelled to its Petitions Unit (see Chapter 3), its stance in Orange Farm towards public protests was antagonistic, as seen in their forcible repression. Nonetheless, the COJ did respond, in a more measured fashion, to the effects of the issues under contention and its root causes. It made concessions in its citywide tariff structure, reworked its policy for indigents, extended services in Orange Farm, and acknowledged the permanence of informal settlements and began planning long-term infrastructure for them. Perhaps the COJ could have been less abrupt with protestors and more proactive in building a more constructive state–society relationship. However, efforts were constrained by enmity with the APF and the escalating water wars solid-ified mistrust between the parties. The COJ and Johannesburg Water struggled to maintain a balance between the need to recover costs for services, protect water as a scarce resource given the city's relatively low annual rainfall, supply free water, and invest in all historically under-served areas under ongoing pressure to be financially self-sustaining.

Antagonistic yet responsive to the poor (2006–2010)

The COJ's maturation period between 2006 and 2010 saw the admin-istration's move to more consistent responses to the hundreds of service delivery protests during this period. However, in Orange Farm, as the water wars shifted from the streets to the courts, the COJ used the police and the JMPD to forcibly, even antagonistically, suppress around 15 per cent of the at least 30 other increasingly violent protests using armoured military vehicles, rubber bullets and electroshock weapons, according to media articles (Pernegger 2016). The escalation in hostility constrained the possibility of building a productive and agonistic relationship between the COJ and dissenters. Nonetheless, the COJ changed its approach and behaviour towards Orange Farm, becoming more responsive, proactive and citizen-centric in dealing with the issues underlying protests. The COJ also fine-tuned its organisational structures, including reducing the number of Offices of the Regions from 11 to seven, with Orange Farm falling now under Region G.

Mayor Masondo, embarking on his second term of office, noted in his *State of the City Address* of 2006 that Johannesburg Water had reduced the unaccounted-for water losses from 40 per cent in 2001 to 32 per cent in 2006 through *Operation Gcin'Amanzi*. Around 43 per cent of households did not pay for any water as they had stayed within their 6 kilolitre free monthly allocation (COJ 2006a, 2006e). Also, for the first time, plans such as the *Spatial Development Framework (SDF 2005–2006)* included Orange Farm as the southernmost point in the city's north–south development corridor (COJ 2005c), and were more consciously 'citizen-centric' and 'customer-centric' (COJ 2006c, p. 35).

Despite the COJ's advances in planning and service delivery, protests in Orange Farm peaked in 2006 at 14 protests recorded (Pernegger 2016). Protestors were angry about the cancellation of planned projects, the city administration's absent or poor communication with residents, councillor bravado, political misconduct, nepotism, and white elephant projects not fit for purpose. Costly and useless projects left incomplete due to contractor bankruptcy and called 'yellow elephants' by Thamsanqa Radebe, Region G's Manager of Urban Management and Service Delivery, also enraged the community (Radebe 2012). Similarly, a nearby councillor's purchase of a yellow Humvee, a pricey sports utility vehicle associated with opulence, inflamed the community and marked the start of increasingly violent protests targeting councillors and their properties (City Press 2011; TimesLive 2010a, 2010b). The Landless People's Movement, a social movement campaigning for housing and land in some informal settlements in Johannesburg (Greenberg 2004), joined the Orange Farm Water Crisis Committee in its water wars for a few months, the two together staging half of all protests in Johannesburg in 2006.

The participation of the Orange Farm Water Crisis Committee and the APF in protests dropped markedly from mid-2006 to 2007. Various factors caused this drop. The Phiri water meter objectors moved the water wars from the streets. They lodged their case in the South Gauteng High Court in July 2006 (*Mail & Guardian* 2009a). Ngwane's departure from the APF led to changes in its leadership (APF 2006a; Ngwane 2011). Many objectors capitulated to *Operation Gcin'Amanzi* and began to pay for the extra water they used over and above their free allocation (APF 2006c). Public participation improved as the South African Local Government Association, allegedly spurred by the APF, built ward committees' capacity for engagement in 2006 (APF 2007b). The COJ approved a revised and extended Social Package Policy in mid-2006, although its implementation was to be delayed. In December 2006, the COJ partly responded to the issues underlying dissensus and approved the increase of the 6 kilolitre free monthly allocation per household to 10 kilolitres. Extra free water was also available on application in circumstances of need (Mazibuko vs City of Johannesburg et al. 2009). These improvements, however, did not stop the Landless People's Movement and the APF from applying to the JMPD for permission to march against housing and land-related evictions. The JMPD, in trying to suppress the incidents of violence associated with the groups, refused their application to march in September 2006 (APF 2006b).

Although the number of service delivery protests by other new groups was at its lowest in Orange Farm in 2007, some were violent. The COJ responded by preparing a more detailed *Regional Spatial Development Framework* for the 2007/08 financial year for Region G, deliberately emphasising specific areas in Orange Farm to address backlogs, poor-quality services, uncoordinated development and poverty (COJ 2007h). Despite Orange Farm's bleakness, it offered its residents positive 'queuing opportunities' for services and a way to 'belong' to the city by helping them to stake their claim, according to Jak Koseff, the Director of Social Assistance within the COJ's Community Development Department since 2007 (Koseff 2012). The COJ's launch of its regularisation policy in April 2008 reinforced this sense of permanence; *regularisation* aimed to formalise most of the land, legal and housing issues in Johannesburg's informal settlements, bar those located on unsafe ground prone to sinkholes, poisoned by toxins or in danger of flooding (COJ 2006e, 2008s).

The COJ was stunned when Judge Tsoka of the Johannesburg High Court ruled in favour of the Phiri water meter plaintiffs in April 2008. Tsoka declared the COJ's meters to be 'unconstitutional and unlawful' (Mazibuko vs City of Johannesburg et al. 2009, p. 49). He also ordered the COJ to double the supply of free water. Mayor Masondo attacked the ruling, claiming the courts had overstepped their mandate and were taking over the government's role (APF 2008; *The Sowetan* 2008).

The COJ appealed the ruling but also stopped *Operation Gcin'Amanzi* in May 2008, reporting that by then the COJ had installed 162,000 meters and saved R359 million in water costs ($46.75 million) (COJ 2011v). As part of its pro-poor approach, the COJ announced that for the upcoming year, it would not increase the cost of the first step of the tariff above the free water step (Fiil-Flynn 2013).

Eliciting the COJ's and the police's sometimes justifiably firmer response to protest events, violent anti-foreigner protests took place during May 2008 in almost every town and township in Johannesburg and South Africa, distracting from the water wars (noted in Chapter 3). Orange Farm, however, experienced no anti-foreigner attacks (Monson et al. 2012). Despite its residents' reservations at foreigners in their midst, interventions in Orange Farm, such as by the COJ's Social Cohesion office and a capacity-building non-governmental organisation, may have prevented attacks there (Everatt 2011). Nonetheless, service delivery protests in Orange Farm after these xenophobic attacks became more spur-of-the-moment, longer-lasting (up to a week or more), with violence directed at people and property. Barricading of the settlement's main roads by protestors became more common. According to JMPD data cited by Duncan (2014a), the COJ frequently denied permission for these gatherings to take place.

Acknowledging the seriousness of the issues underlying protests, the COJ became more proactive at tackling the national and provincial governments' policy vacuum about informal settlements. Hence, the COJ approved an *Informal Settlements Upgrading and Formalisation* programme strengthening its earlier regularisation policy (COJ 2008s), recalled Philip Harrison, the Executive Director of the Development Planning and Urban Management directorate (Harrison 2012). Orange Farm received special attention, being ranked as one of four focus areas in the initial *Upgrading of Marginalised Areas* programme, although it received a paltry 3 per cent of the programme budget (COJ 2008q). In a part-placatory, part-agonistic turn, the COJ managed the service delivery protests' immediate impact by appointing the former politician and activist Thamsanqa Radebe as Region G's new Urban Management and Service Delivery Manager in 2008, nicknamed *Oupa* (Grandfather) as a sign of the Orange Farm community's fondness and respect for him despite his youth. Radebe lived in Orange Farm, had been a local councillor, and was still an active ANC member and civil society activist. His credentials allowed him to play on his multiple roles to tackle insurgency, helping the COJ to stabilise Orange Farm (Pernegger 2020; Radebe 2012). The COJ, recognising that protests were partly due to poverty, introduced its *Expanded Social Package* (ESP), or *Siyasizana*

(We Are Helping Each Other), in 2008. *Siyasizane* provided increased support measures for the poor especially in informal settlements on a one-stop shop basis (COJ 2009h). Communities could also help decide the details of infrastructure-based ward plans in November 2008 (COJ 2008e, 2008f, 2008g, 2008h, 2008i). Mayor Masondo, at South Africa's Human Settlement Summit in 2009, announced a plan to overcome the uncertainty of informal settlement living, with Orange Farm also to benefit, by building 100,000 houses by 2011 and providing security of tenure to residents (COJ 2009j). More integrated spatial and business plans followed: an *Urban Development Framework for the Stretford Node* (COJ 2009i), an expansion of an earlier plan (COJ 2007k), and a *Township Regeneration Strategy* in 2009 (COJ 2009b).

The COJ successfully appealed a part of the Tsoka ruling in the Phiri water meter case. The Supreme Court, in April 2009, reduced the previous court-ordered free allocation (from 50 litres to 42 litres per person per day) but upheld the appeal about the alleged illegality of the meters in favour of the plaintiffs. The Constitutional Court then heard the case. To the dismay of water activists, it ruled in favour of the COJ in October 2009 that prepaid meters were not unlawful (*Mail & Guardian* 2009b). Hence, a few months later, in January 2010, the COJ approved the restart of its *Operation Gcin'Amanzi* (COJ 2011v).

Protests likely spurred changes to national government's grant-funding regime too, which rewarded metropolitan municipalities with larger grants if they submitted appropriate and comprehensive plans for their cities. Accordingly, the COJ's *Built Environment Performance Plan* of 2010 included quantified infrastructure challenges on an area-by-area basis. In Orange Farm alone over the next five years, the COJ determined an overwhelming 'immediate need' of R1.035 billion ($0.14 billion) of capital investment in water, sanitation and other infrastructure, community facilities, and housing (COJ 2010b). The COJ's *Integrated Development Plan* for 2010–2011 again prioritised Orange Farm (COJ 2010h). The COJ identified 'extra-ordinary measures' needed to address Region G's backlogs in its *Regional Spatial Development Framework: 2010/11* (COJ 2010n, p. 14). However, the COJ could allocate only a third of the required funds in its draft five-year capital budget given the needs of other priority areas (COJ 2010b). This budget did not even account for long-term future planning needs, first identified in the *Orange Farm Integrated Development Framework and Business Plan* of 2010 (COJ 2010k).

The planning processes for the *Regional Spatial Development Framework* potentially provided an agonistic space for community voices. However, engagements between city representatives and community members sometimes proved positive but also difficult for officials, according to Liana Strijdom, the senior planner responsible for strategic planning in the city's southern regions. She said 'order, and even respect' characterised some meetings when steered by a respected facilitator, making agonistic, or at least participative, interaction easier. In the absence of such a facilitator, 'aggression and testosterone' could permeate interactions, as in the case of the COJ's outreach for the *Regional Spatial Development Framework* in Orange Farm in 2010, with the threat of violence so tangible and imminent that the engagement had to be aborted and the plan prepared without community input (Pernegger 2014; Strijdom 2012).

Despite the COJ's responsive measures to improve the state–society relationship and address the causes of dissension, Region G's satisfaction levels about sanitation in the COJ's *Customer Satisfaction Survey 2010* (COJ 2011o) were lower than in other regions, and the lowest in three years. Water, too, despite real improvements, was also a source of dissatisfaction due to the threefold increase over the previous three years in the number of water outages. Unsurprisingly, these and other frustrations boiled over in a huge 1,500-strong protest over a number of days in Orange Farm, including opportunistic attacks against foreign-owned businesses, with protestors and the police exchanging stones and rubber bullets, respectively, and leading to 83 arrests (*Mail & Guardian* 2010b; news24 2010).

Standardising responses and planning for protests (2011–2015)

The COJ developed more routine approaches to manage service delivery protests, planned to tackle the underlying issues in Orange Farm and other informal settlements, and built capacity for more agonistic interaction beyond the protests themselves, during the bureaucratisation period between 2011 and 2015. The COJ's services in Orange Farm improved, although some levels were lower relative to elsewhere in the city and the country, outstripping its growth rate. The COJ's long-term plans for Orange Farm's formalisation were more cohesive than before, with quantified investment costs and greater planned capital budget allocations.

By 2011, the official census data (Quantec 2014) revealed Orange Farm's extraordinary growth in population and services since its origins around two decades earlier. Although 98 per cent of Orange Farm's households had direct access to water, better than city (92 per cent), provincial (89 per cent) and national (73 per cent) averages, now a little less than half (48 per cent) had a connection inside the dwelling, with the rest connected in the dwelling's yard. Although 76 per cent of households in Orange Farm had access to free sanitation in the form of flush and chemical toilets, and almost all the rest to other types of sanitation, this rate was far lower than the city (90 per cent) and provincial (87 per cent) averages, but far better than the country's rate of 63 per cent. However, these statistics masked the true status of the access to sanitation in Orange Farm and other informal settlements. Sanitation facilities were often shared ones, poorly maintained, unhygienic and even unsafe. This lack has become linked with rights struggles, as being forced to use substandard facilities undermines the constitutional right to human dignity (Socio-Economic Rights Institute of South Africa 2011).

Almost three-quarters of Orange Farm's 55,624 households were, by 2011, formal structures, with the newer dwellings tending to be shacks in their backyards, pointing to Orange Farm's internal densification and adding to its development challenges (COJ 2010k). This level of formalisation, far better than the provincial and national rates (59 per cent and 65 per cent, respectively), is, however, spread highly unevenly across Orange Farm, with some areas containing as little as 2 per cent and some as much as 44 per cent informal structures. The state has transferred ownership of around 30,000 of Orange Farm's 46,000 plots to their residents (COJ 2010k). Some 94 per cent of Orange Farm plots were by then formally constituted planning-legal areas with state and private sector-led approved land development applications or general plans in place (COJ 2010k).

The COJ had provided Orange Farm, also by 2011, with other services and development initiatives. These included collecting refuse weekly; planting thousands of trees, including orange trees; tarring all main roads and gravelling 34 kilometres of the 81-kilometre road network; and installing street lighting in some places (COJ 2011d). Despite these regularisation measures, levels of other amenities were still lower than the rest of Johannesburg. For instance, Orange Farm had far less libraries per capita as compared to the middle-class suburbs' 'forest of libraries' (Koseff 2012).

Orange Farm's predominantly black population had grown in the two decades since its establishment to 197,030 people by 2011. Most still lived in poverty, with 20 per cent of households receiving no income and a further 71 per cent receiving less than R76,800 ($11,546) per annum. Skills levels were low, with only 4 per cent over the age of 20 having a higher education, lower than the city and provincial averages of 19 per cent and 18 per cent, respectively. The official unemployment level of 15–64-year-olds, while less than the 1996 level, was still 39 per cent, far higher than the city's average of 25 per cent, and was possibly exacerbated by the lower education levels and the distance from job opportunities (Quantec 2014).

Orange Farm's depressed life outcomes have seen scholars and others persist in using implicitly negative terms to describe the area. These communities at the city's periphery were called 'disposable people' (Murray 2008, p. 90), forced to squat there due to their poverty or forcibly moved there by the state from other places where they had been squatting. Orange Farm was labelled as a place of 'permanent informality' by Naidoo (2010, pp. 250–254). Monty Narsoo, a consultant and researcher specialising in housing development and informal settlement upgrading policy in the country for over 30 years and formerly the Deputy-Director General of Housing in the national government, calls Orange Farm 'Jo'burg's orphan' (Narsoo 2012).

The COJ, too, had negative or at least varying attitudes towards Orange Farm, as a place, and towards its residents and their regular protests. Despite Orange Farm's increasingly formalised services and housing, its continued marginal nature, high poverty levels, differential development and high rates of informality led the COJ to use the convenient shorthand of 'informal settlement' to describe Orange Farm (COJ 2011e), thereby defining its illegitimacy even while touting its infrastructure improvements. In the COJ's review of its *2012/2016 Integrated Development Plan* though, it detailed Orange Farm variously as a 'post-apartheid housing scheme', a 'marginalised area', one of the 'individual marginalised areas which also have informal settlements' within them, and as containing 'priority informal settlements' within its boundary (COJ 2013a, pp. 9, 21, 63, 199 and 200 respectively). Certainly, Orange Farm remained a place that is 'still not part of the city', said a senior ANC politician with a number of roles in city politics, especially in Johannesburg's Deep South since 1995 (Anonymous 2012b). Councillor Walters, a councillor for the ANC and a member of the Mayoral Committee managing a variety of political portfolios in the COJ since 1994, too, maintained Orange Farm remained largely 'forgotten' (Walters 2012).

The COJ's attitude towards the citizens of Orange Farm, though, was more mixed. Orange Farm residents were politically important to the ANC as it derived significant support from the area; this support had become more important as the ANC's share of the votes at every election since 1994 had declined. The COJ respected Orange Farm's residents as 'particularly vibrant, resilient and resourceful'

(COJ 2011e). But these residents were also needy due to their markedly lower standards in living conditions, health, education, income and employment levels, evident in the COJ's spatial mapping of its *Indices of Multiple Deprivation*, and were 'marginal' and 'deprived' (COJ 2014a, pp. 66–67). Views towards protest and protestors were rather different. Orange Farm's protestors may have felt their 'struggle is not yet over' and that the COJ has not paid attention to them (*New York Times* 2009). However, Councillor Walters claimed they had been 'heard and listened to by many managers' and been involved in 'plenty, plenty, plenty' consultation (Walters 2012). Other COJ respondents ranged from feeling unafraid of protest and being 'used to it' to considering protest as a 'disease' (respectively, Radebe 2012; Sibaya 2012).

This variation in attitudes to Orange Farm, its citizens and protestors partly explains the COJ's responses to street protest in Orange Farm, which continued throughout 2011 and 2012. The make-up of protests shifted again, with objectors becoming gradually more specific in their demands and no longer mobilising around water issues. Smaller localised issues such as objecting to a shopping centre development in 2011, which the COJ was able to address in an information session with protestors, were less common than protests with wider sets of demands. Some of these demonstrations took place with the JMPD's permission, but very many did not. The increasingly violent protests elicited the JMPD's firm, and sometimes antagonistic, response. However, despite hundreds of mainly women demanding toilets, housing, electricity, social amenities and roads during a three-day protest in June 2012, police remained on standby and did not intervene, and the COJ promised that provincial politicians representing housing, social development and infrastructure development would speak to protestors the next day (ioL News 2012b). Bar these responses from the state, little record of direct and agonistic engagement with protestors was evident. Protestors demonstrated violently for a week in October about the JMPD's demolition of illegal shacks and the area's lack of sewerage and electricity (Pernegger 2016), prompting Radebe to call the protestors 'criminals' (Radebe 2012). However, protestors also increasingly used the COJ's petitions channel, sometimes handing over a memorandum to the COJ during a protest but also submitting these without protesting, at least initially, as in the memorandums about poor service delivery from the South African National Civic Organisation in July 2012 (Pernegger 2016), and community members in November 2012 (ioL News 2012a).

The COJ clearly disliked protests. However, it sometimes took them seriously, with protests again prompting systematic changes to the COJ's plans and operations. For instance, the COJ's *Integrated Development*

Plan 2012/16 stressed the notion of inclusion of all but also aimed, ide-alistically, to 'eliminate protests', and to reduce petitions by 90 per cent from the 2012–2013 levels over three years, through a R15.2 million ($1.99 million) civic education and awareness programme (COJ 2012f, pp. 78 and 320). The COJ also allocated 12 times more budget in 2012 to Orange Farm than it did in 2008 (COJ 2008q, 2012e); this repre-sented a full quarter of its five-year capital budget (COJ 2012f). The COJ identified protests as one of the top ten management risks in its *2013/16 Integrated Development Plan* (COJ 2013b). It also made urgent arrangements for private security guards to protect councillors under attack from protestors (COJ 2013c). The COJ believed it was justified in continuing to emphasise water shortages and the importance of not wasting or losing water, although it no longer mentioned the controver-sial *Operation Gcin'Amanzi* by name (COJ 2014e). Further, the COJ empowered communities by improving its participation outreach and communications channels, including calling for community support of ward committee and petitions processes in its *Growth and Development Strategy 2040* (COJ 2011s).

Despite the COJ's progressive responsiveness to the protests' under-lying issues and operational adjustments, as well as the structured channels of petitioning and planning forums, some Orange Farm resi-dents still felt excluded from decision-making processes. The intensity of protests increased throughout Johannesburg between 2013 and 2015. Orange Farm protestors targeted a local councillor in February 2013, dumping garbage in protest at the COJ's absent refuse collection services in their ward for the previous two months (ioL News 2013c). Service delivery protests in March and again in May 2013 about the lack of recreation facilities, poor workmanship, housing and sewerage incorpo-rated vandalism and looting, specifically aimed at local foreign-owned businesses, leading to 93 arrests in the May incident (ioL News 2013a, 2013b; Xenowatch 2018). The JMPD dispersed protestors blockading the highway next to Orange Farm in November 2015 and fired rubber bullets to allow traffic to flow again (SABC News 2015). These and many other service delivery protests throughout Johannesburg, despite Orange Farm's strong support for the ANC, may have lost the ANC its control of Johannesburg in the 2016 local government elections. Despite still having strong support, the ANC did not receive enough votes to maintain its control over the COJ.

The protestors' escalating use of violence, and possibly even the city administration's own ambivalent attitude towards protestors, and Orange Farm and its residents generally, hampered the COJ's potential for agonistic practices in this period. Perhaps agonistic engagements were unnecessary as the protestors' antagonistic conflict may have been more effective in forcing the COJ to change its governance practices with positive effects on Orange Farm.

Observations

Over 55 episodes of public protest in Orange Farm in Johannesburg's Deep South between 1996 and 2015, ostensibly about water but also about other services, were recorded. They offer critical insights into the state's qualification of the conflict and protestors, its responses to dissensus, and dimensions affecting the state's extent of agonism in its governance practices and conflict management.

Local politicians' and officials' responses to most incidents of protest in Orange Farm were frequently immediate and short-term. Responses tended to address each protest's effects on a one-by-one basis and signified the state's largely anti-conflict mindset. Practices of handling conflict were generally not in keeping with the spirit of agonism as outlined by theorists. Responses included elements of disregard, denial, acknowledgement, disrespect, placation or antagonism, sometimes even simultaneously. Examples of hard-line forcible suppression, especially if protests were violent or even sometimes merely threatening violence, included the COJ's accusations of protestors' unacceptable actions against non-protestors in 2003; the COJ's use of the Red Ants private security firm to forcibly prevent the destruction of water meters and make arrests in 2003; the JMPD's refusal of permission for a public gathering in 2006; and the JMPD's use of armoured military vehicles, rubber bullets and electroshock weapons to quash about 15 per cent of the protests between 2006 and 2010.

The city administration's longer-term responses to protests, however, focused rather on the issue under contention and its root causes. Such responses were less antagonistic and more measured, seeming to address protests collectively rather than on a one-by-one basis, and resulted in incremental changes to the benefit of the citizens of Orange Farm. These responses included the COJ's increase of the free monthly water allocation from 6 to 10 kilolitres in 2005; the new pro-poor pricing structure for the water tariffs in 2005 due to pressure from protestors and activists; *Operation Gcin'Amanzi*'s suspension in 2008 pending the court ruling; and the active incorporation of Orange Farm into the city's plans and budgets, especially from 2008 onwards. Further, state support to all poor households in Johannesburg increased, as seen in the GJMC's introduction of the *Indigency Management Policy* of 1998, the package of free services in 2002, the write-off of arrears in 2005, and the announcement of the expanded social support package of *Siyasizane* in 2008. Also, the COJ improved conflict management arrangements. These included introducing the petitioning channel in 2001 and its strengthening in 2006, and appointing an activist-cum-politician-cum-resident for the Region G office to manage city–citizen conflictual relationships in Orange Farm. However, the city administration's stance on protest was generally negative, as seen in its 2012 plan to eliminate protests along with petitions. Although service delivery in Orange Farm (and other informal settlements) improved over the 1996–2015 period, it seems unlikely this would have been the case if the city administration had adopted more deliberately agonistic practices. Indeed, South Africa's biggest city may have been the first in the country to deliver a full range of free services to poor residents because of its (at times) more mature responses to protest actions.

Prevailing contextual factors significantly influenced the city administration's (lack of) propensity for agonistic governance, with its stance towards protests generally shifting from ambivalence to antagonism in some cases, or increasing responsiveness without agonism in others. Over time, Orange Farm's residents increased considerably in number, became more institutionally cohesive and made demands on the city administration. Orange Farm was no longer a marginal corner of Johannesburg that the city administration could ignore. The city administration itself matured, from a financially fragile transitional administration with short-term objectives into a relatively stable and better-capacitated administration with clearer long-term aspirations and visions. In this context, Orange Farm shifted from its temporary informal settlement status to become a properly acknowledged, formal part of the city. In tandem with these processes, the nature and intensity of the protests changed, as did the protestors and their tactics. The power of protest and these contextual changes compelled the city administration to respond more constructively to Orange Farm's dissenters and their demands, but not necessarily agonistically. The city administration's attitude changed from seeing the marginalised Orange Farm as orphaned from the rest of Johannesburg and as a burden, to adopting a more citizen-centric approach, rather than a customer-centred one, by including Orange Farm more explicitly and ever-increasingly in city budgeting, planning and operations.

Any deliberate state–society engagements aimed at resolving conflicts can result in unanticipated and unsuccessful outcomes as the complexity and variety of protests made it difficult for the state to respond coherently. The protests were also entangled with multiple other unexpressed concerns often extending beyond the scope of local government. In Orange Farm, before 2006, the stated objective of the protests was unfair access to water. However, there were also other underlying resentments and motives expressed by communities and civic agencies mobilising the communities, such as the APF's linking of local protest to a global anti-capitalist agenda. The city administration could respond somewhat constructively to the concerns raised, within the constraints of its cost-recovery goal, although dissenters' obscured objectives meant that a direct and immediate response to the concerns of the protestors was unlikely. However, dissenters must have been at least partly satisfied with the city administration's responses, as households started paying for water in 2006 and water-related protests dropped to their lowest level in 2007. Moreover, after 2006, the stated objectives of the protests became even more varied to include the lack of sanitation, roads and streetlights, housing and land tenure. Other more complex concerns included having a stake in projects and the ward councillor's purchase of an expensive Humvee, as well as more general ones, such as development, corruption-free governance, jobs, and exclusion from human rights. Hence, the agonistic task became massively complex. Here, an agonistic state could mean at best a broad shift towards greater institutional responsiveness and agonistic governance practices, not necessarily linked to any specific protest.

Although the city administration's responses to dissensus were generally not agonistic, these were not necessarily undemocratic. In many cases, the city administration did engage with communities according to governance practices, perhaps more in line with participatory and deliberative democratic approaches and favouring more structured channels for protest than agonism does. These practices were frequently difficult to undertake successfully, as seen in the fruitless *Regional Spatial Development Framework* outreach of 2010. The impulse to reach consensus is strong; hence, typical of participatory democratic regimes, many of the city administration's officials and politicians tended to see protest as a so-called failure of democracy rather than as a signal of its growth. By not appreciating conflict as a useful mode of engagement, the city administration tended to dedicate resources to the pacification of protestors rather than to agonistic engagement with them and citizens more generally.

These points illustrate that the city administration's responses to conflict in Orange Farm undoubtedly matured over time. However, the city administration's appetite for centring conflict in governance was mostly low. When it did respond, even beyond the protest events themselves, it was generally defensive. The role of agonistic practices was minimal in realising the state's real and largely positive improvements, which addressed the fundamental concerns raised by protestors in Orange Farm and other informal settlements to some extent. Any discussion about agonistic practices needs to be situated within the wider debate of how service delivery serves to empower or disempower new citizens in the South African democracy (von Schnitzler 2016), but clearly the city administration missed opportunities to apply agonistic principles to the management of processes of conflict. If it had done so, such practices might have resulted in different outcomes. However, agonistic practices may still hold potential as poverty in the Deep South and Orange Farm will likely continue to drive dissensus for years to come.

5
Informal trading struggle in the Inner City

Informal traders and the city administration

This chapter tells the story of Johannesburg's changes in post-apartheid city governance intersecting with informal trading on Inner City streets. I trace the democratically elected city administration's limited agonistic responses to informal traders' protests despite seemingly favourable conditions for agonistic practices. These limited responses, mainly in initial stages, decreased over time, even though one might reasonably expect a democratic institution to have become more agonistic as it matured. This story details the increasingly antagonistic state–informal trader relationship and the multiple constraints to the city administration's potentially agonistic practices. Before I turn to the city administration's conflict management efforts in Johannesburg, I briefly set out the informal trading sector's make-up, participants, dynamics and background between 1996 and 2015, with these facets still relevant at the time of this book's writing.

Survivalist informal trading is an urban governance challenge in many African cities but also in other cities, including many of the world's wealthiest nations (Graaff and Ha 2015). Informal trading, occurring in the streets, had become widespread because of the structure of countries' economies, low economic growth and barriers to formal employment (Heintz and Valodia 2008). In South African cities, informal traders, typically black, sold goods and services on city centre pavements as high footfall guaranteed trade. These goods and services included hairstyling, food vending, telephony, fruit and vegetables, traditional medicines, cosmetics, toiletries, mobile phones, clothing, shoes, appliances, and household goods. Studies have painted a grim picture of the informal trading sector in South African cities over the last two decades as these traders tended to target low-income consumers and had limited growth prospects (Rogerson 2003). Further, about 85 per cent of metropolitan traders served less than 20 customers per day, reporting a lack of trading infrastructure and business cash flow as impediments to trading (Willemse 2011). In Johannesburg's city centre, the gross daily earnings of 60 per cent of the traders typically ranged between R230 ($35) and R310 ($47), with a ceiling of R352 ($53) (2010 data) (Callaghan 2012). Traders' interests were also poorly represented. Although over 60 informal trading associations have represented traders' interests at different times since the 1990s (Pernegger 2016), only between 15 and 20 per cent of traders belonged to informal trading associations, bringing representivity into question (Skinner 2008). Associations tend to be weak and disjointed, competing with each other for members (Bénit-Gbaffou 2016). Further, six of the seven most dominant associations in the Inner City were less than ten years old and fought 'everyday struggles' and hardly influenced city policy (Bénit-Gbaffou 2014, p. 229).

Ground zero for informal trading is the Inner City, although informal traders operate across Johannesburg. Despite the state's significant formalisation of this sector through the creation of markets and designated spaces and the issuing of permits, such trading continues nonetheless to be referred to as *informal trading* in Johannesburg, and also in this book. The city administration had already designated the Inner City as a special development area in the 1990s. This almost 17 square kilometre area incorporated the traditional city centre, a much smaller 375-block, 49-street area within the wider Inner City (see Map 5.1). Informal trading density was the highest in the city centre and presented the city administration with a significant governance challenge. Although the city centre had been in decline since the 1960s (Beavon 2004), it was still home to many important banks, mining houses, public sector buildings and public transport facilities. Pavements were (and still are) jam-packed with too many traders, even according to traders themselves (Bénit-Gbaffou 2016). Traders targeted pedestrians moving between the city centre's key transport, employment, education and residential sites. The wider Inner City, consisting of industrial, cultural and high- to medium-density residential precincts around the city centre, contained localised concentrations of traders. The number of traders was fluid and counts were unreliable. However, about 6,000–8,000 informal traders operate in the wider Inner City, with 3,723 of these traders operating in the city centre alone (COJ 2013d, 2013e). The associated congestion, litter and disorder of pavement and public spaces was acute, especially in the city centre.

The main actor in the management of this sector was the city administration, which managed about two-thirds of the traders in the city centre, and traders in other Inner City locations through markets. It had built, or dismantled and rebuilt, over 50 formal Inner City markets since the 1990s (COJ 2013e; Pernegger 2016). Traders operated from fixed stalls and demarcated sites in on- or off-street public markets. By law, all traders should comply with informal trading by-laws. However, some traders operated illegally within restricted and prohibited trading areas or sold illegal goods in contravention of the by-laws. The post-apartheid city administration's many departments and entities played complex and contested roles in informal trading management and development (Tomlinson 1999b), with no single part taking respon-sibility for the entirety of informal trading management. Cross-cutting functions included economic policy, operational management, urban management, by-law policing, markets management, property man-agement, facilities management and markets development. They also included transport policy because of the coincidence of informal trad-ing with informally provided mass public transport. Various committees exercised political oversight of informal trading management, such as the Inner City Committee, a political committee advising the Council's decision-making Executive Committee until 2010. The city administra-tion's developmental intentions clashed with by-law enforcement and operations (Rogerson 2016; Socio-Economic Rights Institute of South Africa 2015). Although officials and politicians recognised and even commended traders' entrepreneurialism as vital for their livelihoods and the city centre, the chaotic impact on the 'city beautiful' vision infuriated state actors since the late 1980s (Rogerson 1990, p. 124).

The other main player in the management of city centre traders was the private sector through the Central Johannesburg Partnership, which managed the balance of city centre traders (2013 data) (COJ 2013e).[1] The extent of privately owned landholdings in the city centre outstripped that of other nodes (Johannesburg Land Company 2014). Formal busi-nesses regarded traders as a 'real' and 'perceived' nuisance and a 'serious problem' (*The Star* 2014c; Tomaselli 1985, p. 132). The private sec-tor championed Inner City regeneration through its support for the Central Johannesburg Partnership since 1992 (Central Johannesburg Partnership 2006b). The Partnership created and managed City Improvement Districts, including the management of informal trading in these districts, with evident success (Bénit-Gbaffou et al. 2012).

The tension between the city administration's twin aims of devel-opment and control in informal trading management has long roots. The state's approach to trading was episodically hands-off, repressive and restrictive from the 1920s to the 1980s when but 200–250 traders were allowed to trade in the city centre (Beavon and Rogerson 1986; Rogerson 2003). In the 1980s, however, much of the global economy had liberalised and South Africa's politics began moving towards

Map 5.1 – Informal trading in Inner City

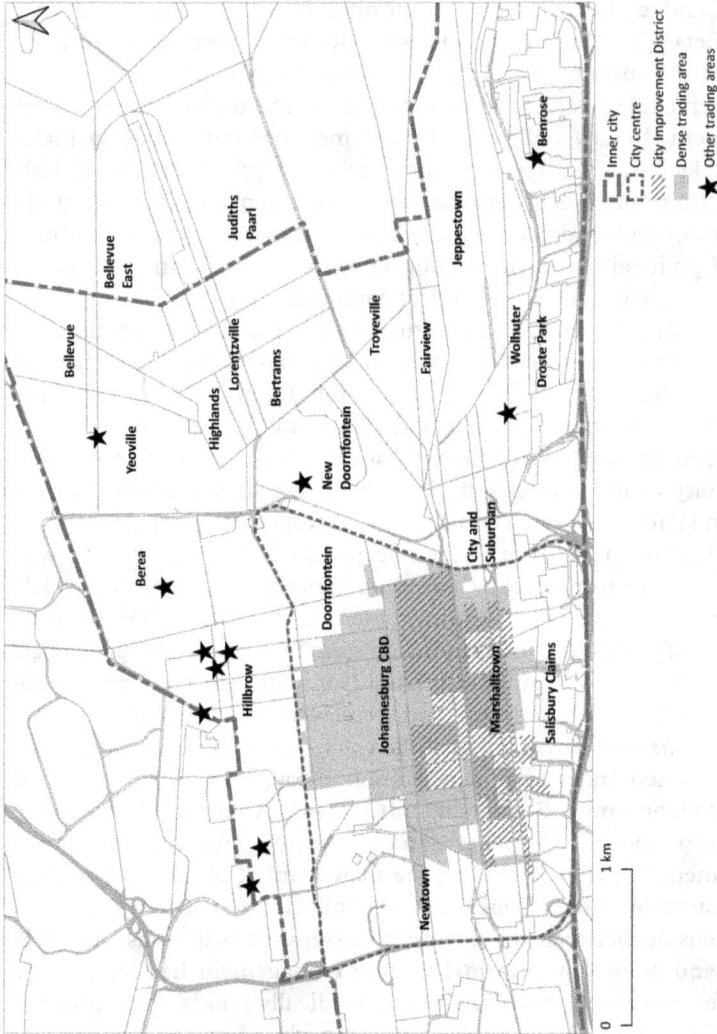

Legend:
- Inner city
- City centre
- City Improvement District
- Dense trading area
- ★ Other trading areas

Areas labelled on map: Bellevue, Bellevue East, Yeoville, Judiths Paarl, Berea, Highlands, Lorentzville, Bertrams, Troyeville, Hillbrow, New Doornfontein, Fairview, Jeppestown, Doornfontein, Johannesburg CBD, City and Suburban, Wolhuter, Droste Park, Benrose, Newtown, Marshalltown, Salisbury Claims

0 1 km

Note: Informal trading is concentrated in the city centre part.

Source: Author's formulation (adapted from COJ 2004g, 2009d; Dinat 2012; Pernegger 2016)

democracy. These changes translated into the state's deregulation and relaxation of some apartheid and economic strictures. For instance, the state declared Johannesburg's city centre as a desegregated free trade area in 1986, opening up informal trading to all races (South African Institute of Race Relations 1988), and scrapped influx control into cities (RSA 1986a). More reforms followed, including the removal of restrictions of the *Businesses Act* (RSA 1991), which delegated the business licensing function to local authorities once they had set up the necessary by-laws and created a hiatus in the legislation governing informal trading activity. These new freedoms sparked a surge in informal trading numbers from around 1988. By 1991, the Johannesburg City Council counted between 1,498 and 2,050 black traders in the city centre (Community Agency for Social Enquiry 1995b). By 1994, city centre traders had increased to between 3,167 and 6,893 traders, the huge fluctuations due to timings of the three surveys done (Community Agency for Social Enquiry 1995a). These increases in trader numbers led to significantly increased congestion on pavements, which the Council was not equipped to manage. Unsurprisingly, tensions over space between the state, the informal trading associations and formal businesses emerged. The Council tackled the informal trading and urban management challenges with a developmental project-based approach and participative engagements, including a strong public participation component with individual traders in project areas (Johannesburg City Council 1994). The Council and the Metropolitan Chamber (discussed in Chapter 3) reportedly engaged in productive, possibly agonistic (as the state brought all civil society and government groups together for the first time) discussions between 1993 and 1997, resulting in co-created 'ground-breaking', 'holistic' informal trading policy (Bobat 2012).

However, despite the 'progressive' tone of these engagements between the city administration, the informal trading associations and the formal business sector, any positivity proved short-lived (Bobat 2012). Some traders resisted aspects of market developments in some of the earliest service delivery protests in post-1994 Johannesburg (Pernegger 2016). The Johannesburg City Council's Informal Trading Market Division's officials, mostly ex-anti-apartheid activists, tried to interact with trading associations by being open to negotiation (Bobat 2012; Sher 2013). However, the associations used mass street marches to force the council to consult only with them rather than individual traders in project areas, claimed the Council's consultant (Muthialu 2012). By 1995, deep interaction with huge numbers of traders had become increasingly impractical and relations with the associations were increasingly prioritised. Further, the disruptive effects of the local government's multiple restructurings overshadowed these earlier agonistic efforts (see Chapter 3).

Partly agonistic within the prioritised Inner City (1996–2000)

The first democratic local government in Johannesburg entered its first five-year term between 1996 and 2000, soon after the November 1995 elections. A period of intense organisational transition driven by the GJMC followed (Tomlinson 1999b). The city administration incorporated responsive, occasionally agonistic, principles in engagements with informal traders. However, increasing prioritisation of the Inner City over the period, and other constraints, gradually eroded this inclination.

As most of the Inner City fell under the control of the new SMLC, its officials bore most of the responsibility for managing the area. The SMLC officials, many coming from the former Johannesburg City Council, had already intensively workshopped and agreed new informal trading by-laws with affected parties in 1995 (Bobat 2012; *Business Day* 1996). These by-laws had been submitted to the Gauteng Premier for approval in January 1996. Inner City traders marched on 18 April 1996 in protest against the GJMC's and MLCs' planned change of focus to 'clean up' the city centre (*Business Day* 1996). Officials said the prominent trading association, the African Council for Hawkers and Informal Businesses, lied when it complained it had not been consulted about the new by-laws. In response to the protestors, the GPG met the city administration and the traders, publicly rebuking the GJMC and the SMLC even though they had consulted the associations (Bobat 2012). The GPG then pressured the GJMC to submit only the first but least controversial phase of the proposed by-laws to it for approval, satisfying the trading associations. This phase of the by-laws dealt with the cleanliness and conduct of traders (GJMC 1997b, 1998b). The GPG approved this phase only a year later (January 1997) (Province of Gauteng 2004). Even though the GJMC had approved an updated informal trading policy in October 1996, common to all MLCs (GJMC 1998b), without by-laws in place its ability to manage informal trading and taxis in the Inner City was limited. A senior politician representing the ANC agreed at the time with the property owners who were sceptical about the city administration's ability to manage informal trading (Anonymous 2012a). Some property owners tried to manage informal trading's impact by supporting the Central Johannesburg Partnership's precinct-based urban management, which included more informal trading management than the city administration could provide. By the end of 1997, the Partnership regulated about 50 city blocks through these managed precincts (Central Johannesburg Partnership 2006a). Meanwhile, the SMLC developed some markets to move traders off pavements.

The city administration wrestled for a new democratic and African vision for the Inner City and solutions to renewal challenges jointly with affected parties (Bremner 2000). To empower stakeholders, the GJMC set up the Inner City Committee in 1997 to make recommendations to the GJMC's Executive Committee. This new committee was unusual as it was area-based but also incorporated public and private sector and informal trader representatives (GJMC 1998a; Tomlinson 1999a; Urban Inc. 2011). Further, in April 1997, the GJMC and the relevant MLCs established the Inner City Street Trading Interim Crisis Committee (known as ICSTICC) to identify 'practical management' solutions for the 'crisis' of informal trading in a partnership approach, considering trader registration and other informal trading management arrangements (GJMC 1997b, 1998a). By now, managed informal trading was seen as critical, being linked to the Inner City's improved urban management in the provincially driven *Mayivuke* (Awake) renewal strategy launched in July 1997 (Beavon 2004, p. 267; Johannesburg Inner City Development Forum 1997; Murray 2008).

Despite provincial and local governments' openness to traders' concerns, local traders took to the streets on 9 July 1997, 'up in arms' about foreign black Africans trading in the city (Human Rights Watch 1998; Peberdy and Talibe 1997). Around 45 per cent of traders were foreign black Africans (Bremner 2000). The trading associations issued a memorandum to the mayor, Isaac Mogase, protesting the SMLC's inclusion of foreigners in its market-related projects. On 14, 15 and 18 August, traders demanded the state remove foreigners from the streets, staging violent marches (Pernegger 2016). The state had no option but to use force to quell the xenophobic violence to protect lives and property; 100 traders were arrested for looting shops and market stalls (Centre for Study of Violence and Reconciliation 2008; Pernegger 2016). In response, the SMLC and traders worked together, quite agonistically, as traders and officials jointly fashioned revised allocation criteria for stalls, favouring local traders (SMLC 1997d).[2] The GJMC also tried to build the associations' capacity by facilitating the trading associations to set up an informal trading umbrella body and providing support for its activities; the resultant Gauteng Informal Sector Forum then engaged the SMLC and the GJMC to discuss development issues (Goldsmith 2012).

However, any agonistic potential was overtaken by local traders' growing resentment against what they perceived to be more profitable foreign traders (Human Rights Watch 1998; Peberdy and Talibe 1997). Again, traders, 500 of them this time, marched against foreign traders in October 1997. Again, they attacked foreigners, not only in

Johannesburg. Similar attacks broke out across the country (Pernegger 2016). The Deputy Minister of Home Affairs, seeming to support local traders, claimed some foreigners, namely refugees, were 'trading illegally' (Human Rights Watch 1998). The GPG's Safety and Security Department seemingly sanctioned 'community arrests' by traders of 'illegal foreigners' (Human Rights Watch 1998). But the Foreign Affairs Ministry declared South Africa had to help those that needed protection in accord with terms of the United Nations and the Organisation of African Unity (*Mail & Guardian* 1997). Foreign traders, victims of the violence, thought such protection was ineffectual (Peberdy and Talibe 1997), even though the army had helped police to quell the violence, and the police had arrested protestors for illegal marching, looting of formal and informal retailers, property damage, and assault (Peberdy and Crush 1998). Unfortunately, this anti-foreigner tension remained unresolved, foreshadowing xenophobic riots across South Africa in 2008.

Almost all the SMLC's investments in informal trading markets and the Inner City Street Trading Interim Crisis Committee's approvals of consultants, which might have contributed to a more managed trading environment, were immobilised by the city administration's 1997 financial crisis (Skinner 1999). Capacity for agonistic engagement was also negatively impacted, as by mid-1998 the SMLC froze staff appointments. With its seven officials, the SMLC could only respond to informal trading hotspots in limited ways (Skinner 1999).

However, the state still prioritised the Inner City, partly as it contained nearly a quarter of Johannesburg's rateable value (COJ 2001a), meaning a substantial portion of its income was derived from the Inner City. The GJMC set up a dedicated Inner City Office in April 1998 (COJ 2001a; Tomlinson et al. 2003). This team experimented with new ways of city governance, in response to funding constraints, boding well for future agonistic interactions as such experimentation is the cornerstone of agonistic practices (Westphal 2014). The Inner City Office used a project-based approach, testing concepts through pilot initiatives, the design of which was informed by much public debate, before developing policies (Gotz and Simone 2001). Despite the by-laws' 'zero tolerance' principle, the city administration had yet to carry out much enforcement due to the by-laws' missing portion and the lack of capacity and slow restructuring processes within the administration (GJMC 1997a). This was soon to change, though, as the city administration, in 1998, approved a plan for a systematic, consistent, dedicated, multi-sectoral team for by-law enforcement as part of the Inner City Office's *Safer Cities* project in anticipation of the GPG's imminent proclamation of the complete set of by-laws applicable to all MLCs in Johannesburg (GJMC 1998a, 1998b). Some 30 months after its meeting with the GJMC and the trading associations, in July 1998, the GPG proclaimed the complete set of by-laws. For the first time in a decade, the city administration had the full legal tools to enforce informal trading conduct. These by-laws now also allowed it to create restricted and prohibited trading areas, confiscate goods, and charge standard penalties across the MLC areas (Province of Gauteng 2004). Enforcement took the form of *blitzes*, meaning concentrated and intermittent operations on a street-by-street basis, by collaborating officials from departments such as the traffic police, building control and environmental health, informing traders in advance (Abrahamse 2012).

Complementing this enforcement, the GJMC's *Inner City Informal Trade Management Plan* of March 1999 planned for the move of informal traders from the pavements into markets (GJMC 1999b, 1999c). The plan focused on public and private sector partnerships to create 5,000 trading spaces in three years. Traders were to pay nominal rentals. Key to the plan's success was to keep the pavements around the markets clear from new incoming traders as the existing traders moved off them into the markets. Hence, the SMLC approved 25 areas in the Inner City as restricted trading areas in March 1999, with the requisite proclamation following in August (GJMC 1999a; Province of Gauteng 1999). Traders protested the GJMC's clearance of traders from the restricted area of Braamfontein, an office precinct within the Inner City, in September 1999, demanding the GJMC recognise the permanence of informal trading on all Johannesburg pavements and the return of all goods confiscated by law enforcement officers since mid-1998. However, Motala (2002) reported the GJMC's officials and trader representatives were able to negotiate rights and responsibilities, with officials recognising the traders' need to build capacity and traders acknowledging the GJMC's requirement for by-law compliance.

The GJMC, too, faced capacity constraints. To provide institutional capacity to implement the *Informal Trading Management Plan*, it set up the MTC in April 1999. The MTC, a stand-alone entity, formed part of the new consolidated city administration arrangements envisaged in *iGoli 2002* (GJMC 1999d). The MTC was initially responsible for the facilities management of markets and taxi ranks, but later also took on development facilitation, marketing and business development (COJ 2004f). Initially, traders were hopeful about real prospects for empowerment, through the ownership of shares in the markets for a nominal investment they thought was affordable (GJMC 1999b). Their hopes were dashed, though, when the city administration had to abandon this part of the plan as it contravened the new Municipal Finance Management Act, in effect shutting traders out of market partnerships (Pernegger 2001).

By mid-1999, the city administration had accommodated over 1,200 traders in about 20 formalised markets in the Inner City for a nominal daily fee (SMLC 1997d). However, this promising start met with increasing resistance from traders, who began to object to the user-pays approach and the inevitable, reportedly quite forcible, street clearances as markets were opened. For instance, traders in the markets and traders operating illegally in surrounding streets opposed the Yeoville Market in the media when it opened in December 1999. This opposition forced the MTC to declare a moratorium on market rents for at least the first three months. As the new Johannesburg unicity was formed, what seemed to have been an effective working relationship between the city administration and trading associations declined steadily, and the COJ's propensity for agonistic engagements with traders dissipated.

Growing antagonism to informal trading (2001–2005)

The newly established unicity city administration, the COJ, tried to intensify the enforcement of the informal trading by-laws during its period of organisational consolidation between 2001 and 2005. This intensification was in response to increasing pressure from the other spheres of government, property owners and the Inner City political committee, impatient for the COJ's implementation of the 1997 *Mayivuke* Inner City regeneration strategy to support their investments and overcome over a decade of unmanaged trading and perceived anarchy. Traders' protests increased, resisting the COJ's enforcement and its ambition to clear pavements by moving traders to markets.

In 2001, Johannesburg's new executive mayor, Amos Masondo, took office and declared the Inner City as one of his six priorities. One of the COJ's institutional responses was to create the Johannesburg Development Agency, which took over most of the functions of the former Inner City Office in April 2001 (COJ 2001a). Another was the development of more markets by the still new MTC. Politicians thought uncontrolled informal trading had become a 'nuisance', 'a danger and a hazard' and a 'free-for-all' (Anonymous 2012a). Trying to tackle trading's so-called chaos meant the COJ had to further strengthen its multisectoral Inner City Task Force to enforce the by-laws. It expanded the team to 30 officials within the wider Office of Region 8, enforcing informal trading and other by-laws, frequently in blitzes in the city centre (COJ 2002f, 2004h).

This increased emphasis on enforcement led to traders' resistance. For instance, 2,000 traders marched in July 2001 protesting the COJ's confiscation of stock and lack of a management plan. This march forced the COJ to negotiate a plan with the Gauteng Hawkers Association, presumably partly agonistically or at least collaboratively, to demarcate trading spaces on pavements, an issue that had been in limbo for a year due to the COJ's lack of resources; the association agreed to help the COJ, resulting in demarcations, which were undertaken in October 2001 with the police's help (Motala 2002).

Soon the *iGoli 2002* plan spurred the COJ to reorganise the enforcement function by incorporating it into the new JMPD on 1 November 2001 (GJMC 1999d). A few months later, in early February 2002, the JMPD, the national police and Home Affairs, with the Inner City Task Force, began to enforce informal trading by-laws in earnest (COJ 2002f). The JMPD quashed protests by disbanding mass meetings, as it did in February and March 2002, but also more forcibly by baton-charging protestors (news24 2002). This antagonism, coupled with the JMPD's alleged 'looting' of traders' stock, prompted the Gauteng Hawkers Association to ask the High Court to grant an urgent interdict against the COJ's enforcement (news24 2002). The court ruled in favour of the trading association. This win compelled the city manager, Pascal Moloi, to comment to the media that the COJ was 'dealing with anarchy' (*Sunday Independent* 2002). The COJ appealed to the High Court, which set aside the order on 20 February, less than two weeks after the original interdict, allowing the JMPD to resume enforcement in the city centre. That same day, traders started to lay charges of theft, harassment and bribery against some JMPD officers (AllAfrica.com 2002).

The COJ's mixed affinity–hostility stance towards traders is plain in its conditional acceptance of traders in the *Joburg 2030* strategy of February 2002 (COJ 2003d). On the one hand, it stated informal trading added a unique 'African flavour' to the world-class city of Johannesburg, but on the other, the extent of trading had to be reduced, the negative image overcome, and zero tolerance enforcement undertaken (COJ 2002c). Some claimed *Joburg 2030* favoured the interests of investors over those of the poor (Emdon 2003). Others, though, argued that to manage the chaos of the many Inner City interest groups was a little-credited and complex task (Lipietz 2004). By February 2002, the JMPD had assembled a dedicated by-law enforcement unit of 115 officers to enforce restricted and prohibited areas and other related by-laws throughout Johannesburg (COJ 2002f).

Joburg 2030's follow-on *Informal Trading Development Programme* in 2002 merged all informal trading plans made since the late 1990s into one citywide plan (COJ 2002a, 2006e). This programme intended to create a system of graded market spaces to accelerate trading's formalisation, from A-grade (formal permanent market structures with dedicated spaces) to D-grade (no structures, no dedicated space on pavement, but a licence to trade). As traders steadily 'graduated' up these grades, from D to C to B to A, the vacated C- and D-grade spaces would be progressively removed, so that within 15 years only A- and B-grade spaces would be available (COJ 2002a). In this way, the COJ would 'shrink' the demand for trading spaces and the number of traders on the pavements (COJ 2002a). Acknowledging the anti-enforcement protests, but also the need for time to organise institutional and resource capacity to implement the programme, the COJ planned to delay rigorous enforcement for a few months until April 2003, when it had implemented enough of the plan.

However, boding poorly for the viability of this new programme, traders stepped up resistance to markets development and management from mid-2002 to the end of 2003 (Pernegger 2016). One protest by traders, against the underlying neoliberal logic of the August 2002 anti-World Summit on Sustainable Development conference, was to impact future protests, which increasingly incorporated statements about the right to trade (Death 2011; Liberty Institute 2002a, 2002b, 2002c; *The Sowetan* 2002). For instance, also in August, despite the MTC's concession in halving Yeoville Market rentals (COJ 2002f), market traders protested against the MTC's operations and rentals (Pernegger 2016).

Because of the COJ's planned delay in enforcement of the informal trading by-laws while the *Informal Trading Development Programme* was being implemented, any enforcement was constrained, forming part of other campaigns, such as the *Nude Ants* campaign (the reason behind the name is unclear) that started on 18 September 2002. *Nude Ants*, a 12-month multipronged campaign with the police, dealt with all by-law violations, including 'illegal trading and other crimes' (COJ 2003a, 2003h). On 2 October, the MTC used the Red Ants private security firm to evict non-paying tenants from Yeoville Market (*Business Day* 2002).

Critical to Inner City renewal was the new Metro Mall market and minibus taxi rank, which opened officially in the city centre in January 2003 (COJ 2002d). Metro Mall was the city's infrastructure solution for informal traders and taxi operators in that part of the city. It integrated informal trading with mass transit minibus taxis in one market–taxi rank facility, catering for about 600 traders, 3,000 taxis and other formal retailers, and was the largest of its kind in Johannesburg (COJ 2002d). The COJ reiterated the Inner City's economic importance for Johannesburg and

Africa in February 2003 by approving the Economic Development Unit's refreshed Inner City renewal plan. Two of the *Inner City Regeneration Strategy Business Plan*'s five pillars tackled areas of severe decline known as 'sinkholes' (not related to the real geological problem on the city's periphery) and the lack of 'intensive urban management' (COJ 2004h). The plan also identified dedicated capacity within the JMPD and the Inner City Task Force to enforce by-laws and restricted trading areas (COJ 2004h).

Mayor Masondo made it clear in his *State of the City Address* in January 2004 that markets were the COJ's way to to limit 'unfettered informal trading' (COJ 2004e), with traders expected to pay for spaces in markets to ensure managed markets were sustainable. The COJ's user-pays principle, initially supported by traders as they would gain shares in the markets, was now more controversial for perpetuating a 'divided city' (Beall et al. 2002). So, when taxi associations in Metro Mall refused to pay their fees in April 2003, jeopardising the MTC's viability, the MTC threatened to lock them out of the rank. They paid up (Pernegger 2020). The COJ's user-pays policy took hold, certainly by the beginning of 2004, as about 85 per cent of taxi associations and traders paid rentals on time (COJ 2004e). Keith Atkins, the MTC's chief executive officer, pointed out the markets' success relied heavily on the JMPD's effective enforcement and clearance of the proclaimed restricted and prohibited trading areas around the markets. The JMPD did not prioritise this enforcement in the same way the MTC did, reportedly disconcerting the MTC's managers (Atkins 2012). In May 2004, the taxi associations again stopped payments. Any concessions by the COJ were not enough for the associations; although the COJ consulted them, 'they just weren't getting to hear what it was they wanted to hear' (Atkins 2012). The COJ never resolved this non-payment, despite repeated consultative engagements chaired by various political leaders. So, the MTC limped along, needing subsidies to stay afloat to counter imminent insolvency, until its closure in 2012 (COJ 2012c; Pernegger 2020).

Also, in May 2004, ending the informal trading by-laws' murky legal status for the last three years as they applied to the former GJMC and the MLCs, the GPG repealed the 1998 informal trading by-laws, replacing them with a set of uniform by-laws across Johannesburg (Province of Gauteng 2004). Although not markedly different from their 1998 counterpart, the JMPD's ability to enforce stricter enforcement, especially in restricted and prohibited trading areas, could no longer be questioned, no doubt causing some apprehension among traders.

The COJ's Economic Development Unit and the MTC tried to speed up development of formal markets to counterbalance enforcement efforts.

They began the stopgap 'cages' initiative in August 2004 (COJ 2004c), semi-permanent cage-like metal mesh stalls to be fixed to the pavements. Traders could fold these cages up at night and lock them, providing much-needed storage space for stock. The cages would allow traders to remain in their existing trading sites rather than relocating them into the less popular off-street markets (Pernegger 2016). Months of planning and negotiations with informal traders, formal businesses, trading associations and other groups resulted in the agreed cage prototype and locations. The COJ manufactured cages in their hundreds. However, after the COJ had only installed but a few, some formal businesses lodged legal challenges against the COJ. These challenges forced the COJ to abort the initiative before it had even completed it (Dinat 2012).

Around this time, too, in late 2004, the JMPD launched the mysteriously named *Operation Token Days*, a 500-day 'high-profile' series of blitzes to enforce multiple by-laws (COJ 2006e). The COJ still favoured Inner City blitzes as they could tackle safety and enforcement issues simultaneously (McMichael 2015). Nonetheless, the JMPD found it hard to carry out enforcement as frequent restructurings had left the JMPD 'totally unstable', claimed a long-standing director within the JMPD (Gerneke 2012). Despite the JMPD's challenges, its enforcement clearly affected traders. Some traders staged violent protests against enforcement, market management and the cages in September and November 2004. However, notwithstanding the COJ's engagements with traders, Councillor Cowan publicly condemned the protestors' bullying, looting and destruction (Cowan 2004). Shortly before Christmas in 2004, 'illegal' traders invaded the MTC's recently redeveloped Commissioner Street market (Atkins 2012). Formal and informal traders objected to the COJ's inability to keep designated areas clear from new incoming traders, which the 2002 *Informal Trading Development Programme*'s success relied on if the COJ was to reduce the scale of informal trading activities. Intending to provide a participatory channel for traders to deal with their concerns, the COJ set up a monthly forum in mid-2005 to consider traders' concerns. Although the forum allowed for possible collaboration between the COJ and traders, traders saw it as a sporadic and superficial vehicle limited to, for instance, issuing updates on the COJ's plans for restricted and prohibited trading areas in terms of by-law procedural compliance (*Mail & Guardian* 2005). However, also unlikely to have supported the forum's agonistic engagements was the JMPD's *Operation Jaywalker*, launched in August 2005 to address the 'culture of lawlessness' on the streets; the JMPD confiscated goods from over 100 traders, arrested 140 people and issued several fines in its first week (*The Citizen* 2005).

The COJ increasingly integrated and stepped up enforcement measures to reduce uncontrolled trading in designated areas in this period. By-law enforcement of all sorts was one of the COJ's top priorities during 2005 (COJ 2005a). The COJ's new emphasis on enforcement did not endear traders to the COJ despite its boosting of some traders' business acumen through skills development initiatives (Radebe 2007). Indeed, the COJ's drive to control and formalise the sector through enforcement and markets provision created even more discontent among traders in the period to come. Animosity between the COJ and traders was also fuelled by the COJ's move away from its initial planned partnership-based market development for informal trading management to a more traditional service provider–customer model.

Zero tolerance approach towards trading (2006–2010)

Despite the COJ's organisational maturation during this period from 2006 to 2010, its zero tolerance relationship with traders became increasingly antagonistic. The COJ's prioritisation of by-law enforcement, registration of traders and management of markets led to more protests. About a third of these protests, mostly in 2009 and 2010, raised concerns about traders' rights to sell on the pavements (Pernegger 2016).

The COJ made relatively minor institutional adjustments only, in 2006 and 2007, to the organisation. The COJ was now able to enforce Mayor Masondo's 'very hard line' to deal with what he saw as 'the shocking levels of disorder in the Inner City' (Harrison 2012). Despite the lack of clarity about the COJ's then new urban management role, the COJ undertook forceful urban management measures in the Inner City. Here, the COJ adopted systematic enforcement of the by-laws on a block-by-block basis, namely tackling one city block at a time rather than its former impromptu blitz approach. The JMPD, working on a 'zero tolerance' basis with the Office of the Region (now part of the larger Region F), impounded 6,709 items of stock and issued 6,884 fines for trading in non-designated areas in Johannesburg over the 12 months ending in June 2006 (COJ 2007a, pp. 58 and 59). The JMPD, in September 2006, launched *Operation Hleka* (Clean-Up). Around 1,300 patrolling officers saturated the city centre and enforced by-laws (*The Star* 2006b). The JMPD also undertook the first blitz of the ongoing multi-year *Operation Thiba* (Prevent or Stop). This operation involved the national police and other regulatory agencies, also acting against 'illegal' traders (COJ 2007e; ioL News 2006, 2009).

Despite the COJ's pursuit, too, of developmental goals for traders in 2006, with training of 1,222 traders in food hygiene and 519 traders in business skills (COJ 2007a), after three weeks of heavy enforcement, traders were fed up. The newly formed Johannesburg Traders Crisis Committee objected to the COJ's alleged criminalisation of traders and corruption within the JMPD (Elias 2006; *The Star* 2006b). The COJ reassured traders of its ongoing commitment to informal traders, evidenced by many meetings and workshops, training, and efforts to beat corruption (*The Star* 2006a). The COJ reminded the Traders Crisis Committee that by-law enforcement benefited all Inner City users (*The Star* 2006a). It continued with the more unpopular enforcement blitzes through the first half of 2007 (*Mail & Guardian* 2007).

Progress on strategic issues lagged, according to Graeme Gotz of the Central Strategy Unit in the Office of the Executive Mayor (Gotz 2012). Gotz thought strained relations between the Central Strategy Unit and the Economic Development Unit accounted for the new *Inner City Regeneration Charter*'s limited attention to informal trading development. The *Charter*, completed in July 2007 (COJ 2007d), was the result of eight months of multi-stakeholder engagements, but dealt with trading 'only to the extent that the *Inner City Charter* unavoidably couldn't not deal with it' (Gotz 2012). The *Charter* promised a completed smart card system as a management, development, enforcement and trader identification tool by the end of 2007 (COJ 2007d). However, the MTC was able to issue only 665 smart cards by August 2008 (Tissington 2009). The Economic Development Unit reported these delays were due to the lack of appropriate up-front planning and policy; unsynchronised internal systems; confusion about the implications of potential changes to restricted and prohibited trading areas; the number of traders included in the smart card system; 'contentious' trader registration processes; and the need to secure the national Home Affairs department's verification of asylum seekers given local traders' antipathy against foreign traders (COJ 2008r).

In October 2007, the politicians considered a revised *Informal Trading Policy for the City of Johannesburg* (COJ 2007b, 2009a). Although the policy may not have been formally approved at the time (Tissington 2009), it largely guided the COJ's approach to the sector from then on. The proposed policy contained an explicit development intention (by providing informal traders markets, linkages with formal traders, training, mentorship and business development), but it also focused on the regularisation and formalisation of the sector in a detailed operational way, allowing trading in designated areas only. By-law enforcement was still a key component of the informal trading policy as well as the prioritisation of the Inner City. The COJ's new regional director of the Office of Region F, Nkosinathi Mthethwa, since April 2007, was reputedly hands-on (COJ 2010c). Responsible for coordinating the delivery and improvement of local services in a multidisciplinary approach in Region F, namely urban management and maintenance operations, social, health, leisure and billing services, he had strong views about the need for enforcement in the inner city and was clearly frustrated. In October 2007, he said inadequate by-law enforcement was a 'disease' and the COJ was like 'a snake without poison' (COJ 2007c). He believed the COJ had to be far tougher on by-law infringers, to the point of making it 'hurt' (COJ 2007c). Mthethwa continued with multi-agency block-by-block interventions, as well as 'spring blitzes' in September and November 2007 (COJ 2007c, 2007i). In December, *Operation Shanyela* (Sweep It Up) targeted Hillbrow to deal with the 900 tons of monthly waste dumped illegally in the Inner City, with informal traders receiving 3,724 refuse bags but also about 86 citations for health violations (COJ 2007f, 2008a). Keeping the pressure on, in February 2008, the JMPD ran another five special enforcement campaigns in the city centre, including issuing citations for trading illegally and health violations; arresting street hairdressers, criminals and undocumented foreigners; and closing illegal liquor outlets, but also giving refuse bags to traders and handing out educational pamphlets (COJ 2008a).

On the developmental side, the COJ trained 1,067 informal traders in food safety and by-law compliance citywide in 2008 (COJ 2008m). On the operational front, though, the COJ was still struggling with the logistics of implementing its smart card management system, extending its completion date to June 2008 (COJ 2008m). Again, Mthethwa re-emphasised by-law enforcement, saying in March that 'if the Inner City fails, the whole city will fall' (COJ 2008k). Predictably, even though two more markets were coming online, with designs reportedly workshopped with and approved by beneficiaries (COJ 2008o), the One Voice of All Hawkers Association marched in protest to Mayor Masondo and the MTC on 24 April, handing over a memorandum calling for an end to the JMPD's 'harassment' and other demands (Tissington 2009). Despite this dissensus, the COJ planned to meet traders on 29 April 2008 to redraft the informal trading by-laws (*The Citizen* 2008). However, violent anti-foreigner protests erupted across South Africa and overtook any informal trading concerns. Again, citizens felt that foreigners took economic opportunities away from locals, which was at the core of much of the xenophobic sentiment (Centre for Study of Violence and Reconciliation 2008).

Even as traders protested, they were also engaging with the COJ on a new *Master Business Plan for Linear Markets for the Inner City of Johannesburg*, announced in October 2008 (COJ 2008p). This plan was the result of many consultative interactions over eight months between the MTC, 700 traders, trader representatives, the private sector, the police, ward councillors, and COJ departments and agencies (COJ 2008p, 2008r, 2009e). Despite stakeholders' concerns that the plan was vague in parts and that budget cuts caused unacceptable delays, the plan aimed to ease trading congestion in the streets and enable by-law enforcement by creating linear markets. Although the plan stated it covered the Inner City, it focused on only the first phase of implementation in 17 of the most congested city centre streets (and the nearby Fordsburg area). Once implemented, this phase would accommodate 97 per cent of the traders in this targeted area, namely 3,298 (COJ 2008p). Future phases of the plan to accommodate the remaining reported 6,815 traders in the wider Inner City were indefinite, with phases to be implemented sometime after the 2010 FIFA World Cup event or when budgets became available (COJ 2008p). The MTC again reiterated its intention to register each trader through the smart card system (COJ 2008p). Traders were to benefit from this stability (Lund and Skinner 2005) and could 'graduate' from the informal to the formal economy (COJ 2008l). Although some were sceptical these benefits could be realised (du Toit 2008; Rasmussen 2007; Rogerson 2008; Simone 2009), the Department of Economic Development and the MTC had nearly completed two more street markets by May 2009 (COJ 2009e) and organised adult basic education and training for 500 traders (COJ 2009f). However, mass actions took place in late 2009 when the South African Informal Traders Forum protested against the COJ's ongoing by-law enforcement and purported human rights infringements in August 2009. In December 2009, the One Voice of All Hawkers Association demanded the MTC's closure, an investigation of the JMPD's alleged corruption and the provision of more trading spaces in the city centre.

At last, the COJ was able to approve its informal trading policy in 2009, developed some two years earlier, after more workshops, including some in February 2009 with traders to elicit their inputs, which were facilitated by COSATU, the Congress of South African Trade Unions, the country's largest trade union (COJ 2009a). This approval also triggered the Department of Economic Development's creation and chairing of a new forum as envisaged in the policy, called the Johannesburg Informal Trading Forum, in 2009. This forum was intended to be a representative partnership bringing together traders, municipal departments and agencies, formal business associations, and political committees to facilitate informal traders' review and input into management matters, as well as to streamline by-laws and their implementation, create a new policy, and advise the COJ on implementation of sites and stalls and operational management (COJ 2010o).

However, traders were less focused on the forum than on expressing anger at being excluded from the benefits of increased trade promised by the upcoming June–July 2010 FIFA World Cup hosted by South Africa (Çelik 2011), as special by-laws were to prohibit informal trading at football events in compliance with FIFA's requirements (Province of Gauteng 2009). Traders, unsurprisingly, protested this exclusion and the COJ's allegedly overly vigorous and corrupt enforcement of the by-laws at least five times between 2009 and May 2010, including a thousand-strong march to Mayor Masondo.

Friction within the COJ also worked against potential agonistic engagements with traders. When the COJ's Mayoral Committee ordered the MTC's then chief executive officer's (Alfred Sam, deceased) reinstatement after his dismissal for alleged misconduct, four MTC board members resigned in protest in August 2010 at the COJ's interference in the MTC's governance (*The Sowetan* 2010). These events undermined the COJ's already tenuous relationship with informal traders, which had high expectations of 'their' government, making emotional appeals to the state to support and protect them, on the one hand, but protesting against its actions, on the other (Anonymous 2012c; City Press 2010; *Mail & Guardian* 2010a).

Sweeping clean and stalemate (2011–2015)

The COJ's bureaucratisation period of 2011–2015 saw the COJ's relationship with traders decline into even further animosity. The COJ became overtly hostile towards unmanaged trading, peaking in its much-publicised, disastrous *Operation Clean Sweep* and subsequent constitutional challenge in 2013, and followed by a trading management stalemate for years thereafter.

When the new executive mayor, Councillor Mpho Parks Tau, took office in May 2011, he declared a new 'business-unusual' approach to service delivery (COJ 2011j). Traders' protests in 2011 became increasingly rights-based (Pernegger 2016). Although the COJ's policy statements supported people's right to make a living, in reality the COJ was less supportive of informal traders, with Matjomane (2013) finding the Informal Trading Forum ineffectual in allowing traders to voice concerns as the forum had become deeply divisive and played the personality-driven associations off one another and met but infrequently, only once in 2011, for instance.

From the COJ's perspective, traders were beyond enforcement. The COJ found the complexity and density of Inner City informal trading overwhelmingly difficult to manage. According to the City Safety Programme's manager in the JMPD (Cachalia 2012), traders knowingly broke the rules. The Public Protector also reported in August 2011 that traders and others had gotten away with by-law violations, leading to 'anarchy' in Johannesburg (*The Star* 2011). Yet the municipal court dismissed around 16,000 of 21,000 illegal informal trading notices issued by JMPD officers as they contained falsified and incorrectly completed information – deliberately so, hinted the media (*The Star* 2011).

After years of negotiations, on 14 March 2012, the GPG promulgated revised *Informal Trading By-Laws*, repealing the 2004 by-laws; these new by-laws underscored the role of designated areas and markets to control trading and were aligned closely to the 2009 policy (Province of Gauteng 2012). The Concerned Hawkers Group and the One Voice of All Hawkers Association made four formal objections and requested permission to march against the by-laws' changes between May and November 2012. The COJ–traders relationship became even more antagonistic when the COJ allegedly reneged in June 2012 on an agreement with associations to use enforcement only as 'the last resort' (*The New Age* 2012).

The inability to cope with the Inner City's continued and long-term decline into a 'slum' frustrated other senior managers and politicians in the COJ (COJ 2012h). To reverse this, Councillor Roslynn Greeff, the Member of the Mayoral Committee for Development Planning and Urban Management, endorsed a *Mayoral Clean Sweep* of the Inner City to the Development Planning Committee in October 2012 (COJ 2012h). The report said the 'old ways of doing things have not worked' in addressing challenges of dirt, crime, congestion, traders operating illegally, building invasions, homelessness, antisocial behaviour, and neglect (COJ 2012h, p. 1). The report proposed the mayor spearhead the initiative (COJ 2012h). The focus would be on getting the basics right, including enforcement in a coordinated way. Thereafter, the mayor would hand the initiative over to the Member of the Mayoral Committee for Development Planning to continue (COJ 2012h). The first *Clean Sweep* operation took place in October 2012 (*The Star* 2012b). This was a limited operation, possibly because of the COJ's institutional restructuring at the time, bound to impact future informal trading management (COJ 2011m). By then, the MTC's role had expanded far beyond its initially envisaged facilities management one. It had become the COJ's implementer of much of the informal trading policy's operational aspects, as well as taxi rank management for the ubiquitous but privately owned informal mass transit minibus taxis. Despite the MTC's widened scope of activities and the clear need for holistic management of the sector, the COJ decided the MTC's functions should be split as the MTC had become too costly to run and did not need to be corporatised as other entities were (COJ 2011m). Economic development functions, staff and budgets were to be moved to the Department of Economic Development, and taxi rank management to the Department of Transport (COJ 2011m). The rest of the functions, namely facilities and property management of the markets, including staff and budgets, were then absorbed into the Johannesburg Property Company in November 2012 (COJ 2012c). This restructuring created a gap in the COJ's management of informal trading.

Into this gap stepped other spheres of government. First, the national government's Department of Trade and Industry, also frustrated about unmanaged trading, signalled intensified enforcement in its *Draft Licensing of Businesses Bill* (RSA 2013) of March 2013. The Bill proposed the state would establish an inspectorate of police, metropolitan police and peace officers, which would have the right to question, search, fine and jail informal traders who broke the law. Unsurprisingly, traders and their associations, formal businesses, political opposition parties, and others objected to the Bill's extreme impracticality, xenophobic stance, sloppiness, expense, and regression to apartheid-style rule (*Mail & Guardian* 2013a). This Bill was still in limbo, neither revised nor officially abandoned, as of early 2019. Then the GPG also stepped in, proposing to develop a uniform policy across the province in talks in July 2013 with a new umbrella body of informal traders (Province of Gauteng 2013). Meanwhile, in Johannesburg, the One Voice of All Hawkers Association stepped up its protests. It planned five marches between June and August 2013, demanding the right to trade and to trading spaces.

The ill-fated *Operation Clean Sweep* story unfolded over a ten-week period starting on 1 October 2013. Bénit-Gbaffou (2018) provides a thorough account of the operation; I have also provided a detailed timeline (Pernegger 2016). To summarise, though, the COJ planned this operation in response to complaints from pedestrians, formal businesses and other members of the public in the Inner City about informal trading's 'unmanaged chaos' (*The Star* 2013a). The operation also targeted crime and grime issues, illegal dumping and littering, building and land invasions, and illegal services connections (*The Star* 2013c). A politically led interdepartmental and intergovernmental multidisciplinary team, with unprecedented levels of coordination, carried out the operation. Team members came from the COJ's Public Safety, JMPD (with a new head since September 2013), the Johannesburg Road Agency, City Power, Joburg Water, Environmental Health, the Johannesburg Property Company and the national Department of Home Affairs. The team even included the South African Revenue Service to address the influx of counterfeit goods on the streets.

The JMPD, purportedly heavy-handedly, evicted between 2,000 and 8,000 traders from the Inner City, clearing both illegal and legal stalls from streets and re-demarcated sites (*Business Day* 2013a; *Mail & Guardian* 2013b; *The Citizen* 2013a; *The Star* 2013a). The COJ verified permits: it had issued only 800 permits to traders for legitimate trading sites but about 2,000–3,000 permits were in circulation, most fraudulent (*Mail & Guardian* 2013b; *The New Age* 2013). Matters between the COJ and traders became strained. Each accused the other of telling lies (*Business Day* 2013a). Traders protested and issued ultimatums to the COJ to stop the operation and allow traders to return to the streets (Socio-Economic Rights Institute of South Africa 2013). The COJ and trader representatives failed to find solutions despite meeting ten times between 25 October and 8 November 2013 (Pernegger 2016). Trading associations had requested the COJ set up a joint operations committee, which the COJ had agreed to on 25 November (COJ 2013g), to consider reallocations of stalls, resolve objections to the permit verifications and allocations, and identify streets suitable for new trading sites. However, talks collapsed when traders accused the COJ of not acting in 'good faith' (Pernegger 2016). The COJ's operation was vilified as being 'anti-poor' (Harrison et al. 2013; Socio-Economic Rights Institute of South Africa 2013; *The Citizen* 2013b).

Traders sought relief from the High Court on 26 November 2013. The court, however, postponed the application, agreeing with the COJ that the matter was not urgent (*Business Day* 2013c). The traders appealed, successfully, to the Constitutional Court, which temporarily interdicted the COJ from further evictions on 5 December 2013 (*The Star* 2014d). The COJ had to allow traders to return to their trading spots in the interim without the JMPD's interference (*The Citizen* 2013c; *The Star* 2013b).

Ultimately, on 4 April 2014, the Constitutional Court ruled the COJ's actions had been procedurally and legislatively flawed and had violated traders' right to trade (*The Star* 2014a). The COJ, forced to respond to the ruling, decided in May 2014 to try a new approach to create a new informal trading plan based on inputs from stakeholders

(COJ 2014c). The COJ then reinstigated discussions in July 2014, for a 'lasting' solution to the ongoing challenges (*The Citizen* 2014a). Talks took place over several weeks between the COJ and Inner City residents, formal and informal businesses, public transport operators, and others (CityBuzz 2014). But by August 2014, despite apparent goodwill, the individual groups' vested interests still continued to hamper any agreements between the parties (*The Star* 2014c).

The GPG's Department of Economic Development also played a role in trying to resolve this impasse. The Member of the Executive Council for Economic Development in the GPG, Lebogang Maile, convened a session of municipalities and 37 informal trading associations on 21 September 2014 (*The Citizen* 2014b). To provide 'financial and non-financial support' to small businesses, including informal traders, the GPG created the *Gauteng Informal Businesses Upliftment Strategy* that aligned with a national version of the plan (GPG 2016b). However, the COJ's new informal trading development plan was still a long way off. Traders also blocked the new African Food and Cultural Hub project in Eloff Street, fearful they would not be allowed to return to their trading sites (*Saturday Star* 2014).

Prospects for agonistic practices by the COJ after the Constitutional Court's ruling were even more remote, given the COJ's launch of *Operation Ke Molao* (It's the Law) in February 2015. This operation seemed to some to be a repeat of *Operation Clean Sweep* (TimesLive 2015; Webster 2015), with the COJ continuing to emphasise by-law compliance at the expense of traders' development. By then, the forum had been completely disbanded and the relationship between the COJ and traders had disintegrated (Bénit-Gbaffou 2016). The COJ was unable to move towards an alternative way of governing informal trading (Bénit-Gbaffou 2018).

Eventually, though, in April 2016, after wide engagement and detailed studies, the COJ's Department of Economic Development gave stakeholders feedback on a final draft informal trading plan (COJ 2016). Internally, the department had integrated aspects of the plan with departments responsible for land use planning, urban management, economic development and transportation. This plan tried overtly to balance traders' development with enforcement. The four-pronged plan's concepts were similar to previous plans, aiming to decongest the most crowded pavements, minimise illegal trading activities, provide extra trading spaces and manage traders. Management arrangements were to comprise trader registrations, agreements with precinct managers, an agreed-upon informal trading forum, special project management capacity, Inner City subcommittee support and dedicated enforcement.

The COJ would even consider self-management options if they aligned with procurement legislation.

However, before this nascent plan could be adopted, the COJ was overtaken by the August 2016 local government elections. The new Democratic Alliance-led coalition prioritised the Inner City. However, the COJ's efforts to resolve unmanaged trading have yet to yield a concrete plan that satisfies all parties as of March 2019 (COJ 2019). Informal trading management remains in limbo.

Observations

The chronology of the city administration's responses to the well over 50 protests by informal traders in Johannesburg's Inner City paints a mixed picture of its responses to conflict over the four periods. Despite a seeming broad orientation towards agonism between the city administration and informal traders in the earlier post-apartheid years, the application of agonistic practices to these processes of conflict by the end of this period is not much in evidence.

In qualifying the conflict about Inner City informal trading, the city administration initially recognised the right of traders to trade and demonstrated qualities boding well for the adoption of an agonistic governance: the new city administration was experimental, took informal trading protests seriously, was willing to engage in partnerships to tackle challenges, and empowered traders' associations to participate in conflictual engagements. However, as the city administration matured and stakeholders demanded a managed informal trading sector, these qualities and the potential for agonistic practice dissipated, with the COJ expressing progressively negative views about anything to do with the perceived (and real) nuisance, chaos, lawlessness and anarchy of informal trading.

The city administration's portrayal of protestors somewhat followed this broad trend towards, if not entirely agonistic, certainly responsive practices. Although it treated traders in the earlier years as vulnerable survivalists in need of protection and as citizens, it also recognised informal trading associations could be disingenuous, untruthful and manipulative. Even as the COJ matured post-2001, it still saw traders as a vital part of the African city, but was also aware they operated illegally, could be bullies, and played on emotions by wanting the city administration's protection while protesting against it at the same time. By 2013, at the time *Operation Clean Sweep* occurred, the city administration saw traders as beyond enforcement: anarchical, dirty, illegal and law-breaking.

The city administration's responses happened at three levels. At the level of the informal trading protest events themselves, we see a similar pattern in its responses to protest incidents elsewhere. Here, if protestors were violent, the city administration forcibly suppressed protest-related violence to protect lives and property. Sometimes it did so with the help of other state actors, such as the army during the xenophobic protests in Johannesburg of 1997 and 1998, as well as those nationally in 2008. Even when protests were not violent, the city administration was as likely to ignore protestors as to pacify them by meeting with them.

Then, when dealing with the effects of the issues under contention, the city administration's responses followed the broad trend of a seemingly agonistic organisation initially that became gradually hostile towards informal trading over time. It displayed some ostensibly agonistic approaches in the immediate post-apartheid period. This support included amending by-laws jointly with traders in 1998; supporting the new umbrella body for trading associations, the Gauteng Informal Sector Forum; and negotiating new stall allocation criteria with traders. Placatory concessions, such as halving the Yeoville Market's rentals in 2002, did not seem to calm protestors for more than a few months. The COJ became more antagonistic and less willing to engage much with informal trading associations until shortly before *Operation Clean Sweep*. During and after this operation, the COJ became increasingly defensive and even hostile, with talks with informal trading associations collapsing. These responses overshadowed the more positive training provision, creation of markets and participation. However, this broad trend contains some inconsistencies: while broadly agonistic during the earlier period, the city administration could also be repressive, as in its enforcement of the Braamfontein precinct of the Inner City as a restricted trading area in 1999. Likewise, even when antagonistic in later periods, it displayed some agonistic, or at least responsive, practices. For instance, the COJ delayed enforcement for a few months in 2003, halted the cages initiative in response to protests from informal and formal traders in 2004, drove intense engagements for the *Master Business Plan for Linear Markets for the Inner City of Johannesburg* in 2008, and facilitated workshops with traders in 2009 led by COSATU, the Congress of South African Trade Unions. Even at the height of its hostility towards traders in *Operation Clean Sweep*, the COJ stopped the operation and engaged, presumably partly agonistically, in many public meetings, even if inadequately.

Lastly, in tackling the root cause of the issues, the city administration was more likely to be responsive towards traders rather than deny the dissensus. It incorporated empowerment principles in its practices with traders, for instance, by using ex-activist officials to build bridges with them; issuing shares to traders (although unrealised in practice); partnering with traders and associations, and landowners, for designing management options, ensuring traders were able to enter into dialogue and make decisions about management options through the Inner City Street Trading Interim Crisis Committee and the Inner City Committee in the late 1990s, and the forums created in 2005 and 2009; granting concessions on rentals and enforcement grace periods; and experimenting on joint initiatives and providing skills training. As the COJ matured, though, it moved away from this more experimental approach to a less flexible one as it sought to standardise its management and enforcement measures. Many of the measures noted in this paragraph and the ones above also point to the city administration's sensitivity to unbalanced power dynamics between the city administration and the traders, and between traders and trading associations. Through its practices, the city administration acknowledged traders were vulnerable and disempowered, creating structures for traders to engage in and partner on management matters, projects and policies. However, over time, these actions dwindled, becoming less effective, as in the COJ's Informal Trading Forum, started in 2009, which traders were to criticise as a mere box-ticking exercise a few years later. On more than one occasion, traders found they had no voice, resorting to the courts in 2002 and 2013 to have their concerns heard.

The practices most closely aligned to agonistic principles, especially in the initial post-apartheid period in the 1990s and early 2000s, resulted in co-created project and policy agreements. However, later on, any agreements tended to be implicit in the city administration's responsiveness, although rarely agonistically so, to the issues underlying the dissensus. Quite often the city administration's responses were deemed inadequate, as in traders' disregard of the forum as an effective space to engage with the COJ on their issues.

How could the state have responded more agonistically, and why did it not? Prospects for an agonistic approach by the newly democratic local-level state reflected post-apartheid goodwill and the global and national shift towards economic liberalism to support job creation. The city administration, imbued with this new spirit of freedom, undertook some, at least partly agonistic, cooperative efforts with traders and associations. However, later efforts revealed the city administration's increasing hostility towards informal traders. Quite why it became so is hard to appreciate, given the context and objectives of post-apartheid governance, the 2008 global economic crisis, South Africa's high unemployment levels and stated policy support for livelihood efforts such as informal trading. I credit this antagonism and the lack of agonistic practices to two main forces influencing the city administration's stance towards conflict management. First, the specific interests and politics of local role-players directed events and resources away from agonistic management after the city administration's financial crisis of 1997 and beyond. The city administration and formal business aspired to make Johannesburg a world-class city, leaving little room for informal trading's perceived disorder. As political and business sentiment hardened towards informal trading's so-called chaos, the COJ intensified by-law enforcement efforts. It also stepped up market development, including tighter revenue controls to ensure their viability. Informal traders resisted these measures and protested more regularly. This deepened levels of mistrust, hostility and aggression between the COJ and informal traders and their associations. Second, internal tensions within the local government group and traders' groups were not cohesive internally. The city administration displayed many internal inconsistencies. Departments, and even individuals, had different approaches, reflecting each other's unresolved attitudes of affinity or hostility towards traders. This meant multiple and frequently contradictory tendencies within the broad trend towards or away from agonism. Traders, too, were also often irresolute in their interests, approaches and demands, making consistently productive interactions with the city administration difficult. Even the fluidity of positions within the trading associations themselves, within the context of their changing internal politics and broader contexts, compounded the management challenge. Ultimately, these mistrusts solidified around *Operation Clean Sweep*, leaving informal trading management in limbo for years.

In closing, consider the local-level state's potential for agonistic practice in this story. The city administration's mindset towards conflict management in the Inner City informal trading sector in earlier years was broadly agonistic, but became steadily more antagonistic in later periods; this broad trend is recognisable in the complex chronology of protests and responses of post-apartheid Johannesburg. Here, wider forces fostered the city administration's initial adoption of agonistic principles in its practices, to experiment, partner and centre conflict in its efforts to manage informal trading. One would expect the more mature and experienced organisation of the later periods to have invested in increased capability for agonistic interaction, yet it did not. Here, the role-players' vested interests, and internal tensions within the informal trading sector and the city administration, constrained the agonistic impulse. Even when individual practices appear agonistic, their hybrid and unclear nature is impossible to disentangle from other collaborative and participative processes, making it difficult to define precisely what is agonistic. Even when an agonistic, or partly agonistic, practice was in play, it did not necessarily automatically resolve issues underlying dissensus, challenging agonism's inherent assumption that centralising conflict agonistically will always lead to beneficial outcomes. However, in the context of the Democratic Alliance-led coalition city that followed between 2016 and late 2019, and over two decades of democratic governance, this Inner City informal trading struggle story is still far from complete.

Notes

1. The Central Johannesburg Partnership became Kagiso Urban Management in 2003 and then Urban Genesis in 2010.

2. I worked as the SMLC's Manager of Economic Empowerment and Business Support between 1996 and 1999, which included the management and development of the informal trading sector.

6
Billing backlash by middle-class suburbia

Strife in middle-class suburbia

The last in this trio of city strife stories explores the suburban middle class's backlash against the city administration's so-called billing crisis. The crisis began with the city administration's antagonistic approach to boycotting ratepayers and ended with its experimental and proactive responses to customers. The battle was long-lasting because of the city administration's enduring technical difficulties encountered with the billing system. The middle class's backlash against the billing crisis embarrassed the city administration until it had no option but to respond with corrective measures and various conflict management tactics. Party politics further complicated this struggle. Although scholars overlook middle-class battles, tending to focus on other post-apartheid protests by low-income communities, exploring middle-class protest provides further insight into the city administration's conflict-related practices across different groups, spatial locations, and types of service delivery.

The selected suburbs reveal a small but powerful middle-class group of protestors, forming part of a larger historically white middle-class area stretching from Johannesburg's historic city centre northwards. Although this suburban area's combined footprint is 28 square kilometres, similar in size to Orange Farm's 31 square kilometres (Quantec 2014) (see Chapter 4), its population is much smaller, roughly a quarter of its size. At 45,061 people, it represents but 1.4 per cent of all city households (2011 data) (Quantec 2014) and could not be more different than Orange Farm. This middle-class residential area was well established already by 2001 (Selzer and Heller 2010), having grown northwards in phases between the early 1900s and 1970s along main transport routes between the city centre and the initially speculative Sandton business node in the north. Each part of this area has its own distinctive character, created by developers and prevailing planning trends (Mabin 2014). Although a few high streets dot the area, its dominant economic centres are Rosebank and Hyde Park, with Sandton at its north-eastern edge (for the 17 suburbs included in the study area and its main features, see Map 6.1). The label *middle class* in Johannesburg is somewhat imprecise as it includes wealthy groups considered 'upper middle class' and the 'middle middle class', which have consolidated spatially in the northern suburbs since 1996 according to Selzer and Heller (2010), as well as their more downmarket southern-based blue-collar middle-class counterparts (Harrison and Zack 2014; Mabin 2014). Even parts of the historically black Soweto can be identified as middle class or emerging middle class (Phadi and Ceruti 2011), and share some service delivery concerns with this selected middle-class area.

The selected middle-class area falls amidst Johannesburg's most elite areas (Mabin 2014). As home to South Africa's wealthiest people, and with the highest property values in the city and the country, the area contributes significantly to the city administration's income in the form of property taxes, or 'rates' (BusinessTech 2012, 2014). Importantly for this story, this middle-class area's suburbs were all represented by Democratic Alliance councillors. This political dynamic was to prove challenging for the ANC-led city management until the August 2016 local government elections when the ANC lost control of Johannesburg to a Democratic Alliance-led coalition. Although this area has witnessed changes in population growth and racial composition between 1996 and 2011, these were less marked than other parts of the city. This area is also far wealthier relative to the rest of the city and the country. Citizens' economic prospects and resources here are better too, with superior levels of employment, education, car ownership and access to the Internet. The unemployment rate here was only 3 per cent in 2011, far lower than the city and provincial rates of 21 per cent and the national rate of 22 per cent (Quantec 2014). These demographics created area-specific protest dynamics distinct from low-income protests. State actors within the city administration hardly seem to consider protests from the middle class as protests, relative to those originating in low-income areas. Indeed, neither did I when I started my research, and it was only the coincidence of the middle class's expressions of dissatisfaction in the media, reporting on the thousands of billing complaints, that helped me recognise these three stories are linked.

Contrary to Schreiber's (2013) view that South Africa's middle class does not protest, Pernegger (2016) has documented several of its protests. Although the middle class uses different logics compared to low-income protestors, it also seeks to change the level of participation in democratic governance (Fuentes and Frank 1989). Still continuing with the theme of resistance to the actions of the local-level state, 6,000 pet lovers objected to the COJ's draft *By-Laws Relating to Dogs and Cats* in 2006 (Anonymous 2012d). Communities in Rosebank and

Map 6.1 – Suburbs in selected middle-class area

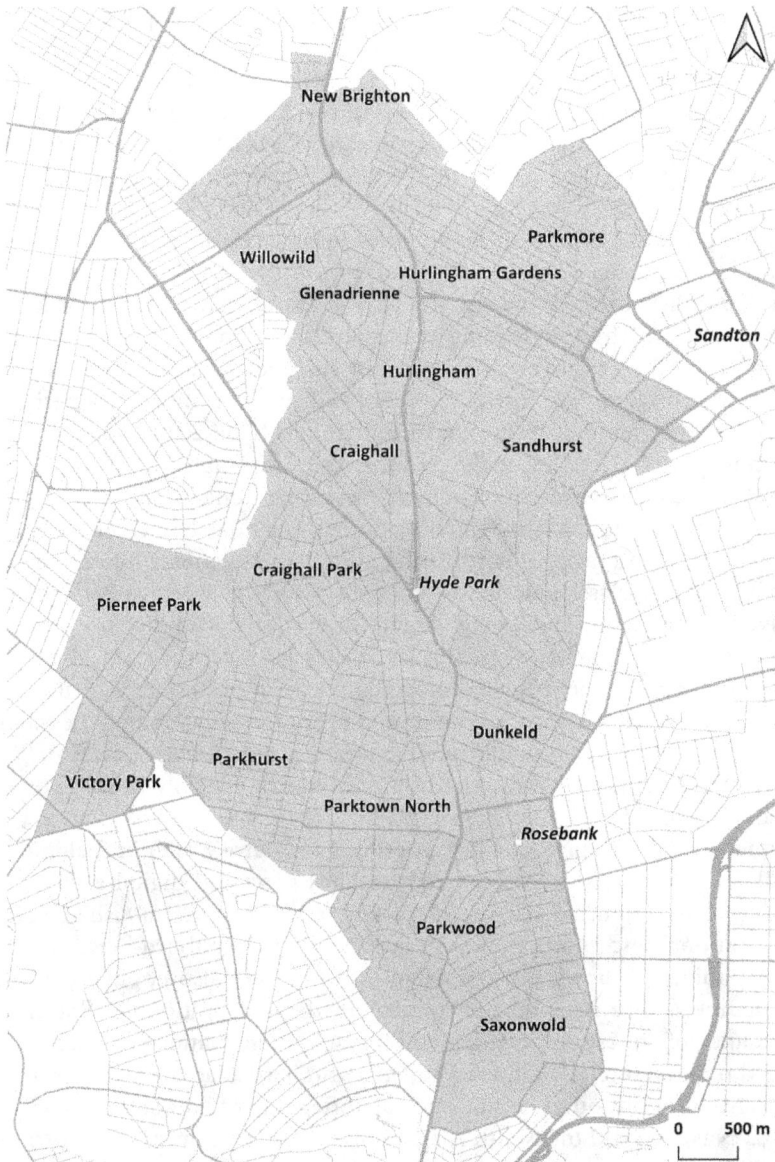

New Brighton

Parkmore

Willowild

Hurlingham Gardens

Glenadrienne

Sandton

Hurlingham

Craighall

Sandhurst

Craighall Park

Hyde Park

Pierneef Park

Dunkeld

Parkhurst

Victory Park

Parktown North

Rosebank

Parkwood

Saxonwold

0   500 m

Note: Includes 17 suburbs of Saxonwold, Parkwood, Parktown North, Rosebank, Dunkeld, Parkhurst, Hyde Park, Craighall, Craighall Park, Sandhurst, Hurlingham, Hurlingham Gardens, Glenadrienne, New Brighton, Parkmore, Pierneef Park and Victory Park.

Source: Author's formulation

Saxonwold successfully resisted the COJ's proposed public transport project along Oxford Road between 2008 and 2012 (news24 2011; Rea Vaya 2008). Potholes and traffic congestion frequently outraged motorists, and still do today (ioL News 2011d, 2020; iTWeb 2011e). The alleged closure of a local library incensed residents in 2011 (*The Star* 2012e). Shopkeepers and residents contested the COJ's installation of paid parking in the high street of Parkhurst between 2012 and 2014 (ioL News 2014).

In the protests I observed, the middle-class protestors favoured protesting in the media – and social media – through articles written by news journalists and other activists, almost exclusively over the picketing tactic used by low-income communities. Using the media was a high-profile but relatively low-cost and sustainable tactic over long periods, often taking the form of a concerted media campaign, a petition or a memorandum, by groups or individuals (Cox 2012). Even the local newspaper, *The Star*, facilitated this tactic through MetroWatch, a weekly local government watchdog featuring Johannesburg's service delivery failures. MetroWatch's editorial agenda shamed the city administration into action by featuring complaints (generally common to many middle-class households) that the COJ's call centre had not resolved within a month of being lodged (Cox 2012). Middle-class protestors very rarely staged a street protest or a sit-in; if they did, these were not violent, except in one instance where a protest turned into a scuffle between factions within the protesting group (Look Local 2011b). Notwithstanding their relative wealth, middle-class protestors rarely went to court, or threatened to go to court, possibly because of the costs involved.

Other media coverage was just as critical as MetroWatch in fuelling middle-class protests, which centred on hard copy and digital articles by investigative journalists, reporters and opinionistas, published in local, national and international newspapers, trade publications, and blogs. Radio talk shows and television features were also popular protest channels. The two most prominent media corporations in South Africa and Johannesburg, owning newspapers, radio stations and satellite and terrestrial television, are Primedia and Tiso Blackstar (formerly Times Media), but other media, such as Independent Newspapers and Media, Naspers, and the South African Broadcasting Corporation, also provided important protest forums for the middle class.

Although a single complaint by an individual may not constitute a protest, it can be a precursor to one. The malcontent makes a complaint to a specific authority (such as to the COJ's call centre or petitions system, or to the Presidential Hotline) expecting a response or redress.

Should the authority not address the complaint, the malcontent will find another way, usually publicly, to bring the issue to the authority's attention. Such a complaint is easily escalated by the media, especially when enough people (including those controlling news agendas) share the same concern. Their collective rage and sense of betrayal, injustice and powerlessness can escalate this dissatisfaction into a protest, in the same way tensions rose with traders in the Inner City and Orange Farm residents. The protesters thus act collectively to resolve their issue (DeHoog et al. 1990; Grégoire and Fisher 2008; Ward and Ostrom 2006).

In Johannesburg, the full extent of such protests was not easy to see; such protests might even have seemed insignificant to the city administration at the time as they were driven by only a few activists purporting to represent a larger community (Peacock 2012). However, state actors stressed that the city administration had to provide resources to manage these middle-class protests, especially as the media has the potential to exaggerate a matter (Anonymous 2012d). An example of such a protest, and the feature of this story, is the billing crisis. As with most customer-focused organisations, Johannesburg's billing system is an important indicator of the perceived and actual financial health of the city administration. This financial health translates into much-needed cash in hand and cheaper loans to develop and maintain areas throughout the city. Any dissensus about the billing system must then have a potentially negative effect on all residents.

Antagonism towards rates boycotters (1996–2000)

The first post-apartheid city administration met with a rates revolt when it implemented its 'one city, one tax base' policy during the transition period between 1996 and 2000, and was deeply non-agonistic, even antagonistic, towards the middle-class protestors. Although the city administration made some minor concessions during the rates revolt, its interactions with the middle class were mostly antagonistic. The city administration decentralised the billing functions to the individual MLCs in 1997 and then re-centralised billing when it formed the unicity in 2000. These restructurings of the billing function would contribute to the billing crisis that was to stretch from 2001 to 2013. The middle class had already been alienated from the city administration during the rates revolt of the 1990s and was impatient with billing struggles. Prospects for future agonistic engagements during this period declined due to the apparent mutual hostility and the city administration's denial of a billing crisis.

Central to the rates revolt was the 'one city, one tax base' concept; popularised by the black resistance struggle (Pillay et al. 2006), the concept was the cornerstone of new local government in South Africa (Van Ryneveld 2006). The concept manifested in the Johannesburg city administration's strong localised redistribution agenda (Reddy 2003). Turning the 'one city, one tax base' slogan into reality drove the state to restructure resources to facilitate city integration (Visser 2001). However, the processes to do so were far from perfect (Powell 2012). Pre-1994, the jurisdiction of the selected middle-class suburbs had fallen under three councils, namely Sandton, Randburg and Johannesburg. When the new democratic GJMC and the decentralised MLCs were created in November 1995, these middle-class suburbs fell then under the Eastern and Northern MLCs' management (comparison of over-lays of spatial data from Beavon 1997; COJ 2001a, 2003f, 2003g). The Eastern MLC residents were already disgruntled at losing their bat-tle earlier in 1992 for a form of city administration that would enable them to avoid the redistribution policy (Clarno 2013). The Eastern MLC's contribution was a significant 43.6 per cent, or R642.92 million ($109.07 million), of the city's total annual rates revenue of R1.47 bil-lion ($0.25 billion) (1998 data) (Emdon 1998). Moreover, its payment level was near 100 per cent while Orange Farm's was 5 per cent and Soweto's was 27 per cent (Tomlinson 1999b).

The middle class's fears were realised when, in an antagonistic move in July 1996, the GJMC and the Eastern MLC sharply increased rates without any prior discussion (COJ 2001a). The GJMC aimed to stand-ardise rates across the municipal area and redistribute the revenue to develop the poorer southern and western areas of the city (Clarno 2013; Emdon 1998). The Sandton Ratepayers Association and 30 other res-idents' associations and the formal business sector were outraged at the GJMC's unfair increase of between 150 and 358 per cent (Clarno 2013; Wilson 2019). They did not think the city administration could spend funds wisely (Bell and Bowman 2002; Tomlinson 1999b) due to the MLCs' irresponsible spending since January 1996 on the assump-tion that the GJMC would cover any shortfalls (COJ 2006e). So, they embarked on the 'Sandton rates boycott', or 'rates revolt', as the city administration dubbed it (COJ 2006e; Lipietz 2008).

Antagonism between the city administrators and protestors was obvious in Clarno's (2013) and Camay and Gordon's (2004) detailed accounts of the rates revolt. The city administration's initial talks with the Sandton Federation of Ratepayers Associations (SANFED), in November and December 1996, were so filled with rancour that a stale-mate arose. The provincial government's interventions worsened the impasse (Camay and Gordon 2004). Another group, Fedsure, representing ten corporations including Fedsure Life Assurance and other property, investment and insurance businesses in Sandton, protested through the High Court in December 1996 and later the Supreme Court of Appeal. Fedsure argued the increase was neither procedural nor lawful (Fedsure Life Assurance Ltd and Others vs Greater Johannesburg Transitional Metropolitan Council and Others 1998b).

This conflict teaches us valuable governance lessons on how not to be agonistic, drawing on Camay and Gordon (2004). Namely, the local-level state's stance towards SANFED and Fedsure perpetuated the ongoing deadlock: protestors thought the GJMC was unsympathetic and the GJMC accused SANFED of being hysterical (Camay and Gordon 2004). The provincial government 'undermined rather than promoted resolution' (Camay and Gordon 2004, p. 27). Further, from the protestors' perspective, the state was uncommitted to resolving the problem, was prejudiced, and divided the members of the team tasked by the GPG to resolve the impasse (Camay and Gordon 2004). The ANC may have felt it had the moral high ground but the MLCs' and the GJMC's leaders failed to detach themselves from political bias in interactions with protestors. The media painted the GJMC as bullying tyrants (Clarno 2013) and as acting unfairly (Camay and Gordon 2004).

In July 1997, the GJMC transferred the billing function to the MLCs. This move was disastrous for the GJMC as it then found it impossible to get a full picture of its cash position (Tomlinson 1999b). In August 1997, the GJMC was under severe financial pressure and had to borrow money to fund its cash flow (Camay and Gordon 2004). Responsive to opposition parties' censure, the GJMC also did not apply the annual rates increase in July 1997 (Camay and Gordon 2004).

The rates revolt soured the relationship between the city administration and the middle class. Although the city administration was sensitised to what the powerful middle class held as important (Beall et al. 2000), it also alienated it. Whether differing political inclinations (Camay and Gordon 2004) or racial dynamics (Clarno 2013) drove the conflict, the relationship was now fraught with anxiety and acrimony. Rather than seeing protestors as citizens, the city administration found it easier to see them as customers. The bill for services became 'the symbol of communication between local government and its citizens' (*Business Day* 2001). Indeed, the revenue department saw citizens as 'account numbers, without which they are not recognised at all' (Hunter and Phakathi 2010, pp. 6–7). This boycott may even have masked the billing crisis's early warning signs. Even when the city administration did respond more obligingly, it was not enough to break the impasse, and may have made it worse. For instance, in August 1997, the Eastern MLC refused customer payments against bills with mistakes, afraid to admit tacitly that these amounts were inaccurate, but proceeded to cut off services for non-payment anyway (Camay and Gordon 2004). These billing inaccuracies and the city's hard-line approach to non-payment, despite its mistakes, further damaged the city administration's reputation and relationship with middle-class suburbs (Peacock 2012).

The rates revolt also had a financial consequence, in tipping the city administration into financial crisis in October 1997 (COJ 2006e; Lipietz 2008), and ultimately into full-scale restructuring of the administration (Emdon 1998). The financial crisis was not only due to the non-receipt of the boycotted payments, but also due to the city administration's hands-off revenue management approach, difficulties with the new property valuation roll, the high level of spending of funds it did not have, and ever-increasing capital expenditure demands (COJ 2006e). This financial squeeze continued into 1998. By June 1998, the boycotting ratepayers owed the city administration R180 million ($30.54 million) (Emdon 1998). Ultimately, the Constitutional Court settled the rates revolt in October 1998. The court upheld an earlier High Court ruling that the city administration's actions had been lawful and procedural, although the judges' decision was split (Fedsure Life Assurance Ltd and Others vs Greater Johannesburg Transitional Metropolitan Council and Others 1998a, 1998c). The boycotters then had no choice but to capitulate and began to repay the outstanding rates to the city administration (Camay and Gordon 2004).

In 1999, the GJMC proposed the *iGoli 2002* plan to tackle its financial and organisational challenges with a new form of city administration (GJMC 1999d). The new unicity of the COJ was a consolidation of the GJMC and the four MLCs. The new COJ was reorganised into six new central departments and 11 Offices of the Regions (COJ 2006e). Also, in 2000, the COJ began to centralise the separate financial systems that fell previously under the MLCs (*Mail & Guardian* 2011a), which in turn comprised data in different formats derived from 13 former administrations (COJ 2006e). At the same time, though, the COJ then also separated and corporatised specific services into 14 new service delivery entities (COJ 2006e). The combined COJ employed 26,720 staff across the city, about ten staff per 1,000 citizens (Emdon 1998). The main new entities of City Power, Joburg Water and Pikitip supplied electricity, water and refuse removal services, respectively. Each entity developed its own revenue, financial management and billing systems, and even call centres (COJ 2006e). The individual systems were not harmonised with the COJ's departmental systems (COJ 2006e). Further, the entities'

systems contained disjointed data and used different software pack-
ages. Some even encompassed inbuilt defects (COJ 2006e). External
state departments, which impacted on the COJ's billing responsibilities,
namely the Registrar of Deeds and the Surveyor General, were also not
aligned to the COJ's requirements (Hunter and Phakathi 2010).

Initial attempts by the COJ to integrate these disparate decentralised billing systems and functions failed. Successful integration relied
on the transfer of clean data from each billing-related department and
entity to a common system. However, data were unchecked, corrupt,
incompatible and inconsistent. The COJ lacked a sufficiently methodical
approach. Further, parts of the city the COJ had never billed before and
other fast-growing areas needed accurate data to support billing too. The
integration scheme failed as it did not account for these factors (Peacock
2012). By now, the 1997 financial crisis, the COJ's high debt repay-
ments and the Fitch credit agency's less-than-ideal ranking of the city
administration as BBB+ in 1999 meant that effective billing and clean
audits, on a base of new and improved financial systems, were needed to
reduce the costs of long- and short-term borrowings (COJ 2006e).

The COJ gave the disgruntled middle class the impression for years
that the billing challenge was a simple matter that could be speedily and
simply resolved with some information technology expertise (ioL News
2002b). It is unlikely that the COJ recognised sufficiently at that time that
the billing system was part of a much larger enterprise redesign needed
to support the COJ's multibillion-rand business operations. The start
of work on the billing system came in the form of the GJMC's award
of a R500 million ($62.83 million) five-year contract to Sebedisana in
October 2000 for information technology services to centralise, integrate
and update the city administration's computer and data needs (iTWeb
2003, 2007, 2009a). Sebedisana was a joint venture between Masana
Technologies and IBM South Africa, with Masana Technologies as
the junior partner (iTWeb 2007; van den Berg et al. 2006). Masana
Technologies was a relatively new company set up in 1997 and incorporated into the Peu Group in 1999 (Peu Group 2015). Peu was later to be
implicated in an irregular multibillion-rand prepaid meter contract with
another municipality in 2013 (*Daily Maverick* 2013).

Johannesburg strives to channel complaints (2001–2005)

The new COJ unicity, having realised the billing system was unstable due
to the different data platforms and the restructuring of Johannesburg's
local government, focused on digitising and integrating the existing billing and other operations in the consolidation period between 2001 and

2005 across its organisations. Debt recovery also became a pressing need to support the COJ's financial sustainability. The limits of the COJ's piecemeal billing arrangements became apparent in the 20,000 inaccurate bills in 2001, 176,000 calls to the call centre and 40,000–70,000 incorrect bills in 2002, and the 53,152 new queries and 381,660 billing valuation mismatches in 2004, resulting in thousands of complaints. Although the COJ created formal channels for complaints and provided project-based solutions to address complaints and affirmed respect for customers, its attitude to customers varied between denials of the billing 'crisis' in the media and responsiveness in dealing with customer complaints.

By January 2001, customers owed the COJ R3.6 billion ($0.48 billion); the COJ turned to debt collection agencies to improve collection rates (ioL News 2001). About 20,000 inaccurate accounts were discovered in March 2001 when they were transferred to the new City Power database, which hampered collection efforts (news24 2001). This discovery led to many complaints about billing by customers. As the COJ had attained a positive cash balance for the first time in four years in March 2001 (news24 2001), such inaccuracies might have seemed trivial to it. By mid-year, though, despite the improved collection rate of 86.9 per cent for the 12 preceding months, a large deficit still remained (COJ 2006e).

To improve city services, the COJ launched a new call centre, Joburg Connect, on 1 December 2001. The call centre was to receive and route all complaints about service delivery, including billing, but in effect provided a formal channel for protests. The call centre expected a call rate of 50,000 complaints per month, according to the spokesperson for Mayor Masondo (ioL News 2002b). Revealing the sudden escalation of billing problems, Mayor Masondo said 76 per cent of the call centre's 176,000 calls received in its first month were about billing (COJ 2002g). By now, the media were closely watching the COJ's actions, reporting on 23 January 2002 that a third of the COJ's then 500,000 customers had incorrect bills (ioL News 2002b). Customers were frustrated, too, by the ineffective call centre (ioL News 2002b). Between 40,000 and 70,000 customers in Sandton, Randburg and other northern suburbs did not receive bills because of a one-off problem with postal services, according to Dan Painter, the head of revenue (ioL News 2002b, 2002c).

Responding to complainants, Mayor Masondo acknowledged the call centre's growing pains (COJ 2002g). In his *State of the City Address* on 31 January 2002, he promised the public the COJ would clear up the billing problems (COJ 2002g). He said the Mayoral Committee had approved the appointment of consultants, PriceWaterhouseCoopers, to audit the Revenue Department. Also, the COJ was overhauling the revenue management team. This was the first of the COJ's commentaries on the billing system, which highlighted that the COJ gave it the highest operational priority. Commentaries also provided explanations to the public, advised customers on ways to engage with the city administration to resolve their queries, and defended the COJ's actions.

By mid-2002, the COJ had improved the billing system incrementally. It had streamlined operations and targeted initiatives in a project-based approach (COJ 2006e). However, the COJ encountered problems with systems consolidation and staff shortages, and was unable to match systems with the scale of the city's growth (COJ 2006e). This lack of progress earned the COJ the nickname of 'Blunderburg' in the press in July 2002 (ioL News 2011c). Six months later, the COJ reported a still considerable debt burden; the COJ would have to write off the unrecoverable portion of its by then R4 billion ($0.46 billion) debt, reported the city manager, Pascal Moloi, in December 2002 (City Press 2002). Concerned that customers would see this as an excuse not to pay their bills, Mayor Masondo warned defaulters they would face service cut-offs and legal action if they did not pay (City Press 2002).

In early January 2003, Mayor Masondo reminded citizens their payments were the COJ's 'lifeblood' in his *State of the City Address* (COJ 2003h). He appeared satisfied that the COJ's improvement measures were taking effect. By May 2003, the call centre had improved performance over threefold since February 2002 (COJ 2006e). By mid-2003, new queries and backlog ones, those older than 30 days, were steadily declining (COJ 2006e).

Around this time, the COJ began to reconcile billing system data with valuation roll data to determine the gap between what the COJ charged ratepayers and what it should charge them (COJ 2006e). This reconciliation was a critical step in ensuring a clean audit. As a result, the number of new queries shot up (COJ 2006e) and the number of backlog queries increased again (COJ 2006e). In mid-2003, Keith Sendwe, the chief executive officer of the newly formed Revenue Shared Services Centre, the COJ's institutional structure to manage billing queries, noted meter readings challenges. He also noted the high rate of non-payment by large companies, parastatals and residents in wealthy suburbs (*Mail & Guardian* 2003). Despite these non-payments, the COJ still collected over R100 million ($15.02 million) in the last few months of 2003 from government institutions alone (*Mail & Guardian* 2003).

In September 2003, Councillor Parks Tau, then the Member of the Mayoral Committee for Finance, denied billing was a crisis, saying only about 20,000 of the COJ's 1.2 million ratepayers were affected (COJ 2003d). Ironically, a few months later and reportedly in error, the COJ cut off water to the ANC's headquarters for five days in December and summonsed it to court for non-payment of water and rates charges (*Mail & Guardian* 2004).

Despite these problems, the COJ's performance by the end of 2003 satisfied Fitch, which improved the COJ's rating as A-grade investment quality (COJ 2006e). Mayor Masondo again denied the media's claims of a billing crisis in his 2004 *State of the City Address* on 29 January, saying complaints of bad service were one-offs (COJ 2004e). However, obviously responding to dissatisfaction with billing, he started his speech by announcing plans for revenue and billing improvements, including the appointment of senior managers for the Revenue Shared Services Centre and imminent placement of board directors (COJ 2004e).

Despite these measures, the COJ experienced another surge in new billing complaints in March 2004. Customers logged 53,152 new queries, representing 7.1 per cent of the COJ's accounts; the number of backlog queries also rose (COJ 2006f). This crisis with billing administration was exacerbated by increasing non-payments due to rising consumer debt (COJ 2006e). Even President Thabo Mbeki, on a campaign trail in March, was taken aback about the COJ's so-called 'chaotic practices' (*Mail & Guardian* 2004). At last, Revenue and Customer Relations Management Department officials admitted, if only among themselves over the next eight months, that the problems indeed constituted a 'billing crisis' (COJ 2006f). Although public criticism of billing was prominent, the COJ's first bond, worth R700 million ($109.70 million), was oversubscribed by 3.8 times in April 2004 (COJ 2006e). The media's coverage of the billing crisis also did not hinder the COJ's intended collection of R7.4 billion ($1.12 billion) cash for the year (Engineering News 2004b), meeting its 93 per cent payment level target (COJ 2006e).

Reacting responsively to the thousands of protestors, Mayor Masondo reported in May 2004 the COJ had put corrective measures in place to deal with the queries (Engineering News 2004a). These included dedicating the executive director of the Finance Department, Roland Hunter, on a full-time basis to fix the billing system (COJ 2006e), making improvements in meter reading and ensuring staff accountability (Engineering News 2004b). Also, in May, the COJ suspended Sendwe for alleged 'non-performance' and 'irregularities' (Engineering News 2004a).

In June 2004, the comparison of the valuation roll and the billing system revealed 381,660 data 'mismatches' between the sets of data (COJ 2006f), provoking even more complaints. Also, in June, Sendwe resigned and Hunter stepped in as the acting chief executive officer of the Revenue Shared Services Centre (*Daily Sun* 2004; *Engineering News* 2004a). The number of backlog queries had again risen to 49,975, or 6.1 per cent of the COJ's customer base, by June 2004; three months later, the COJ had been able to make significant progress, with only 27,867 queries (representing 3.6 per cent of all customers) still unresolved (COJ 2006e, 2006f). The national government, also concerned with the spate of protests across the country, launched *Project Consolidate*, a short-term national support project to help local government address a variety of service delivery backlogs, including billing (*Mail & Guardian* 2006; RSA 2004).

Mayor Masondo said customers deserve respectful treatment and are 'never, ever wrong' in his *State of the City Address* on 27 January 2005 (COJ 2005a). Such a statement might have set the stage for agonistic interactions, but these did not materialise. He also reported progress in reducing billing queries; the COJ had reduced these by 39.3 per cent and it was continuing data correction efforts (COJ 2005a).

By then, the COJ had realised the piecemeal approach was ineffective, and it needed a programme to provide a single billing and customer interface system in a bottom-up and thorough approach. So, the COJ conceptualised *Phakama* (Rise Up or Arise) in March 2005. Kick-starting *Phakama*, the COJ started integrating multiple business units, services and the customer in a centralised data management system (COJ 2006e). To do this, the COJ used the SAP system.[1] In about mid-2005, the COJ awarded a five-year contract to Masana Technologies, this time as the lead contractor. The award, to consolidate and upgrade Johannesburg's billing system, was for R208 million ($31.17 million) (*Mail & Guardian* 2011a). Masana Technologies then subcontracted some of this work to other information technology firms such as IBM and Dimension Data (*Mail & Guardian* 2011a). By June 2005, billing matters had dramatically improved. Customers logged only 6,881 new queries per month, with only 6,252 backlog complaints outstanding (COJ 2006e). The COJ had succeeded in greatly reducing the mismatch between valuations and billing. However, it had yet to finalise 40 per cent of the data mismatches, namely 156,862 of 381,660 records (COJ 2006f).

The COJ continued to prioritise billing. In July 2005, the COJ's city scorecard for the 2005/06 financial year stated the COJ was to prioritise fixing incorrect billing and slow clearance certificate issuances (issued when properties change hands) (COJ 2006e). Further, the COJ was to pay special attention to improving operations supporting the 'single customer interface' (COJ 2006e) by, for example, providing call centre operators with scripts (COJ 2006e). The COJ also planned to migrate 170,000, or 30 per cent, of Joburg Water's revenue base to the COJ's revenue management unit as part of the broader integration of all billing functions (COJ 2006e).

Hostility and billing bugs (2006–2010)

By now, the COJ had begun the move to a more holistic and stable billing and information technology platform that allowed for the needed integration of operations across the organisation's various departments and entities. The COJ recognised its planned *Phakama* programme, conceptualised in 2005, was risky for its reputation and finances. However, the COJ's significant change management and business re-engineering to create the common billing platform during the maturation period, between 2006 and 2010, was to impact more negatively than anticipated on customer satisfaction and payment levels. The COJ had already dealt with most of the complaints logged in the previous period. But the 2009 collapse of *Phakama*'s information technology contractor, Masana Technologies, the 2010 migration of 744,852 accounts to the new system, and an increasing backlog of problems older than 30 days, including inflated electricity charges and unfair electricity cut-offs, led to activism by a customers' advocacy group and politicking by the main opposition party. Both groups claimed the COJ was hostile and arrogant.

In March 2006, Mayor Masondo, then in his second five-year term, publicly reassured citizens that billing was under control and not in crisis in his *State of the City Address* (COJ 2006a). Behind the scenes, though, the COJ recognised service was 'unacceptable' as thousands of new complaints were still being received. The COJ pledged to substantially improve billing within 12 months through *Phakama*, launching its detailed blueprint in May 2006 (COJ 2006a, 2006f). This meant the COJ had to standardise each financial and administrative step in all its business operations' billing systems before it could integrate them in the new system (COJ 2006e).

The COJ understood this integration to be fraught and uncertain. The Revenue and Customer Relations Management Department's business plan anticipated negative national television and local newspaper coverage as a moderate to major risk and possible reputational damage as a major risk (COJ 2006f). The COJ predicted unresolved complaints would increase from 0.67 to 1 per cent by the end of June 2007 (COJ 2006f). Inaccurate billing also jeopardised the COJ's revenue collection, observed Mayor Masondo in his *State of the City Address* for 2007 (COJ 2007j). The middle class was satisfied, at least for the next two and a half years, given the media's lack of coverage on the billing crisis. By February 2009, Mayor Masondo reported that data cleansing was underway (COJ 2009h). By July 2009, though, the public again became infuriated about the billing crisis. *Carte Blanche*, a weekly show on paid satellite television popular with South Africa's middle class for broadcasting investigative documentaries, featured incorrect bills and service cut-offs in an exposé called 'Bills and Blunders', starring Democratic Alliance councillors, Masana Technologies and the COJ (*Carte Blanche* 2009; *Daily Maverick* 2009).

Masana Technologies filed for voluntary liquidation in August 2009, triggering the automatic termination of its contract with the COJ (iTWeb 2009b). The company reported it could not pay creditors because the COJ had not paid it on time (Balancing Act 2009). At the time the contract was cancelled, in September 2009, the COJ reportedly owed Masana Technologies R64 million ($8.41 million) (Balancing Act 2009). COJ officials and politicians thought Masana Technologies had misjudged the size of the contract and did not have the right management expertise (ANC 2010). The COJ arranged for Dimension Data and IBM to manage the contract for 12 months from October 2009, with Dimension Data taking over most of the staff of Masana Technologies (COJ 2011i; iTWeb 2010).

A group that campaigned vigorously against the city administration's poor billing services was the Johannesburg Advocacy Group (JAG). The JAG was an independent voluntary group set up in 2009 to represent middle-class individuals and residents' associations (JAG 2014). Proving useful for the middle class's billing activism in Johannesburg, the JAG's founder, Lee Cahill, was an experienced strategic marketing consultant. She had an extensive network of television and radio broadcasters, newspapers and other media within Primedia and the Times Media Group (Cahill 2015). The JAG launched a petition and a Facebook page in September, called for a rates boycott, and demanded a 'City Charter' from the COJ (Cahill 2009; *The Star* 2009).

The Democratic Alliance also challenged the ANC-led city administration's political leaders. The provincial ANC intervened, appointing a task team in November 2009 to manage the political risk and *Phakama*'s contractual difficulties. The task team prepared a confidential report on billing, among other problems (ANC 2010). This report highlighted the unsatisfactory management of the outsourcing of information technology (ANC 2010). The report also raised concerns about insufficient contract management capacity within the COJ to manage the billing system contract, high programme risks, unrealistic revenue data, and a communication breakdown between the COJ and the services entities (ANC 2010).

Nonetheless, the COJ had to proceed with its commitment to change the billing system. So, the COJ piloted the SAP implementation programme *Go Live* on 16 November 2009. The pilot was phased to minimise problems (COJ 2006d, 2010f, 2011v). By December 2009, the COJ had completed the two-month roll-out of *Phakama*'s first phase in Johannesburg's western suburbs (COJ 2009g, 2010l). Based on hundreds of listeners' calls to Talk Radio 702 about problematic electricity bills (*Daily Maverick* 2009), billing problems were still present even though the service provider had reportedly fixed the faults (iWeek 2011). By the end of 2009, the COJ had been able to bill R13.3 billion ($1.80 billion) (Hunter and Phakathi 2010). By then, though, the impact of the renewed billing crisis had not yet manifested in the COJ's annual reporting. The COJ was still able to announce a clean audit for the 2008/09 financial year on 27 January 2010, although it would be the last one for the next few years (COJ 2010d). Ongoing billing problems, despite the COJ's claims to the contrary and frequent power outages (mostly related to national generating capacity shortages), continued to incense the middle-class communities (COJ 2009g, 2010l).

Mayor Masondo announced, in the 2010 *State of the City Address* on 11 March, the COJ had allocated a further R170 million ($22.78 million) for *Phakama*'s final stage and the associated Land Information System (COJ 2010a). The COJ had recently implemented *Phakama*'s second phase of 50,000 accounts in areas north of the study area, including Midrand and Ivory Park, with few hitches (COJ 2010m). However, *Phakama* was seriously over budget, with the Member of the Mayoral Committee for Finance, Councillor Tau, reporting in mid-April the 'nightmare' contract's value was R700 million ($95.15 million), R350 million ($47.58 million) over budget, due to 'honest mistakes made in good faith' (*Business Day* 2010). Nonetheless, the COJ received an industry gold SAP Quality award for *Phakama* in June 2010 (COJ 2010i). Further, the COJ reported, in its annual performance report, the integration of system, people and processes resulted in successes for the year ending mid-2010. Successes included the COJ's delivery of bills to 95 per cent of customers, answering of calls by call centre operators within 70–75 seconds, and the issuing of 94 per cent of refunds and 85 per cent of clearance certificates within 30 days (COJ 2010f).

By 30 June 2010, the COJ had incorporated its entire database into the single SAP billing system (COJ 2010g, 2011v). Challenges, though, were experienced again with the migration of some accounts to the COJ's Revenue Department (COJ 2010e), resulting in another peak in billing complaints. Billing queries older than 30 days then numbered 20,823, or about 1.7 per cent of the COJ's estimated 1,200,000 accounts. Two-thirds, or 13,699, of these queries related to City Power issues alone (Hunter and Phakathi 2010). The COJ contracted EOH Mthombo, a business technology solutions service provider, for a 12-month period from 1 July 2010. EOH Mthombo undertook post-implementation enterprise resource planning and end user training and billing system development (COJ 2012d). While EOH Mthombo geared up, its contract overlapped the work of Dimension Data and other service providers who continued to provide services until March 2011 (COJ 2012d). By July 2010, the COJ had switched 744,852 accounts to the new system (PoliticsWeb 2011b). In August 2010, the COJ continued to capture accounts and Mayor Masondo announced a new 'unified' 24-hour call centre to help customers (COJ 2010j). By October 2010, the COJ had completed the process of moving all accounts to the new system.

However, according to the Democratic Alliance, this process was a complete failure (EWN 2010). The process was not at all smooth and took years longer than planned to complete (Mohlakwana 2012). Customer complaints escalated greatly in this period (EWN 2011k). The COJ reported many of the complaints in recent months were due to bills not received or containing hugely inflated electricity charges (EWN 2011g; *Mail & Guardian* 2012). The COJ hoped to fix these bills by the end of 2010 (EWN 2010). The JAG urged customers in November 2010 to complain again. Avenues for complaints included the Presidential Hotline, the National Consumer Commission and Public Protector, among others (JAG 2010). The JAG tried to publicly shame the COJ into acknowledging it had a problem. In a deeply hostile turn, even though the COJ had not yet resolved the problem with inflated bills, the COJ unfairly issued 13,404 final payment notices and cut services to 8,333 customers in December 2010 (COJ 2011p; EWN 2011g). The Democratic Alliance accused the COJ of being 'arrogant' and 'indifferent' (ioL News 2011b).

Defensive at sabotage and secret agents, step change (2011–2015)

The COJ fine-tuned billing and other operations during the bureaucratisation period, between 2011 and 2015, serving more customers with
less staff. Customers logged 65,000 new complaints about inflated bills,
bringing the October 2011 backlog to 136,000 complaints; staged a
sit-in and a street protest; and took court action against service cut-offs.
Customers complained again in 2012, with thousands of complaints
logged by the Presidential Hotline and at a Democratic Alliance-hosted
Open Day. The COJ became increasingly responsive and experimental
in its interventions, including payment concessions, a partly agonistic
engagement resulting in court-approved service cut-off procedures,
proactive customer relationship media management, and successful
troubleshooting of *Phakama*'s implementation. However, the effects
of the billing crisis were still to be felt during this period. The COJ
was unable to get clean audits for three years in a row or achieve full
payment levels. Despite political interventions, the ANC's allegation
of sabotage and denial of a billing crisis, coupled with voters' concerns
at South Africa's enduring inequality, unemployment, service delivery
protests and corruption, led to the middle-class areas' declining support
for the ANC.

By 2011, the COJ was working leaner, with in effect less staff than 15
years earlier, namely six staff per 1,000 citizens, or 28,017 staff, across the
city administration (calculation based on COJ and population data in 2011)
(COJ 2013c). The JAG released about 35 press statements protesting billing issues from 14 January and made radio and television appearances
(Cahill 2015; JAG 2011, 2014). Low staff morale, internal tensions, inaccurate data and a pervasive silo mentality also negatively affected customer
interactions (Hunter and Phakathi 2010). The COJ's revenue staff even
allegedly downed tools on 19 January in exasperation at long customer
queues (Look Local 2011a). Angry customers, affected by the December
service cut-offs, even staged a sit-in protest at the COJ's offices on 21
January, demanding bills be fixed (JAG 2011; TimesLive 2011a).

The COJ was responsive but also defensive. Mayor Masondo
explained *Phakama*'s complexities (COJ 2011p). He empathised with,
and apologised to, struggling customers (COJ 2011u). He acknowledged management problems. By then, data cleansing had resulted in
all 1,040,648 customers (or most of them) receiving proper bills (COJ
2011u). Billing was difficult and complex, Mayor Masondo explained,
but the COJ was not 'heartless' (iTWeb 2011f). Instead, the COJ was
'people-centred' (PoliticsWeb 2011b). He reiterated billing was not

in crisis (TimesLive 2011a), but the middle class disagreed (Grootes 2011). The COJ's call centre operators admitted they were on a go-slow, calling radio stations in frustration at the almost always non-working computer system on 1 February (EWN 2011j).

The regional ANC, too, was concerned about unresolved billing and potholes. At a special meeting on 3 February, the Gauteng province's 14 ANC mayors agreed there were a few billing 'glitches' but the media had blown matters out of proportion (ioL News 2011a). The ANC's provincial secretary, then David Makhura, alleged sabotage had caused the billing problems (*The New Age* 2011). The Democratic Alliance, tongue in cheek, complimented its 'secret agents' for infiltrating the COJ to cause the billing crisis and called for Mayor Masondo's resignation (TimesLive 2011b, 2011c). The middle class felt the ANC dismissed its concerns because it did not protest in the street (EWN 2011d). So, the JAG held a street protest outside the COJ's revenue offices on 18 February 2011, but protestors numbered less than the 500 protestors the JAG had hoped for (itWeb 2011a; *Mail & Guardian* 2011b). Responsive to the street protest, Vicky Shuping, the COJ's executive director of Billing and Revenue since 2008 (ioL News 2011c), said the COJ was 'hearing the noise' (*Mail & Guardian* 2011b). The COJ's responses included a new one-way hotline, with call centre operators calling complainants, to deal with the 65,000 queries about inflated billing logged since January (COJ 2011f, 2011k). The COJ also extended the northern suburbs' customer centres' operating hours and set up a 60-person dedicated team (COJ 2011g, 2011k). The COJ was seemingly dismissive at the JAG's inability to provide 'a single genuine complaint' at a meeting (EWN 2011c), but was more responsive in a press release, saying, on 22 February, that it was 'listening' and would not cut off services for accounts that were wrong (COJ 2011h).

The COJ continued responding to protesters, apologising more than once in March (COJ 2011a; TimesLive 2011b). Mayor Masondo announced remedial measures, including a discount scheme for unresolved queries and debt settlements (COJ 2011a). Mavela Dlamini, the then city manager, announced Gerald Dumas, Joburg Water's former head, would replace Shuping as Billing and Revenue's new executive director (TimesLive 2011b). Dumas reported the billing problem would be fixed within six months (EWN 2011m). By 17 March, the COJ had resolved 28,000 of the inflated bills (EWN 2011b, 2011m). In April, Mayor Masondo again reiterated there was no crisis; rather, the media publicity had reminded the COJ to be 'even more customer-centred' (COJ 2011a). The COJ also announced a moratorium on service cut-offs for queries outstanding for more than three months (EWN 2011h).

By April, the COJ had resolved over half, or 35,353, of the 65,000 queries logged (COJ 2011l), and a further 5,000 new ones (EWN 2011e). A
month later, two days before the local government elections on 18 May
2011, the COJ declared it had resolved nearly 80 per cent, or 51,388,
of the original 65,000 queries (COJ 2011f; EWN 2011l). However, the
Democratic Alliance's 'concerted and well-executed' media campaign
to discredit the ANC-led city administration helped the Democratic
Alliance to increase its share of the 2011 vote (Democratic Alliance
2011; PoliticsWeb 2011a).

After the 2011 elections, the new executive mayor, Councillor Parks
Tau, said at his inauguration that it would 'not be business as usual'
(COJ 2011b). Billing was a problem, he acknowledged. In mid-2011,
the COJ was disappointed to hear of its qualified audit, the first poor
outcome in four years, for the 2009/10 financial year (COJ 2011n).
Dlamini, the soon to be outgoing city manager, pointed to other billing inaccuracies due to accounting method changes (COJ 2011n). To
stabilise the billing system and deal with auditing requirements, the
COJ extended its contract with EOH Mthombo for another month
(COJ 2012d). The COJ's 'experiential marketing' had overcome some
negative service quality perceptions through radio, print, billboards
and advertorials (COJ 2011c). Also, the COJ had weeded out more
problem bills by spatially matching 94 per cent of properties with the
Land Information System (COJ 2011c). The COJ also closely moni-
tored the call centre, provided more training, set up a problem-solving
multisectoral task team and paid staff overtime wages to resolve queries
(COJ 2011c). On 3 August, Mayor Tau said he was still 'not completely
happy' but that billing had stabilised (EWN 2011f).

However, the claimed billing stability proved elusive. On 25 August,
the COJ suddenly charged 7,000 customers with lump sums for refuse
collection bills overlooked for two and a half years (iTWeb 2011c).
By the end of October 2011, outstanding complaints peaked again at
136,000 logged (*Mail & Guardian* 2012). Payment levels also declined.
The COJ had cash reserves to cover only 12 days of operations on
10 November (iTWeb 2011b). The COJ had no option but to campaign for large-scale arrears recovery, with service cut-offs. The COJ
also planned to improve accuracy and centralise billing data with more
'customer-centricity' in its launch of the *Revenue Step Change Programme*
and associated 'roadmap' on 22 November (COJ 2011j; EWN 2011i;
Fin24 2011). *Step Change* included accountability measures for senior
management and staff, call centre changes, adoption of smart metering,
development of customer services standards, and a focus on clearing the
backlog of billing queries and objections to valuations.

By late November, middle-class customers complained about the COJ's poor process management of mass service cut-offs (EWN 2011a). Also, 13 companies, members of the Property Owners and Managers Association, lodged an urgent case on 5 December 2011 in the High Court against Mayor Tau and Trevor Fowler, the new city manager since 3 October 2011 (Schindlers Attorneys 2011a, 2011b). The case sought to stop the COJ's improperly handled cut-offs (COJ 2011r; iTWeb 2011d). Despite the hostilities, the COJ and the litigants were able to agonistically negotiate an 'amicable' agreement of court-endorsed rules on 15 December (COJ 2011q; Property Owners and Managers Association vs City of Johannesburg Metropolitan Municipality et al. 2011). These rules clarified the COJ's actions to be taken in billing disputes and cut-off processes and the customer's obligation to pay whether he or she had logged a query or received a bill or not (COJ 2011q; Property Owners and Managers Association vs City of Johannesburg Metropolitan Municipality et al. 2011; Schindlers Attorneys 2013a).

In January 2012, the COJ received a second qualified audit, for the 2010/11 financial year, due to billing inconsistencies (Fin24 2012). Even Dumas acknowledged then the billing situation was a 'crisis' (COJ 2012g). The COJ said it would set up an escalation team by the end of February 2012 (iTWeb 2012a). On 19 March 2012, Mayor Tau met Obed Bapela, the Deputy Minister in the Presidency for Performance Monitoring and Evaluation, and Humphrey Mmemezi, the Member of the Executive Council for Local Government and Housing, about the 8,000 calls customers had made to the Presidential Hotline since the previous April (EWN 2012a, 2012b; ioL News 2012c). Deputy Minister Bapela was satisfied the COJ had already addressed 5,000 of these complaints (EWN 2012b). The COJ said it still hoped to finalise the remainder of the 65,000 queries logged before 2011 by the end of the year (EWN 2012d).

The COJ again raised the alarm on 20 March 2012 about rising non-payment levels (COJ 2012b; EWN 2012b). The COJ prepared to send out 22,000 final demand notices to defaulters that had not already logged queries on their accounts, but allowed them to make zero-deposit repayment plans or reverse interest if they paid up (COJ 2012b; *The Star* 2012d). Mayor Tau emphasised the importance of improving revenue collection to support the COJ's planned spending of R100 billion ($13.01 billion) on Johannesburg's needs over the next decade (COJ 2012a). By mid-2012, the COJ had appointed Primedia to counter billing's negative press publicity (COJ 2012d). By then, the billing system for rates and services had become the prime management and collection tool of R24 billion ($2.94 billion) revenue, or 68 per cent, of the COJ's annual income (COJ 2012d). The COJ's Open Day for 'key and corporate accounts' on 20 June drew together affected departments and 900 customers and resolved many queries. However, competing media houses were less impressed with *Step Change*, reporting the COJ's inability to stick to its own 'roadmap' deadlines on 13 July (*The Star* 2012d). After repeated requests to the COJ, the media obtained 'roadmap' documents on 20 July, but project management experts deemed them vague, incomplete and not fit for purpose (*The Star* 2012c). The COJ responded on 9 August that it was not obliged to publicise *Step Change*'s more detailed operations (*The Star* 2012a).

The COJ also claimed it had made significant inroads into the queries backlog. Only 1,200 queries logged before November 2011 were not yet resolved, it reported (ioL News 2012d). The Democratic Alliance refuted this claim, hosting its own 'Open Day' on 18 August and gathering over 3,000 billing-related queries (ioL News 2012d; Truluck 2012). The COJ refused to accept these 'queue-jumping' complaints (Democratic Alliance 2012; Truluck 2012). So, the Democratic Alliance began to hand these complaints to the Auditor General on 10 September (iTWeb 2012b). That same day, Premier Mokonyane announced progress on billing; she claimed the COJ had resolved 95 per cent of received complaints, though nearly two years after the complaints had been initially reported (EWN 2012c).

The COJ's challenges, though, were not over. The media reported on 15 January 2013 the COJ had allegedly incorrectly closed some residents' open tickets, thus exposing them to unlawful service cut-offs (Schindlers Attorneys 2013b). The COJ again received a qualified audit, its third, for the 2011/12 financial year, on 31 January (*Business Day* 2013b). The Auditor General could not verify R867.3 million ($97.20 million) of water- and electricity-related revenue due to the COJ's reliance on estimated rather than actual meter readings and another R695.8 million ($77.98 million) for refuse removal due to discrepancies between source and billing data (iTWeb 2013b).

By February 2013, the problems were at last resolved. Even the Democratic Alliance's Councillor John Mendelsohn conceded billing queries in 2013 seemed less than the year before (iTWeb 2013a). Certainly, by March, the COJ's efforts seemed effective when Mayor Tau reported billing system improvements, a reduction in unresolved complaints, shorter call centre waiting times, and an increased revenue collection rate (COJ 2013f). Customer dissatisfaction levels had also declined markedly from the 31 per cent who had been dissatisfied or very dissatisfied in 2011 to 22.9 per cent in 2013 (Gauteng City-Region Observatory 2015); by July 2013, the COJ was ranked the best of the ten municipalities in the province for billing services (Gauteng City-Region Observatory 2015).

Eventually, in January 2014, the COJ achieved a clean audit for the 2012/13 financial year (*Business Day* 2014b; COJ 2014b). For the first time in 12 years, the mayor did not mention billing in his annual *State of the City Address* (COJ 2014e). However, the ANC's erosion of support nationally due to enduring inequality, unemployment, service delivery protests, scandals and corruption, and the middle class's increasing support of the Democratic Alliance meant the ANC could not attain sufficient majority votes in the 2016 local government elections to control the city administration in Johannesburg. Although the billing crisis was largely over, the new Democratic Alliance-led coalition in Johannesburg was not immune to billing problems. For instance, in February 2017, coming full circle, the COJ tried to regionalise the system and change billing cycle dates, leading to 97,000 incorrectly issued statements, which took at least 18 months to resolve amidst allegations of sabotage (this time levelled by the Democratic Alliance at the ANC) and firing of staff and politicians (Democratic Alliance 2017; eNews Channel Africa 2018; iTWeb 2017).

Observations

Prospects for agonistic practices in the billing crisis were few. The city administration seems to have underestimated the extent of change management and business re-engineering required for an integrated billing and information technology platform when the different parts of the local-level state were amalgamated and then restructured more than once. The difficulties the city administration encountered were further aggravated by deepening hostilities between the city administration and the middle class.

The historical context leaves a shadow over the present. Contemporary relationships and interactions do not happen in a temporal vacuum, but rather the legacy of past interactions shapes them considerably. Before the billing crisis had emerged, the rates revolt, between 1996 and 1998, had already soured the relationship between the ANC-led city administration and the mainly white middle-class protestors, driving an antagonistic wedge between them and marking future interactions about billing with mistrust and acrimony.

The ANC-led city administration's interactions with protestors, agonistic or not, were mediated through party politics with the main opposition party. The ANC faced significant political embarrassment when the Democratic Alliance, representing all the wards in the selected middle-class area, repeatedly accused the ANC of underplaying billing problems. The ANC met with party political ridicule when it alleged the sabotage of the city administration's billing system in February 2011. The Democratic Alliance exploited the crisis in its 2011 and 2016 municipal election campaigns. The ANC's political leadership at the provincial level had to intervene to mitigate negative political sentiment about the party and the city administration. The ANC-led city administration was largely unaffected by the outcomes of the 2006 and 2011 local government elections, but the billing crisis may have partly accounted for the ANC's loss of political control of Johannesburg shortly after the 2016 local elections. Certainly, the city administration had to mediate the billing crisis through the filter of party politics to avoid the near collapse of the city administration's relationship with the middle class, as in the rates revolt of the late 1990s. Likewise, the Democratic Alliance had to concede billing issues were resolved by early 2013. Unlike in the Inner City and Orange Farm, where the ANC enjoyed political support, party politics in the middle-class area created an added dimension to the billing protests that perhaps limited agonistic interactions more than it did in the first two stories.

This story of strife highlights difficult issues in the relationship between the city administration and this specific middle-class community. The ANC-led city administration was ambivalent towards the middle class's protests. However, it was also dependent on the middle class, given its disproportionately significant contribution to the city's revenue and access to resources and business networks relative to low-income residents' contribution. Although the middle class was largely white in 1994, its grievances also began to be shared by a new and growing black middle class. Racial undercurrents may also be evident here, observed initially in the rates revolt. Simplistically, white nationalism resulted in the black struggle against apartheid. The new (largely) black ANC-led city administration had to continue to struggle against the white middle class, which had likely voted for the ANC's main opposition party, the Democratic Alliance, to ensure a fairer distribution of services across the now unified city. Local government's notions of the citizen as customer complicated an already complex billing relationship between the city administration and the citizen, and somehow sat at odds with agonistic practice, which sees interaction as an opportunity to strengthen the state–society relationship and empower citizens, even if no resolution is reached. Notably, middle-class groups were just as ready as low-income ones to feel anger and injustice at unmet expectations.

The real issue at stake in the city administration's interactions with citizens is whether the processes of conflict yielded constructive outcomes for the citizens' benefit, irrespective of the extent of agonism in practice. This was harder to construct, having had to rely more on written accounts, as my interview material was thinner for this story compared with the others. Clearly, though, the city administration employed a range of diverse and inconsistent stances, along an antagonistic–agonistic spectrum, towards processes of city strife. Stances towards citizens included antagonism; denial, with frequent statements there was no crisis; denigration, as when the ANC dismissed their activism as it did not take place in the streets; vexation; and defensiveness. However, moving towards the agonistic end of the spectrum, the city administration also recognised protestors' legitimacy as evidenced in many apologies; responsiveness and openness to criticism; and change embodied in the acknowledgement (eventually) that it had heard customers. The city administration had to make constructive attempts to resolve the problems or risk facing further difficulties with unfavourable audits, low credit ratings, reduced income levels and poor election outcomes. However, the effectiveness of outcomes was variable due to technical and other difficulties. The city administration's many attempts did not necessarily draw on agonistic practices. Efforts included implementing the *Phakama* programme to address the consequences of frequent institutional restructurings and the consolidation of different billing systems. However, *Phakama* itself created other numerous technical and managerial issues, and encouraged more protest, in turn needing other interventions to resolve them. One positive outcome for citizens was the court-endorsed rules for service cut-offs resulting from the partly agonistic interaction with the Property Owners and Managers Association in 2011. Responsiveness to protestors' concerns included other outcomes: the COJ's operational and structural changes to the institution and to billing and revenue policy; establishment of the one-way hotline; extension of the call centre's opening hours; hosting of Open Days; discounting of debt settlements by offering repayment plans and interest reversals on paid-up accounts; political and managerial prioritising of the billing matter; intensification of the *Phakama* programme; and acknowledging the media and customers for compelling the city administration to act with more customer-centricity.

The notion of agonism seduces us with the promise of brokering constructive engagement in processes of conflict. However, agonistic practices in this story of strife were decidedly minimal, although some degree of responsiveness by the city administration to the middle class's criticisms was evident. Amidst the city administration's repeated denials of the billing crisis, it tried to be deliberately constructive, if not agonistic, in measures addressing billing problems. Ultimately, the city administration was successful in responding to the middle-class malcontents' billing backlash. Surveys showed improved customer satisfaction by 2013, with the COJ ranked as the best-performing municipality for billing systems in Gauteng by 2013. Moreover, this story also shows us that agonism (or lack thereof) in practice is not only bound in how the state interacts face-to-face in individual processes of conflict. Rather, the overall tone of the local-level state in its conduct and approach to conflictual issues around the billing crisis could easily be regarded as antagonistic, or at least non-agonistic, as manifested in multiple statements made through many channels.

Note

1. SAP is the German-made System, Applications, Products business enterprise software used internationally.

7
Agonism's possibilities

Taking stock

Protest is on the rise globally, with the state–society relationship at a seemingly all-time low (della Porta and Mattoni 2014). In South Africa, too, open public conflict, especially the mechanism of the service delivery protest, has become a near norm of engagement between low-income and even higher-income middle-class citizens and the state (Alexander 2010; Ballard et al. 2006). South African authorities tend to view such conflict, which is beyond the framework of formal democratic processes, as being a threat to democracy, or at least as something negative and harmful (Everatt 2010; von Holdt et al. 2011). Mouffe (2000) argues conflict is needed to ensure a healthy democracy, but some international observers argue conflict signifies the apparent failure of democratic governance and institutions (Atkinson 2007; Misra-Dexter and February 2010). Certainly, the conflict underlying service delivery protests in South Africa cannot be quashed or simply managed away. Rather, it needs to be brought out into the open, and appropriate responses and processes planned, with agonism being potentially a useful tool in seeing conflict differently.

Mouffe's (2000) agonistic conflict, meaning the conflict between adversaries that mutually and respectfully recognise the legitimacy of each other's view, is seen as a positive force for change, producing outcomes beneficial to ordinary citizens. This positive and generative potential seems largely absent in the state's response to service delivery protests in South Africa. Though governance needs to account for increasing levels of dissensus, the current approach tends to follow the precepts of participatory and deliberative democracy, which emphasise the attainment of agreement and the placation of conflict. By going to the heart of the notion of agonism, that dissensus underpins democracy rather than its more familiar counterpart of consensus, agonism offers an alternative way for the state to consider the meanings of protest and conflict.

Translating an antagonistic state–society interaction to an agonistic one within contexts of democratic rule could steer conflict towards more productive outcomes (see Chapter 2). Although there is a growing and lively literature on agonism, it is mostly at the theoretical level.

The exploration of agonism in practice is mostly missing, namely an understanding of the extent to which agonism is currently practised and what real instances of agonism might say about more fruitful state–society strife in further contexts. The literature on agonism says that the state–society relationship could be framed differently by using conflict creatively and constructively to produce better democratic outcomes for citizens. This is a hopeful and positive claim, but how can the state realistically conduct agonistic practices in a messy and complex world where agendas are sometimes competing or hidden? Even if two parties are genuinely committed to the ideals of agonism, they are but two of many interacting actors that must operate within rapidly changing contexts and configurations of power and political interest. This complexity has been explored from the perspective of local state actors in post-apartheid Johannesburg. But the city administration, like other spheres of the state in South Africa and elsewhere, is not at all an integrated entity, but is rather a set of complex, fragmented institutions and practices with uneven power and abilities, making any consistent approach improbable, let alone an agonistic one. This book does not suggest agonism is unattainable, but uses examples of local government responses to conflict to consider the possibility for an (invariably imperfect) agonism broadly and at the level of individual practices.

This book's overarching question asks: What is the practical potential of applying concepts of agonism to the state's governance practices in future? Although I set out to look for agonistic practices in Johannesburg, what I found was that even a simple chronology of post-apartheid protests in the city did not exist. Neither was there any definitive description of what agonism might look like on the ground. Further, determining the city administration's reactions to conflict was incredibly difficult. Ultimately, I identified over 450 service delivery protest incidents, 96 per cent originating in low-income areas and about shortfalls in basic services, housing and land, and informal trading. The rest of the protests were about less clearly defined, multi-issued or locally specific issues, or were arguably less visible protests originating from the middle class. I then narrowed my focus to three thematically and spatially varied stories of state–society strife: about water service delivery in Orange Farm, informal trading in the Inner City, and billing in selected middle-class suburbs. The stories showed how the different parts of the city administration responded to protests and the extent to which these responses incorporated agonistic aspects. Despite constructing these stories from multiple sources, including scholarly publications, official reports, the media and extensive interviews, there are gaps due to the lack of appropriate data. Nonetheless, in this in-depth narrative of the city administration's management of conflict, a picture emerged of its qualification of each conflict, portrayal of protestors, responses to claims, power dynamics, and agreements reached, providing insights to this challenging inquiry that are relevant for Johannesburg and beyond.

These case studies suggest agonism was not this state's norm of engagement in post-apartheid Johannesburg. Indeed, Johannesburg shows, in addition to the diversity and particularity within even one part of the city and one part of the city administration, how difficult it would be to propose any consistent conflict management approach by the state towards strife, never mind an agonistic one. The deployment of any agonistic practice was constrained by multiple factors, including adverse contexts, the extreme difficulty in practising agonism in multi-actor configurations, and an unwillingness to move beyond the traditional modes of engagement in processes of conflict (which had to do with political interest, a genuine lack of financial and other resources, or simply a lack of knowledge). However, while evidence of agonistic practices is disappointingly infrequent, some agonistic processes, either contradicting or complementing other modes of engagement, do provide insights into the possibilities for agonism for a more fruitful strife. This could be particularly relevant in encouraging local governments to recognise the creative potential agonism provides, particularly during times of financial difficulty. The state could apply broad agonistic principles at the organisational level to improve its approach to the management of strife, especially the adoption of Wingenbach's (2011) 'ethos of agonism'. The translation of agonism into practice, however, remains largely theoretical, conceptual, ambiguous and insufficiently tested empirically, although the same could be argued about the deliberative and participatory democratic approaches to governance.

The agonistic city?

How did this state, in its management of strife, qualify conflict? The Johannesburg city administration had a largely anti-conflict mindset, despite protest being regarded as a democratic right in South Africa, aligned with significant new freedoms of movement, association and speech. Contradictorily, the ANC-dominated state seemed torn. On the one hand, it was the party that brought about South Africa's political transition and struggled agonistically for transformation. On the other, it negated post-apartheid service delivery protest as illegal at worst or ill-advised at best. The city administration, led by the ANC in the periods reviewed, rather than taking advantage of the seemingly fertile ground to experiment with agonistic practices in dealing with service delivery protests, suppressed, pacified or eradicated them (Dawson 2010b; Death 2010). Even when it was not negative about conflict, it remained largely ambivalent. For instance, in Orange Farm, it saw protests as a risk to the story of good governance it wanted to project, and therefore wanted to eliminate them. However, it was not unaware of the humanitarian aspects underlying the conflict, but felt justified in implementing initiatives to save water, recover costs and provide limited free water, balancing these against the challenges of water scarcity, the user-pays policy directive and the right to water. In the informal trading story, although the city administration initially recognised the informal traders' right to trade, it increasingly viewed all related aspects as a nuisance, chaotic and anarchic. The city administration failed, too, to regard the billing issue as a crisis and was unsympathetic to the middle-class complainants; rather than acknowledging the crisis, it treated the issues as teething problems until 2012. These negative qualifications of conflict are not a uniquely South African trait as other governments in democratic states have also been reluctant to engage with conflict and tend to focus on measures to address the perceived lack of order arising from frequent protests (della Porta and Reiter 1998).

What is apparent in the city administration's public statements and speeches is their portrayals of protestors as customers, rather than as citizens, and frequently in negative terms. Orange Farm residents were net spenders of city finances and other resources, and the settlement was a liability, temporary and not part of the city; only infrequently did the city administration treat residents with respect. Informal traders were seen variedly as economic survivalists, guilty of acting illegally, manipulative, vulnerable but also bullying, looting and progressively more lawless and beyond enforcement. Despite seeing the middle-class malcontents as vital for the financial sustainability of the city and as a customer relationship management priority, the city administration also saw middle-class complainants as wealthy, hysterical, hostile, the enemy, secret agents, insurrectionary, and as non-paying customers and debtors. Even when considering the impact of socio-economic geography on the city administration's service provider–customer approach, and the nature of the protests against shortfalls in basic or added-value services dependent on groups' race and income profiles and historic relationships with the state, which in turn affected the dynamics of responses, the local government was less responsive to protest events than it was to their underlying issues, ultimately always addressing the latter, even if not immediately, or fully.

The city administration responses to protestors' claims unfolded at three levels, each differently. These patterns of responses were only apparent when considering protests over long periods of time. Short-term responses to protest events were often reactive, aggressive or denialist. However, such antagonistic responses were not necessarily the final stopping point for the city administration. The city administration responded differently to the effects, and root causes, of the issues under contention. Examples of such longer-term responses include policy changes, new projects and changes in operations, and were more likely to include limited instances of agonistic practices.

First, to the service delivery protest events themselves, the city administration's response was immediate, typically within hours or days, and ranged between denial and placation when protests were peaceful with (often token) promises of meetings to be held between protestors and politicians. For instance, the city administration adopted approaches of denial seen in its use of language allegedly denigrating electricity and water anti-prepaid meter activists and its insistence to middle-class protestors that there was no billing crisis. However, if protestors threatened violence, they met with the city administration's hostility. This hostile retort sometimes inflamed protests, turning them violent. Then the city administration, with or without other parts of the state, frequently suppressed protests, often forcibly, and criminalised violent protestors. This was the case when protestors damaged municipal water meters, stopping any negotiations; when permission was refused for a public gathering during a period of frequent, threatening and violent protests about water services and land in 2006 in Orange Farm; when violent anti-foreigner protests took place; and later, when informal traders' mistrust solidified around *Operation Clean Sweep* in the Inner City.

Second, to the effects of the issue under contention, the city administration's responses showed it did not deny protestors' claims. Although responses may not always have been made immediately after the service delivery protest incidents, thus entrenching a belief the city administration was unresponsive, there are numerous cases where it did respond, typically within weeks or months of the date of the protest. Responses incorporated multiple conflict-handling tactics. The deep details of Johannesburg's chronology of protest showed the city administration made numerous small concessions and incremental changes – though not necessarily following agonistic processes – and that protestors perceived to be too little, too late. In Orange Farm, the city administration became increasingly aware of the need to invest in the area: it installed prepaid meters despite their unpopularity, but provided concessions such as debt write-offs and more empowerment measures, and changed its operations and water policies in 2005 and 2008. The city administration's early willingness to engage agonistically with informal traders in the late 1990s became increasingly less so over time. Even as the city administration created markets in consultation with traders' groups, it became aggressive and repressive in its zero tolerance by-law enforcement, overshadowing the more positive training and infrastructure provided, culminating in *Operation Clean Sweep*'s overt aggression. With billing, the defensive city administration grudgingly and gradually accepted there was a crisis by stepping up concessions, responsiveness, displays of empathy and customer-centric messaging, although it was at times disparaging too. Sometimes responsive and hostile reactions unfolded simultaneously as different parts of the city administration responded. For instance, the city administration delayed implementing informal trading by-laws but forcibly quashed violent and potentially violent street protests in the Inner City. In the billing crisis, it issued termination orders for electricity services to middle-class defaulters but also offered them incentives to settle debts. Overall, the city administration's mindset towards the position of conflict in democracy over time did not display a linear progression towards agonistic practice, but rather an irregular series of moves towards and away from it. Nonetheless, that did not mean the city administration did not set out to deliberately not manage conflict or that it was unresponsive towards protestors.

Thirdly, to the root causes of the issues driving protests – frequently intractable challenges such as poverty or shifting expectations around service delivery operations – and because the cumulative weight of repeated protests had become impossible to ignore, the city administration's responses tended to be more comprehensive, taking months and years to implement, but ultimately benefiting residents and addressing the concerns that protestors raised, even if only in part. However, if agonistic practice means to embrace conflict rather than avoid it, then there were few cases of deliberately agonistic engagement between the city administration and the protestors. Indeed, the city administration was generally reactive. One of the city administration's tactics was to concede to protestors' concerns by changing its policies and behaviours. This is apparent in the case of Orange Farm, which the city administration increasingly prioritised along with other informal settlements by providing progressively greater budgets, plans and infrastructure, and increasing the amount of free water and other free services to poor residents. The city administration made elaborate and costly changes to internal systems to improve billing, initiated the *Phakama* programme, invested progressively more resources in the system, escalated the billing crisis politically, and provided more information to the public. The case of informal trading is less clear-cut; even so, the city administration modified governance practices in response to protest. Here, the city administration changed its policies, increased capital budgets to deal with issues under contention, and instigated special forums, such as the Informal Trading Forum in 2009, to debate challenges, even if it did not always do so successfully. The city administration also provided trader empowerment initiatives and skills training, gave concessions on rentals and enforcement, and consulted on initiatives. However, over time, it also became increasingly less experimental and deepened hostilities towards traders. Although much of the responsiveness in these stories was not necessarily agonistic, the city administration was more likely to engage agonistically when responding to the root causes of issues.

How did the city administration tackle power dynamics? Perhaps because of the scale and number of state–society relationships, the city administration expressed a marked preference for structured channels of engagement. The city administration was able to respond more readily to protests made through formal channels across all the examples. Service delivery protests are a form of conflict that operates outside, although not necessarily in contradiction to, the city's framework of democratic and formal spaces and channels for engagement. These formal structures included participatory processes in planning, petitioning, one-on-one meetings with politicians and officials, and other channels provided by the city administration, including political committees.

However, when these formal structures were inadequate in the face of increasing protest, the city administration also provided special-purpose channels to routinise some conflicts, which supported agonistic, or at least consultative, practices. Street and other forms of public protests, such as protestors' use of the media or appeals to other spheres of government, discomforted and embarrassed the city administration and pressured it to respond. Although the city administration sometimes struggled to accept the validity of these protests in the short run, or to deal with the scale of conflicts on a one-on-one basis, over the longer run, the city administration's operations and systems did change to capacitate it to engage more with dissensus. Examples include the call centre for complaints, and the Petitions Unit. In many instances, this form of channelled protest merely placated protestors or created the appearance of a responsive administration or was used to co-opt protestors and suppress real conflict. However, in other instances, such channels were a genuine attempt by the city administration to engage with the issues under contention, especially where no response may have led to continued street protests or media campaigns. In the Orange

Farm case, the city administration's appointment of Thamsanqa 'Oupa' Radebe was not just a placatory measure or a way to enhance its legitimacy, but was also a real attempt to build its capacity to engage with protestors by choosing an official that protestors could readily identify with. In the billing case, the city administration hosted Open Days for specific groups of complainants.

These standard and special-purpose channels, however, did not always work, or work well. For instance, access to these channels was unequal, with well-resourced protestors best placed to take advantage of structured channels such as petitioning, although less-capacitated objectors did also use them. Channels were seen as ineffective by some residents. Despite increased engagement with the city administration, protestors in low-income areas such as Orange Farm still felt excluded from the city administration's decision-making processes and that the pace of change was too slow and continued to resort to street protest as a relatively low-cost (for them) tactic. Likewise, although the city administration created structures for engagement about policy and projects as in the informal trading forum, traders thought its efforts were mere tokenism. Sometimes an engagement worked only when it was forced on the city administration. For instance, the threat of court action pressured the city administration to engage with the Property Owners and Managers Association, presumably partly agonistically, about rules to declare billing disputes, and electricity and water disconnection processes. Forcing change in this way could be tricky and did not always yield satisfactory outcomes for protestors. In some cases, the extra-municipal channel rebounded on protestors, as in the court actions about the Sandton rates boycott, and the Constitutional Court ruling of 2009 that prepaid meters were not unlawful, which was a blow to Orange Farm and other anti-prepaid meter protestors.

What were the forms of agreement reached, or the outcomes if there was no agreement? State–society strife in democratic Johannesburg resulted in changes to the city administration in the form of typically incremental outcomes rather than sweeping changes. Their combined effect over time could be significant. For instance, progressively larger allocations of capital budget for infrastructure investments in Orange Farm were made by the city administration since its incorporation into Johannesburg's boundaries in 1995. However, although the literature proposes incremental decision-making as the best outcome of agonistic conflict management (Gunder 2003; Mäntysalo et al. 2011; Wingenbach 2011), in reality changes tend to be incremental anyway, whether or not agonistic practices were in evidence, possibly because planning for appropriate interventions and changes in policies tends to be slow, and the cost of implementation of solutions is high. Rather, the city administration took the underlying conflict on board, when it did not suppress, placate or deny it, and adjusted operations, many of which ultimately benefited citizens. When agonistic practices were used, as in the Petitions Unit's 'walk with them' approach (Kute 2012a), or the court-forced interaction with the Property Owners and Managers Association about rules for service cut-offs, joint agreements were possible, and the local government was able to gain critical and useful insights from protestors about possible solutions to service delivery challenges. Even in the story of informal trading, despite the city administration's antagonism in the later years, its early agonistic engagements with traders enabled some co-created project and policy agreements.

Agonistic practices were used to deal with mainly intractable problems, which underlay contention. For instance, the city administration made institutional modifications such as appointing former ActStop activists in the 1990s in a conscious and deliberate attempt to build capacity to improve relations with potentially adversarial informal traders. The city administration set up the Petitions Unit, adopting its 'walk with them' approach (Kute 2012a), providing a formal agonistic space to ensure issues entered into political decision-making processes (as advocated by Bäcklund and Mäntysalo 2010). Also, at the peak of protests about water and other services and housing in Orange Farm in 2008, the city administration appointed an Orange Farm resident and ex-activist, Thamsanqa 'Oupa' Radebe, to create a bridge with protestors. In other initiatives, the city administration made operational changes as in its overt codification of project-based conflict management for the *Rea Vaya* bus rapid transit service.

In the literature, there is a possibly misleading assumption that agonistic strife leads to positive outcomes and is more beneficial than other sorts of participatory and consultative processes. Although the accumulated literature-based evidence points to agonism's benefits, there is nothing definitive about it. Responsive practices can lead equally to poor outcomes and negative unintended consequences. For instance, the city administration's response in the form of the problematic *Phakama* programme to the middle class's numerous billing complaints and its initial ineffective performance led to new and different billing problems, deepening the conflict. In another case, the city administration unintentionally became the owner of a dilapidated building in the Inner City, the very situation it sought to overcome, when it tried to provide for temporary accommodation for residents evicted from another building targeted for redevelopment. Even where the city administration responded proactively to protests, outcomes invariably contained both negative and positive aspects. Negative aspects included residents' increased mistrust of the city administration, costly litigation in the courts, and unintended outcomes that did not ultimately benefit residents. However, the few agonistic practices yielded enough positive outcomes to be cautiously optimistic about agonistic conflict management's prospects.

Drawing a conclusive link between agonistic strife and outcomes is difficult. Quantifying the actual effect of conflictual processes on behaviour or policy, whether agonistic or not, especially where the outcomes may be indirect or may evolve over the longer term, is challenging when the city administration may have made certain changes based on prompts other than those flowing from conflictual interactions. Further, differentiating between outcomes that reflect agonistic practices and those that reflect other kinds of democratic practices, including electoral, participatory, consultative and deliberative engagements, which form part of agonistic interactions according to some scholars (Knops 2012; Tambakaki 2009; Vink 2007; Wenman 2003; Westphal 2014), also problematic. Even if one could disentangle agonistic practices fully from the processes of strife, the difficulties in drawing a conclusive link between agonistic strife and outcomes is difficult. Outcomes may, for example, be the consequence of agonistic interactions acting together with other processes.

Beneficial outcomes are not always necessarily apparent to dissenters. This was the case in the billing crisis where the city administration's multiple attempts to address the crisis were dismissed by the middle-class protestors as not enough, and in Orange Farm where the state's significantly upscaled investments did not stop service delivery protests. The protestors' negation of outcomes may be due, though, to their expectations shifting over time, meaning any responses would be deemed incomplete. However, the idea that the state can ever completely satisfy residents, through pacification, concessions, sincere or manipulative engagement, or other ways that follow agonistic democratic principles, is ultimately unrealistic as it is the agonistic state's responsibility to always keep the space open for conflict.

Why did the state not respond more agonistically? Arguably, many more constraints, challenges and complexities than opportunities made agonistic practices difficult to realise in Johannesburg's governance. Various aspects of these constraints mainly inhibited, but sometimes advanced, the city administration's potential for agonistic responses.

Context can limit agonistic interactions. Interacting parties did not engage in isolation from broader networks of relationships and power.

The prevailing context shaped the intent, nature and consequences of interactions in ways that limited or empowered agonistic interactions. There are many examples of this: in the late 1980s, there was an unusual willingness to interact more agonistically with informal traders, even during apartheid's repression. This, however, had a lot to do with the ideological shift internationally seen in Reagan's and Thatcher's emphasis on economic freedoms and the gradual shift to a democratic South Africa. In Orange Farm, the broader context of the national government's pressure on municipalities to be financially self-sustaining through initiatives such as the *Masakhane* campaign combined with the city administration's extreme cash shortage, the 1997 financial crisis, and the need to implement *Gcin'Amanzi* compelled the city administration to adopt a tough stance towards residents' protests about the payment for services.

Historical relations can inform the state's current capacity for agonistic conflict. Conflicts and interactions do not happen in a vacuum, but are influenced significantly by what has happened in the past. The most weighty history in South Africa is that of the anti-apartheid struggle and the seemingly agonistic engagements that brought South Africa to its transition to democracy. This history points to both the productive role of conflict and the power of agonistic interaction in creating positive change, and could surely support a more agonistic ethos in governance today. The city narrative here, though, does not offer enough evidence to suggest that such an ethos is still possible today despite the country's transformative history. An excellent example of relations shaping governance was the effect of the Sandton rates boycott of the late 1990s, exacerbating the financial crisis faced by the city administration in the 2000s, souring the future relationship between the middle class and the city administration. The reluctance of the ANC-led city administration to then engage agonistically, or otherwise, with the middle class in the billing crisis related to this history to an extent. When the main opposition party, the Democratic Alliance, took advantage of this conflict in its electioneering, mass politics added another layer of party political complexity, making it almost impossible for the city administration to resolve the billing conflict as purely a technical problem. A history of mistrust endured and even deepened in other relations also, despite embryonic agonistic approaches reflecting post-apartheid goodwill in the 1990s, as seen in the enmity between informal traders and the city administration, culminating in the 2013 *Operation Clean Sweep*. Even the shock of the 2013 Constitutional Court interim ruling against the city administration did not shift the way the city administration related to traders.

Juggling and satisfying many demands limited agonistic practices in Johannesburg. The major constraint may simply have been the enormous variety and complexity of conflict that needed to be managed within the narrow frame of service delivery, notwithstanding protestors' other motives such as mobilising resources, claiming identities and reshaping the democratic state according to their ideals. Even under the most cooperative of circumstances, relationships between the parties with such divergent interests could be tricky to manage. The element of conflict brought greater complexity and new risks to governance. With willingness and skill, agonistic engagements might have been possible, but would have been difficult to sustain as the broader environment was not supportive. An added challenge in many cases was that there were not necessarily only two parties in a conflict, but multiple parties that had some interest in the conflict as well, even if they were not directly related to the conflict. The city administration's need to attend to, and balance, multiple contending interests, including its own, and make trade-offs between them, added a huge complexity to the interaction. In the case of informal trading, for example, it was not just the city administration and the informal traders that clashed, but also the formal businesses, the property owners and the many users of the Inner City environment, with diverse interests, from maintaining property values to walking freely on Inner City pavements. In the case of billing, the interests of the middle class were often mediated through the Democratic Alliance's pursuit, as the main political opposition party, of boosting electoral power and serving its constituents, as well as the city administration's own drive for income and increased focus on billing's technical and contractual difficulties. In Orange Farm, the city administration sought to not only provide free water, but also to protect water as a scarce resource. Some state actors overtly recognised conflict management as a vital mechanism to balance these competing priorities as in the case of the apparent inability of the city administration to balance resources and rights in the matter of social housing in the Inner City. The protestors' shifting expectations and unclear demands meant outcomes were frequently short-lived, with the city administration required to constantly renegotiate the scope of its services as residents lodged objections against formerly accepted service standards. For instance, the Orange Farm protestors' demands for the provision of free water shifted to also including housing and other unspecified demands from 2006 onwards.

Institutional dynamics complicated agonistic practices. Although writers (such as Gunder 2003; Pløger 2004) claim the state has more power and resources than the weaker adversary and so should take the lead in facilitating agonistic engagements, the state is not all-powerful in reality. The huge complexity of relationships within and between the institutions of the city administration made agonistic practices hard to implement and sustain. The city administration was far from being one cohesive organization, but was rather a multibillion-rand organisation with over 100 departments and 30 agencies, each with its own driving force frequently at odds with others. Internal dysfunctions, tensions and a lack of harmonisation made consistent and synchronised handling of activities and mediation between paradoxical goals and responses related to conflict a hugely complex task. One example was Joburg Water's emphasis on earning revenue for the provision of water services to customers while other parts of the city administration emphasised the allocation of minimum free water to citizens. Another example was the JMPD's non-enforcement of the informal trading by-laws in the Inner City, thus reportedly compromising the viability of self-sustaining markets. In addition to the city administration's multiple and diverse positions making consistent and sustained agonistic practices difficult, so too did the fluid institutional dynamics related to post-1994 restructurings. Challenges at various times included weakened capacity, an inward focus, growing sensitivity to criticism and a loss of institutional memory. These factors undermined the potential for agonistic state–society strife. The complexity of governance did not only relate to the city administration itself, but to the multi-sphere form of government in South Africa. For instance, one sphere of government may have been interacting antagonistically with society while another was interacting agonistically, as in the informal trading associations' appeal to the provincial government in the 1990s when they felt aggrieved by the city administration's actions, resulting in more agonistic responses from the provincial government; the risk for the state, though, is increased state-on-state friction.

While institutional dynamics are important, individuals also matter in constraining or amplifying agonistic practices. The negative reactions of some individuals to conflict limited the extent to which the city administration was able to adopt agonistic practices. However, some individuals' ability to tap into their 'inner agonism' and empathy (McManus 2008; Morrell 2014) significantly widened the city administration's prospects to govern agonistically. In the Johannesburg case, some state actors used their institutional authority or persuasive powers to promote agonistic practices, such as Radebe, who responded agonistically to protestors in Orange Farm while at the same time the overall approach of the city administration largely constrained agonistic engagement.

The city administration's mindset about conflict affected interactions. Despite the role of conflict in producing positive outcomes in recent South African history, state actors often had a fear of conflict and a strong desire to avoid or suppress it. This may have something to do with the influence of international public administration approaches such as New Public Management and its emphasis on the role of the citizen as a customer rather than as a citizen. Caught up in the task-based aspects of service provision, and constrained by lack of knowledge and resources, the city administration's possible acknowledgement of conflicting interests was subordinated to service delivery's technical considerations. In terms of this mindset, the city administration was more familiar with consensus-seeking, logical, rational, participatory and deliberative democratic practices and tactics of avoidance, denial and placation of protestors than with the passion of agonistic practices (Fung 2003). Among individuals, negative views of conflict dominated, with some personally or professionally fearful of threatening and violent protests, seeing conflict as endangering effective urban governance. Far fewer saw conflict as an inescapable part of governance and as a necessary force to drive productive change, had personal and professional views of conflict not necessarily aligned to those of the organisation, and sometimes consciously held contradictory views at the same time. The challenge of agonistic state practice is that such practice is not a mere administrative function, but requires a particular and quite rare form of leadership to steer the processes of interaction with adversaries (Westphal 2014). However, in the context of the city administration's reported high turnover rates of officials and politicians, those with the willingness, courage and experience to engage agonistically were present for short periods only.

Reflecting on the chronology of protests, although it raises as many questions as answers, clearly the city administration engaged in conflict in multiple ways. However, what is much less clear is to what extent those practices of engagement were agonistic. Agonism's potential lies in its 'empowerment' and not merely 'governance' of citizens (Pløger 2004), and ability to shock state institutions out of political complacency (Schaap 2006). Yet this book shows that although the city administration's practices attempted to take citizens' needs into account, these practices, sometimes constructive or well-intended, were not necessarily intentionally or deliberately agonistic. Such practices were hard to decipher on the ground as our understanding of agonism in practice is incomplete despite having identified potential agonistic practices (see Chapter 2). Also, information was frustratingly incomplete, with accounts of conflicts and protests tending not to record the state's responses. The study established that agonism is indeed present to some degree in the interactions between the city administration and protestors. Gauging its extent, though, is difficult as the definitional issues are still unclear. Even Mouffe (2013) acknowledges that agonism can consist of many diverse practices, making for difficult definition and identification of agonistic practices. Does the broad use of agonistic principles qualify the governance practice as agonistic? Or are detailed aspects of agonism required in governance practices, and if so, how many, and in what mix, and how often? Excluding entirely from the definition of agonism any processes of interaction about conflict that do not deliberately involve all possible practices may be very limiting as some practices do display some components of agonism, though minimally and unknowingly, but which nonetheless resulted in outcomes that might not have materialised if the conflictual interaction had not happened. If the city administration's approach was agonistic, how different would its practices have been? Perhaps more resources would have been directed into facilitating capacity-building of weaker adversaries and empowerment of citizens; building resources for more sophisticated negotiation, imaginative inquiry into conflictual issues and problem resolution; and creating more effective and appropriate policies and changing them faster when needed.

What are agonism's practical possibilities?

Although Mouffe's concept of agonism was less in evidence than hoped for in the study of state–society strife in Johannesburg, in considering the evidence presented in the Johannesburg case, the notion of agonism nonetheless lends itself to five main practical possibilities that the state can adopt in governance practices in conflict management, described in order of priority.

First, agonism suggests the state can adopt its principles as an ethos of governance. The case of service delivery strife in Johannesburg points us towards specific practical possibilities of agonism in day-to-day governance. This case shows us that the single biggest value agonism might bring, despite its ambiguities, lies in raising awareness of the potential design of agonistic practices of the state as empowerment of citizens and not simply their governance (Pløger 2004). Agonistic practices are designed to treat city inhabitants as citizens and partners by building state–society relationships, rather than as mere customers of the state as it goes about its business (as in the New Public Management approach). The state could deliberately adopt an 'ethos of agonism'

(Wingenbach 2011), particularly valuable for difficult situations or for when conventional approaches have failed (Tambakaki 2014). Namely, the state could acknowledge that an agonistic ethos may allow it to view state–society conflict with a different mindset, open to conflict's generative ability to formulate constructive outcomes from state–society strife. What does this mindset mean for day-to-day governance? The literature implies specific essentials for the state to adopt that reflect the agonistic mindset. The state could purposefully manage state–society strife according to agonism's principles. The state could carry out practices of empowerment by supporting weaker adversaries and overtly clarifying within the institution common understandings of issues of power and distinctions between different groups in each conflict. The state could be open to hosting, or facilitating the hosting, of conflicts. The state could intentionally strive to demonstrate a real agonistic respect for others and acknowledge the different interests lying beneath the conflict. The state could articulate comprehensively who benefits and does not benefit from policy choices arising from conflict management engagements. The state could appreciate that protests and dissensus will never end as concerns can never be completely addressed. However, that the state might not adopt an agonistic ethos of governance may have to do with its reluctance to centre conflict and its lack of knowledge about agonism's principles.

Second, the state could adopt a managing, not resolving, conflict mindset. The agonistic state, at its highest levels, acknowledges conflict in all its forms. It accepts Mouffe's (2013) centrality of dissensus in governance practices, rather than liberal democracy's more familiar notion of the centrality of consensus. Then, seeing conflict as inevitable, it could develop the mindset that it will manage conflict but not necessarily resolve it. With this mindset, the state can maintain or build on its channels for protest knowing there will be continual strife, but be open to the voiced desires of communities to influence state action, accommodate shifts in power relations, fight the capitalist democracy's innate inequities and raise awareness of the issues under contention (Mouffe 2013). Integral to that approach is the state's acknowledgement that agonistic principles are an asset to state–society interaction, making for more positive and constructive relationships with citizens, whether in low-income or middle-class communities, potentially resulting in outcomes that better serve its citizens. However, this critical agonistic approach would represent a major move away from the state's current preoccupation with the concern that conflict is detrimental and destructive and needs eradication. The state could recognise the impossibility of reaching consensus, thus avoiding the pessimism and frustration of state actors that agreements reached with adversaries appear to be short-lived only. The state could accept that almost all agreements need repeated brokerage over time as contexts and needs change. Agonistic governance means being aware that partial, incremental and iterative agreements are typical of agonistic practices (Gunder 2003; Mäntysalo et al. 2011).

Third, having adopted the above two points, agonism can serve as a foundation for the state to widen its repertoire of practices by drawing on examples from elsewhere, although more research is clearly needed to close the gap between theory and practice. To be practical, the state could consider combining agonistic practices with other current public management and deliberative or participatory democratic governance approaches. The state could ensure that agonistic skills, particularly in change management, ethics and care, are grown within its various institutions for conflict management (Gunder 2003; Sager 2013). The Johannesburg case studies raise questions, inviting further speculation. How much agonism does a practice have to contain to be called agonistic? How many practices must be agonistic for an institution to be called agonistic? This aspect is not at all clear in the literature. However, some agonistic principles must enjoy more primacy than others must, especially the all-important broad orientation towards agonism. However, we saw that as city strife unfolded over time, conflict management practices were not linear, contiguous or consistent. Rather, they were marked by a high degree of irregular and contradictory aspects. Within this context, any practices that might have been categorised as agonistic seem largely but not exclusively accidental, pointing to the lack of definitive understanding of what makes practices agonistic. Perhaps such practices can be classified as agonistic only if the state deliberately, knowingly and intentionally undertakes them as such, all the time or at least part of the time. Even if they unequivocally contain one or more easily recognisable principles of agonistic practice, if the overall mindset was not agonistic, then it might be challenging to label such practices as agonistic. Without the latter, the extent of agonism in practice will likely be curtailed.

Fourth, agonism can serve as an ideal in improving governance practices, but with limitations. Agonism could support the state's tackling of wicked problems underlying intractable conflicts. Agonistic practices, or even deeper deliberative ones incorporating agonistic aspects, might result in more imaginative solutions co-created by the state and society. However, an important limitation lies in how any institution can practically measure its performance of utilising agonism at broad or detailed levels of engagement. Mouffe's (2000) agonism has been developed with no practical applications in mind, and the few existing case studies show the translation of its theoretical aspects into practice is difficult to realise (Hillier 2002; Nonhoff 2012). Johannesburg highlights that the relationship between processes and outcomes is not straightforward. Developing standard rules for agonistic practices for the state to follow in the hope that improved processes foster improved outcomes may not guarantee good outcomes (Forester 2011). Because of agonism's limitations, many scholars agree agonism cannot exist on its own and must be mixed with other traditional democratic practices to facilitate decision-making (Beaumont and Loopmans 2008; Gürsözlü 2009; Knops 2007, 2012; Tambakaki 2009; Vink 2007; Wenman 2003; Westphal 2014). However, what ideal proportions of mixes might be used remains unclear. Further, managing urban conflict is risky, and even other traditional practices can and do fail.

Lastly, what agonism does not show us, but is evident from studying Johannesburg, is that the state can recognise the presence of antagonism as an opportunity to drive change. The place of antagonism in agonistic thought is limited to the notion that the conversion of antagonism to agonism is always desirable and always possible. It seems unlikely to imagine any constructive agonistic engagement is possible without some intervening step to calm antagonism and immutable antagonism. Neither Mouffe nor the city administration have explicitly defined antagonism or immutable antagonism. Only subjective understandings of antagonism exist, with some observers seeing antagonism and others seeing agonism, and some who see conflict as a sign of democracy's apparent failure while others see it as a sign of its health. Although the state's handling of service delivery protest in Johannesburg implies an emerging and partial definition for immutable antagonism, namely when polarised positions become cemented and compromise institutional stability, as in extreme enmity or physical violence where lives and property are at risk, this definition may not be valid for all institutions of the state and at all times. In Johannesburg, the local-level state tended to treat service delivery protest incidents as antagonistic, responding by pacifying or quelling them, depending on the level of real or threatened antagonism displayed. When these protests became immutably antagonistic, they were quelled, usually with force. However, the city administration's definition of immutable antagonism, even antagonism – whether immutable or less entrenched – is not nearly so clear when it comes to dealing with issues underlying the conflicts and their effects. Rather, concerns about physical risk to the institutions of the state may be replaced by other risks, namely financial, reputational and political, driving the timing and nature of its responses. Even when these risks were identified (even sometimes uncomfortably great), they did not necessarily result in the city administration's responsive, never mind agonistic, interactions with dissenters. Further, the state can effect changes benefiting residents even without engaging with society. Indeed, positive outcomes were triggered by antagonistic state–society strife as the city administration tried to placate protestors or avoid future protests by proposing outcomes that responded to protestors' concerns. However, the opportunity to empower residents, an important aspect in building state legitimacy and fostering a positive state–society relationship as agonistic practice promises us, would be missed. Certainly, ignoring conflict altogether seems inappropriate. But so does fetishising it. The risk of not dealing with dissensus at each level – to the protest incident, the effects of the issue under contention and the underlying cause driving the contention – is that the antagonism becomes immutable. Deciding not to engage in a conflict is as significant as the decision to engage in it. Costs of either decision should be quantified. If the state's responses do not draw on agonistic principles, the change might take years to effect and the state–society relationship can become characterised with mistrust. However, an agonistic approach, alone or with other approaches, might accelerate positive changes and improve the state–society relationship, and possibly impact positively on wider relationships too.

Final reflections

Is it possible to simply impose the idea of agonism on to a multiplicity of conflict management practices? Clearly, the city administration's efforts to resolve conflict through repression and denial proved unsustainable. However, it also cannot be seen as weak and easily conceding to demands given its role of balancing the long-term well-being of all residents. Despite the deep study of conflict in Johannesburg, and scholars' examples of what agonism might look like in practice, agonistic practices were the exception rather than the rule, even when the broad orientation may have been pro-agonism. Johannesburg's many varied and vibrant conflicts over the post-apartheid years led by low-income and middle-class groups show how state actors have truly tried to grapple with conflict within contexts that are quite constraining. Many responses have in fact been made, not only at the level of individual protests events and to the effects of the issue under contention, but also to the root causes of these conflicts, such as poverty.

Agonism remains an ideal, in the same way that democracy does. Agonistic governance practices may be helpful in achieving democratic aims, by ensuring divergent voices are respected in decision-making.

Democracies are built on difficult histories, layered with race, class and caste abuses, with intense conflicts unfolding in ever-more complex contexts, making governance seem trickier than ever before. The conflicts, here narrowly framed as service delivery protests in Johannesburg, also incorporate deeper conflicts about nation-building and identity. By not trying to repress conflict, agonistic practices could keep the space open for especially deep conflict to have more productive and generative outcomes. Such practices were less viable at the level of individual protests in Johannesburg, especially when these put lives at risk. Yet an overtly managed agonistic approach might inform and even improve current democratic processes of governance at all levels of responses to protestors' claims. Although these agonistic processes may overlap with other participatory, consultative and deliberative democratic processes, agonistic processes place conflict squarely on the agenda by not disregarding or fetishising conflict as a tool for positive transformation.

What are the practical possibilities of applying agonism to governance practices of the state in cases of open state–society conflict? These findings potentially provide conflict management insights for local governments and other levels of the state in South Africa and globally. Although I cannot presume these insights would map on to the experiences of other cities and states, they do serve to raise awareness of the extraordinary complexities of any state's interactions in urban strife. These insights can help define the scope for the state to incorporate agonistic governance practices despite the difficulties in operationalising agonism, thereby improving democratic outcomes. Most significantly, the state seems to lack the mindset and knowledge required to place dissensus at the centre of democracy and governance rather than consensus, and to engage agonistically in strife, using conflict as a creative and constructive force for change.

This book also highlights other important findings, such as cases where practices of agonistic governance were attempted, albeit nominally and inconsistently. Indeed, the outcomes of conflict management processes were highly variable, sometimes having unintended consequences, sometimes succeeding, sometimes not. This points to the state's ability to engage in strife in creative and constructive ways, even if not consistently agonistically. The reality of the myriad contextual factors that negatively influence the state's ability to engage agonistically in state–society strife, thus limiting the potential for favourable outcomes, is not factored in in the literature on agonism. Possible strategies and practical examples of how institutions have overcome these constraints are lacking, making the power of agonism in practice to address difficult conflicts uncertain and potentially as limited as any other conflict management approach. Nonetheless, the exploration of conflict in Johannesburg shows that the state can draw on the ideals of agonism to perceive and manage conflict in ways that might diverge from current practice. However, this would require the state's deliberate intention and attention to the improvement of its current conventional approaches for the conciliation of processes of conflict. The notion of agonism does not sufficiently consider the role of the state in facilitating positive and creative solutions to conflict, although its efforts may well contain traces of agonistic practices, and it discounts the role of antagonism in also driving generative change.

Ultimately, I conclude that agonism is difficult to put into practice, partly because conflict itself is challenging to incorporate in governance. The limitations of the practical application of agonism is discouraging given its significant promise for responding more positively to conflict. Nonetheless, the stories detailed in this book demonstrate that the state, in this case Johannesburg's city administration, incorporated elements of agonistic practices in its responses to conflict, particularly in response to the underlying intractable problems driving conflict. The state could expand on these emerging practices of agonism to realise democratic objectives. However, the absence or presence of agonistic practices does not account solely for successes or failures of governance. Agonistic interaction might not be enough to address deficiencies in state–society relationships where there are multiple, often antagonistic, conflicts that expose both society's and the state's real limitations. However, if the state recognises the potential in positioning conflict centrally, and respects protestors' views, it can build on emerging agonistic practices to find alternative ways to address conflict to the extent that it is appropriate. The state can then increase its ability to creatively and constructively use conflict to drive positive change, gain a wider appreciation of the issues under contention, and empower residents to improve their urban context, thereby improving democratic outcomes in cities and countries with resource constraints and strife.

References

Abrahamse, U. 2012. *Greater Johannesburg Transitional Metropolitan Council's First Coordinator of Street Trading By-Law Enforcement in the Mid-to-Late 1990s after a Stint as Head of Security and Mayoral Programme Coordinator for Johannesburg's Eastern MLC*, Johannesburg, interview with author, 9 November.

African National Congress. 1995. *Nelson Mandela's Speech at the Launch of the Masakhane Campaign, Marconi Beam, Koeberg*, 25 February. Available: www.anc.org.za/show.php?id=3519 [Accessed 17 June 2014].

———. 1997. *ANC Daily News Briefing: ANC on the Masakhane Peoples Weekend*. Available: www.e-tools.co.za/newsbrief/ [Accessed 1 May 2012].

———. 2010. *COJ Provincial and Regional Task Team Report.*

AfriGIS. 2014. *South African Demographic Maps Online, with Select Variables at Province, Municipal, Ward and Sub Place Level, Statistics South Africa Data on Population Census 2011; Imagery Copyright from NASA; Map Data Copyright 2014 from AfriGIS (Pty) Ltd.* Available: http://census2011.co.za/ [Accessed 9–14 July 2014].

Agüero, J., Carter, M. R. and May, J. 2007. Poverty and inequality in the first decade of South Africa's democracy: what can be learnt from panel data from KwaZulu-Natal? *Journal of African Economies*, 16(5), 782–812.

Alexander, P. 2010. Rebellion of the poor: South Africa's service delivery protests – a preliminary analysis. *Review of African Political Economy*, 37(123), 25–40.

Alexander, P., Runciman, C. and Maruping, B. 2015. *South African Police Service (SAPS) Data on Crowd Incidents: A Preliminary Analysis*, research report, University of Johannesburg (Social Change Research Unit).

Alexander, P., Runciman, C., Ngwane, T., Moloto, B., Mokgele, K. and Van Staden, N. 2018. Frequency and turmoil: South Africa's community protests 2005–2017. *South African Crime Quarterly*, 63 (March), 27–42.

AllAfrica.com. 2002. *South Africa: Joburg Hawkers Lay Charges against Metro Police*, 20 February. Available: http://allafrica.com/stories/200202210017.html [Accessed 13 December 2014].

Allmendinger, P. and Haughton, G. 2010. Spatial planning, devolution, and new planning spaces. *Environment and Planning C: Government & Policy*, 28(5), 803–818.

ANC Daily News Briefing. 2006a. *Scores Injured as Police and Coloured Protestors Clash*, 6 February, pp. 59–61. Available: www.anc.org.za [Accessed 29 April 2012].

———. 2006b. *SE SOWEJOCA D' Called Off*, 6 February, pp. 67–68. Available: www.anc.org.za [Accessed 29 April 2012].

Anciano, F. 2012. Agents of change? Reflecting on the impact of social movements in post-apartheid South Africa. *In*: Dawson, M. and Sinwell, L. (eds.) *Contesting Transformation: Popular Resistance in Twenty-First Century South Africa*. London, Pluto Press, 143–165.

Anciano, F. and Piper, L. 2018. *Democracy Disconnected: Participation and Governance in a City of the South*, London, Routledge.

Anonymous. 2012a. *African National Congress Activist and Trade Unionist, with Leadership Roles in Politics in Johannesburg since the Late 1990s*, Johannesburg, interview with author, 12 November.

———. 2012b. *Senior ANC Politician with a Number of Roles in Johannesburg's ANC-Led City Administration since 1995*, Johannesburg, interview with author, 1 October.

———. 2012c. *Senior City of Johannesburg Official Responsible for Public Transportation Working in the City Administration for a Few Years*, Johannesburg, inerview with author, 15 November.

———. 2012d. *Senior Legal Official in the City of Johannesburg*, Johannesburg, interview with author, 26 October.

Anti-Privatisation Forum. 2003. *Appeal for Solidarity*, 9 September. Available: http://apf.org.za/spip. php?article33 [Accessed 3 August 2014].

———. 2005a. *JW Tariffs for 2005–2006*. Available: http:// apf.org.za/spip.php?article150 [Accessed 24 June 2014].

———. 2005b. *Narrative Report 2004–2005*. Available: http://apf.org.za/spip. php?article147&lang=en [Accessed 4 November 2012].

———. 2005c. *Statement on Johannesburg City Council's 'Indigent' Arrears Write-Off*, 16 May 2005. Available: http://apf.org.za/ spip.php?article100 [Accessed 24 June 2014].

———. 2006a. *APF Office Bearers Consolidated Organisational Report to the 2006 AGM*. Available: http://apf.org.za/spip. php?article197&lang=en [Accessed 4 November 2012].

———. 2006b. *In Defence of the Right to Freedom of Expression and Assembly! APF Press Statement*. Available: http://ccs.ukzn.ac.za/ files/news2006-1.pdf [Accessed 7 September 2015].

———. 2006c. *Lessons from the War against Prepaid Water Meters: The Struggle against Silent Disconnections Continues*. Available: www.saha. org.za/apf/final_ppm_research_ report_2006.htm [Accessed 4 August 2014].

———. 2007a. *Anti Privatisation Forum Affiliates 2007*, 14 December. Available: http:// apf.org.za/spip.php?article218 [Accessed 4 August 2014].

———. 2007b. *Narrative Report for the South Africa Development Fund Covering the Period November 2006–August 2007*. Available: http://apf.org.za/spip. php?article222&lang=en [Accessed 4 November 2012].

———. 2008. *Coalition Against Water Privatisation: Response to Mayor's Attack on Court Judgement*. Available: http://apf.org.za/spip. php?article290&lang=en [Accessed 15 October 2012].

Atkins, K. 2012. *Chief Executive Officer of City of Johannesburg's Metropolitan Trading Company from Mid-2001 to Early 2005*, Johannesburg, interview with author, 1 September.

Atkinson, D. 2007. Taking to the streets: has developmental local government failed in South Africa? *In*: Buhlungu, S., Daniel, J., Southall, R. and Lutchman, J. (eds.) *State of the Nation: South Africa 2007*, Cape Town, Human Sciences Research Council, 53–77.

Bäcklund, P. and Mäntysalo, R. 2010. Agonism and institutional ambiguity: ideas on democracy and the role of participation in the development of planning theory and practice – the case of Finland. *Planning Theory*, 9(4), 333–350.

Balancing Act. 2009. *South Africa: City of Johannesburg Owes Tech Supplier Millions*, 11 September. Available: www.balancingact-africa.com/news/en/issue-no-471/ computing/south-africa-city-of/en [Accessed 14 May 2015].

Ballard, R. 2005. Social movements in post-apartheid South Africa: an introduction. *In*: Jones, P. and Stokke, K. (eds.) *Democratising Development: The Politics of Socio-Economic Rights in South Africa*, Leiden, Martinus Nijhoff, 77–99.

Ballard, R., Habib, A. and Valodia, I. (eds.). 2006. *Voices of Protest: Social Movements in Post-Apartheid South Africa*, Scottsville, University of Kwa-Zulu Natal Press.

BBC News. 2009. *South Africa Vows to Stop Riots*, 23 July. Available: http://news.bbc.co.uk/2/hi/africa/8164956.stm [Accessed 9 June 2013].

Beall, J., Crankshaw, O. and Parnell, S. 2000. Victims, villains and fixers: the urban environment and Johannesburg's poor. *Journal of Southern African Studies*, 26(4), 833–855.

———. 2002. *Uniting a Divided City: Governance and Social Exclusion in Johannesburg*, London, Earthscan.

Beaumont, J. and Loopmans, M. 2008. Towards radicalized communicative rationality: resident involvement and urban democracy in Rotterdam and Antwerp. *International Journal of Urban and Regional Research*, 32(1), 95–113.

Beavon, K. 1997. Johannesburg: a city and metropolitan area in transformation. *In*: Rakodi, C. (ed.) *The Urban Challenge in Africa: Growth and Management of Its Large Cities*, Tokyo, New York and Paris, United Nations University Press.

———. 2004. *Johannesburg: The Making and Shaping of the City*, Pretoria, University of South Africa Press.

Beavon, K. and Rogerson, C. 1986. The council vs. the common people: the case of street trading in Johannesburg. *Geoforum*, 17(2), 201–216.

Beinart, W. and Dawson, M. (eds.). 2010. *Popular Politics and Resistance Movements in South Africa*, Johannesburg, Wits University Press.

Bekker, S. and Fourchard, L. (eds.). 2013. *Politics and Policies: Governing Cities in Africa*, Cape Town, Human Sciences Research Council Press.

Bell, M. E. and Bowman, J. H. 2002. Property taxation challenges in post-apartheid South Africa. *Land Lines*, 14(3), 8–11.

Bénit-Gbaffou, C. 2008. Introduction: the place of participation in South African local democracy. *Transformation*, 66/67, i–viii.

——— (ed.). 2014. *A Political Landscape of Street Trader Organisations in Inner City Johannesburg, Post Operation Clean Sweep*, Johannesburg, University of the Witwatersrand (School of Architecture and Planning: Centre for Urbanism and Built Environment Studies).

——— (ed.). 2015. *Popular Politics in South African Cities: Unpacking Community Participation*, Cape Town, Human Sciences Research Council Press.

———. 2016. Do street traders have the 'right to the city'? The politics of street trader organisations in Inner City Johannesburg, post-Operation Clean Sweep. *Third World Quarterly*, 37(6), 1102–1129.

———. 2018. Beyond the policy-implementation gap: how the City of Johannesburg manufactured the ungovernability of street trading. *Journal of Development Studies*, 54(12), 2149–2167.

Bénit-Gbaffou, C., Motaung, T., Sibiya, N., Malemagoba, N., Munzhelele, P. and Manganya, K. 2012. *Unpacking Street Trading Management in the Retail Improvement District (RID)*, Johannesburg, Johannesburg, University of the Witwatersrand, School of Architecture and Planning.

Bennet, M., Mason, J. and Schlemmer, L. (eds.). 1986. *Servicing the Nation: Local and Regional Government Reform*,

Durban, University of Natal (Centre for Applied Social Sciences: Indicator Project South Africa).

Björkdahl, A. and Buckley-Zistel, S. (eds.). 2016. *Spatializing Peace and Conflict: Mapping the Production of Places, Sites and Scales of Violence*, London, Palgrave Macmillan.

Black Sash. 1989. *Nearly an A–Z Guide to Homelessness on the Witwatersrand*, Johannesburg, Black Sash Transvaal Region Urban Removals and Homelessness Group, and Community Research and Information Network.

Blake, R. R., Mouton, J. S., Barnes, L. B. and Greiner, L. E. 1964. Breakthrough in organization development. *Harvard Business Review*, November. Available: https://hbr.org/1964/11/breakthrough-in-organization-development [Accessed 4 October 2011].

Bobat, S. 2012. *Policy Specialist and then Deputy Director of Economic Development within the Johannesburg City Council's Urbanisation Department between 1993 and 1997 Working on Local Economic Development and Urbanisation Matters*, Johannesburg, interview with author, 3 December.

Bond, P. 1998. Privatisation, participation and protest in the restructuring of municipal services: grounds for opposing World Bank promotion of 'public–private partnerships'. *Urban Forum*, 9(1), 37–75.

———. 2004a. Johannesburg's water wars: Soweto versus Suez. *Le Passant Ordinaire*, 48(611), 1–3.

———. 2004b. *South Africa's Resurgent Urban Social Movements: The Case of Johannesburg, 1984, 1994, 2004*, Durban, Research Report No. 22.

Bond, S. 2011. Negotiating a 'democratic ethos': moving beyond the agonistic–communicative divide. *Planning Theory*, 10(2), 161–186.

Bonner, P. and Nieftagodien, N. 2008. *Alexandra: A History*, Johannesburg, Wits University Press.

Booysen, S. 2007. With the ballot and the brick: the politics of attaining service delivery. *Progress in Development Studies*, 7(1), 21–32.

Breen, K. 2009. Agonism, antagonism and the necessity of care. *In*: Schaap, A. (ed.) *Law and Agonistic Politics*, Farnham, Ashgate, 133–146.

Bremner, L. 2000. Reinventing the Johannesburg Inner City. *Cities*, 17(3), 185–193.

Brown, J. 2015. *South Africa's Insurgent Citizens: On Dissent and the Possibility of Politics*, London, Zed Books.

Burawoy, M. and von Holdt, K. 2012. *Conversations with Bourdieu: The Johannesburg Moment*, Johannesburg, Wits University Press.

Business Day. 1996. *Jo'burg Council to Clean up Trading in the CBD*, 4 April, p. 6.

———. 2001. *Not So Fast on Public Utilities (Reproduced in Municipal Services Project. 2002. Municipal Services: Narrative Final Report (Appendix C). Municipal Services Project, Occasional Paper. Cape Town)*, 15 April. Available: www.municipalservicesproject.org [Accessed 13 November 2011].

———. 2002. *Evictions Not Legal, Yeoville Hawkers Say*, 2 October. Available: http://allafrica.com/stories/200210020065.html [Accessed 13 December 2014].

———. 2010. *Ratepayers to Cover Cost of 'Mistakes' in Choice of Contractor*, 16 April. Available: www.bdlive.co.za/articles/2010/04/16/ratepayers-to-cover-cost-of-mistakes-in-choice-of-contractor;jsessionid=06095D03EB94C17010 10A6AF0051C7AB.present2.bdfm [Accessed 11 April 2015].

———. 2013a. *Evicted Joburg Hawkers Talk of Hidden Agenda*, 28 October, p. 1.

———. 2013b. *Johannesburg Metro Saddled with Qualified Audit – Again*, 31 January. Available: www.bdlive.co.za/national/2013/01/31/johannesburg-metro-saddled-with-qualified-audit--again [Accessed 17 May 2015].

———. 2013c. *Judgment Reserved in Dispute between Johannesburg and Informal Traders*, 27 November. Available: www.bdlive.co.za/national/2013/11/27/judgment-reserved-in-dispute-between-johannesburg-and-informal-traders [Accessed 11 October 2014].

———. 2014a. *Battle for Gauteng Will Get Under Way in Earnest*, 12 May, p. 3.

———. 2014b. *City of Johannesburg Officials Upbeat after Unqualified Audit*, 31 January. Available: www.bdlive.co.za/national/2014/01/31/city-of-johannesburg-officials-upbeat-after-unqualified-audit [Accessed 17 May 2015].

BusinessTech. 2012. *Where the Mega-Rich Live in SA*, 11 December. Available: http://businesstech.co.za/news/general/28307/how-the-other-half-lives/ [Accessed 23 June 2015].

———. 2014. *Most Expensive Suburbs in Joburg*, 7 February. Available: http://businesstech.co.za/news/general/52584/most-expensive-suburbs-in-joburg/ [Accessed 23 June 2015].

Byrne, J. (ed.). 2012. *The Occupy Handbook*, New York, Little, Brown & Company.

Cachalia, N. 2012. *City Safety Programme Manager in the Office of the Chief of Police in the City of Johannesburg's Metropolitan Police Department since 2006*, Johannesburg, interview with author, 12 October.

Cahill, L. 2009. *Joburg Rates Boycott*, 1 September. Available: http://petitions.tigweb.org/joburgratesboycott [Accessed 28 April 2015].

———. 2015. *Lee Cahill: Communications Consultant, Writer and Editor*. Available: whoswho.co.za/lee-cahill-398874 [Accessed 8 June 2015].

Callaghan, C. 2012. The effect of financial capital on inner-city street trading. *Journal of Economic and Financial Sciences*, 5(1), 83–102.

Camay, P. and Gordon, A. J. 2004. *Sandton Rates Dispute: Local Government Restructuring and Financing of Equitable Services*, Johannesburg, Co-Operative for Research and Education (CORE), South African Civil Society and Governance Case Study No. 5.

Cameron, R. 1995. The history of devolution of powers to local authorities in South Africa: the shifting sands of state control. *Local Government Studies*, 21(3), 396–417.

———. 2002. Central–local financial relations in South Africa. *Local Government Studies*, 28(3), 113–134.

———. 2015. Public service reform in South Africa: from apartheid to New Public Management. *In*: Massey, A. and Johnston, K. (eds.) *The International Handbook of Public Administration and Governance*, Cheltenham, Edward Elgar, 135–157.

Carte Blanche. 2009. *Bills and Blunders*, Episode 26, 26 July. Available: www.imdb.com/title/tt1484190/fullcredits/ [Accessed 22 November 2015].

Çelik, E. 2011. The exclusion of street traders from the benefits of the FIFA 2010 World Cup in South Africa. *African Journal of Business & Economic Research*, 6(1), 62–86.

Central Johannesburg Partnership. 2006a. *CJP Background: CJP as Urban Manager*. Available: www.cjp.co.za/background.php [Accessed 14 October 2014].

———. 2006b. *CJP Background: Structure*. Available: www.cjp.co.za/background.php [Accessed 14 October 2014].

Centre for Civil Society. 2014. *Praxis News Wire: SA Social Protest Observatory 2003–2012, News Articles in PDF Format.* Available: http://ccs.ukzn.ac.za/default.asp?2,27 [Accessed 27 March 2014].

Centre for Study of Violence and Reconciliation. 2008. *Burning the Welcome Mat.* Available: www.csvr.org.za/index.php/media-articles/latest-csvr-in-the-media/2342-burning-the-welcome-mat.html [Accessed 17 October 2014].

Centre for the Analysis of South African Social Policy. 2009. *South African Index of Multiple Deprivation (SAIMD) 2001 at Datazone Level, Online Database, Statistics SA Census 2001 Data, Environmental Systems Research Institute (ESRI) Datazone Geography.* Available: www.casasp.ox.ac.uk/imd.html [Accessed 7 August 2014].

Chambers, S. and Kopstein, J. 2008. Civil society and the state. *In:* Dryzek, J. S., Honig, B. and Phillips, A. (eds.) *The Oxford Handbook of Political Theory,* Oxford, Oxford University Press, 363–381.

Chigwata, T. C., O'Donovan, M. and Powell, D. M. 2017. *Civic Protests and Local Government in South Africa, The Civic Protests Barometer: 2007–2016,* Working Paper Series No. 2.

Chipkin, I. 2013. Post-bureaucracy: an intellectual history of the transition from the apartheid bureaucracy to the modern public service. *Public Affairs Research Institute, Friedrich-Ebert-Stiftung, and Mapungubwe Institute for Strategic Reflection: African State-Formation and Bureaucracy in Comparative Perspective,* 16–18 September, Johannesburg.

City of Johannesburg. 2001a. *Johannesburg: An African City in Change (The City of Johannesburg Council),* Cape Town, Struik Publishers.

———. 2001b. *Progress Report on Orange Farm New Wave Consolidation Programme 2001, Report to Mayoral Committee (Item 7),* Housing.

———. 2001c. *Spatial Development Framework,* Development Planning, Transportation and Environment Department (Development Planning and Facilitation Directorate).

———. 2002a. *Annexure A: Informal Trade Development Programme* (document status unconfirmed).

———. 2002b. *Annual Report 2001/02: Vision.*

———. 2002c. *Joburg 2030,* Corporate Planning Unit, 00-620-28636-9.

———. 2002d. *Metro Mall Poised to Open for Business,* 12 July. Available: www.joburgnews.co.za/july_2002/metro_mall.stm [Accessed 6 September 2012].

———. 2002e. *Residents May Petition against Increases,* 19 April. Available: www.joburgnews.co.za/april2002/tariffs.stm [Accessed 1 May 2012].

———. 2002f. *The Rise and Rise of Hawking in the City,* 30 September. Available: www.joburg.org.za/index.php?option=com_content&view=article&id=134:the-rise-and-rise-of-hawking-in-the-city&catid=130&Itemid=212#ixzz3Lf CUPtYa [Accessed 4 May 2011].

———. 2002g. *State of the City Address 2002.* Available: http://joburg.org.za/index.php?option=com_content&task=view&id=718&Itemid=2 [Accessed 9 April 2015].

———. 2003a. *Annual Report on the City of Johannesburg: 2002/03.*

———. 2003b. *Annual Report on the City of Johannesburg: 2002/03 (Chapter 4: Council Speaker).* Available: www.joburg-archive.co.za/city_vision/annualreport2002-03/chapter4.pdf [Accessed 1 May 2012].

———. 2003c. *Executive Mayor's Mid-Term Report: December 2000 – June 2003 (Good*

Governance, Development & Delivery: A World Class African City). Available: www.joburg-archive.co.za/2003/coj-report/CoJMidReportMainForeword.pdf [Accessed 9 June 2013].

———. 2003d. Mayor Delivers Mid-Term Report, 23 September. Available: www.joburgnews.co.za/2003/sept/sep23_midtermreport.stm [Accessed 1 May 2012].

———. 2003e. Regional Spatial Development Framework (RSDF), City of Johannesburg: Administrative Region 11 (Review of the 2001 Approved LIDP), June 2003.

———. 2003f. Regional Spatial Development Framework: Administrative Region 3.

———. 2003g. Regional Spatial Development Framework: Administrative Region 5.

———. 2003h. State of the City Address 2003. Available: www.joburg.org.za/index.php?option=com_content&task=view&id=717&Ite [Accessed 29 April 2012].

———. 2004a. Final Offering Circular for ZAR1 000 000 000,00 11,95% Unsecured Bonds Due 13 April 2010. Available: www.joburgnews.co.za/2004/april/coj_circular.pdf [Accessed 1 May 2012].

———. 2004b. Local Economic Development: Resource Document for the City's Regions 2004, Department of Finance and Economic Development.

———. 2004c. Progress Report on the Informal Trading Development Programme, Report to City of Johannesburg Council, Item 23, 2004-08-26, Economic Development Unit.

———. 2004d. Social Services Package, Palmer Development Group for Corporate Services.

———. 2004e. State of the City Address 2004: Ten Years of Democracy in Johannesburg.

Available: www.joburg.org.za/index.php?option=com_content&task=view&id=4933&I [Accessed 1 May 2012].

———. 2004f. Strategic Review 2004 (Input Document Number 5: Review of Joburg 2030 & Related Documents), Johannesburg, Shisaka Development Management Services for Metropolitan Trading Company.

———. 2004g. Urban Development Zone Tax Incentive: Johannesburg Inner City – Submission to National Treasury, Finance and Economic Development, 10 June (Application: Final Submission).

———. 2004h. Urban Development Zone Tax Incentive: Johannesburg Inner City (Submission to National Treasury) – Annexe AA8: Johannesburg Inner City Regeneration Strategy Business Plan, Financial Years 2004–2007, Finance and Economic Development Department.

———. 2005a. 2005 State of the City Address. Available: www.joburg.org.za/index.php?option=com_content&task=view&id=4933&I [Accessed 29 April 2012].

———. 2005b. Municipal Service Subsidy. Available: www.joburg.org.za/index.php?option=com_content&view=article&id=162:municipal-service-subsidy&catid=66:social-programmes&Itemid=114 [Accessed 20 June 2014].

———. 2005c. Spatial Development Framework (SDF 2005–2006).

———. 2006a. 2006 State of the City Address. Available: www.joburg.org.za/index.php?option=com_content&task=view&id=714&Ite [Accessed 29 April 2012].

———. 2006b. Growth and Development Strategy 2006, Office of the Executive Mayor.

———. 2006c. Joburg GDS & 5-Year Integrated Development Plan: Presentation, Johannesburg, Office of the Executive Mayor (Central Strategy Unit).

———. 2006d. *Programme Phakama Blueprint*, RevNews: Newsletter of the Revenue Management Unit, 27 May.

———. 2006e. *Reflecting on a Solid Foundation: Building Developmental Local Government, 2000–2005*.

———. 2006f. *Revenue and Customer Relations Management Department (R&CRM): Business Plan June 2006–July 2007*.

———. 2007a. *Imagine Tomorrow: Annual Report 2006 – Part 1*. Available: www.joburg.org.za/2007/pdfs/ar20067_p1.pdf [Accessed 12 December 2014].

———. 2007b. *Informal Trading Policy for the City of Johannesburg*.

———. 2007c. *Inner City Captain Is Hands On*, 9 October. Available: www.joburg.org.za/index.php?option=com_content&task=view&id=1730 [Accessed 9 October 2014].

———. 2007d. *Inner City Regeneration Charter*, July 2007.

———. 2007e. *Metropolitan Police Department: Projects – Project Thiba*, 19 March. Available: www.joburg.org.za/index.php?option=com_content&id=702&limitstart=2 [Accessed 14 October 2014].

———. 2007f. *Operation Shanyela Targets Dirty Hillbrow Streets*, 18 December. Available: www.joburg.org.za/index.php?option=com_content&view=article&id=2014:2007-12-18-operation-shanyela-targets-dirty-hillbrow-streets&catid=67:press-releases-2007&Itemid=258 [Accessed 9 October 2014].

———. 2007g. *Proposed Protocol for Dealing with Community Protests: Report to COJ Executive Team, Dated 13 November 2007*, Johannesburg, Development Planning and Urban Management: Office of the Executive Director.

———. 2007h. *Regional Spatial Development Framework (RSDF 2007–2008): Administrative Region G (Review of the Approved 2006/7 RSDF: Annexure to the City of Johannesburg Spatial Development Framework – Submitted as a Component of the IDP in Terms of the Municipal Systems Act, 2000)*.

———. 2007i. *Spring Blitzes Air out Inner City*, 21 September. Available: www.joburg.org.za/index.php?option=com_content&task=view&id=1651 [Accessed 9 October 2014].

———. 2007j. *State of the City Address 2007*. Available: www.joburg.org.za/index.php?option=com_content&task=view&id=3538&It [Accessed 24 April 2012].

———. 2007k. *Stretford Node Urban Development Framework*, Annemarie Loots for City of Johannesburg.

———. 2008a. *By-Law Management Unit, Presented to Johannesburg Business Forum*. Available: www.joburg-archive.co.za/2009/pdfs/economic_development/bylaw_management_unit.pdf [Accessed 5 September].

———. 2008b. *City Condemns Alexandra Violence*, 14 May. Available: www.joburg.org.za/index.php?option=com_content&task=view&id=2486 [Accessed 2 October 2015].

———. 2008c. *City of Johannesburg Economic Development Policy and Strategy Framework: Main Report*.

———. 2008d. *City Sets up Alex Operations Centre*, 16 May. Available: www.joburg.org.za/index.php?option=com_content&task=view&id=2503 [Accessed 2 October 2015].

———. 2008e. *Draft Ward Development Plan 2009/10, Region G: Ward 1*.

———. 2008f. *Draft Ward Development Plan 2009/10, Region G: Ward 2*.

———. 2008g. *Draft Ward Development Plan 2009/10, Region G: Ward 3*.

————. 2008h. *Draft Ward Development Plan 2009/10, Region G: Ward 4.*

————. 2008i. *Draft Ward Development Plan 2009/10, Region G: Ward 5.*

————. 2008j. *Expanded Social Package Policy & Strategy: Eligibility Mechanism and Operational Structure for Poverty-Targetting [sic] Subsidies and Services Delivered by and in Colloboration [sic] with the City of Johannesburg.* Available: www.joburg-archive.co.za/2009/pdfs/expanded_social_package_policy.pdf [Accessed 19 March 2014].

————. 2008k. *Extending the Hand of Kindness,* 4 March. Available: www.joburg.org.za/index.php?option=com_content&task=view&id=2252 [Accessed 9 October 2014].

————. 2008l. *Integrated Development Plan: Revision 2007/08,* Central Strategy Unit.

————. 2008m. *Joburg's Mayor Presents the 'State of the City'.* Available: joburg.org.za/index.php?option=com_content&task=view&id=2233&Itemid=114 [Accessed 29 April 2012].

————. 2008n. *Joburg Aims to Integrate Migrants,* 15 August. Available: http://joburg.org.za/index.php?option=com_content&task=view&id=2852&Item [Accessed 2 October 2015].

————. 2008o. *Johannesburg Inner City Charter: Independent Review of Inner City Charter Commitment Progress (Final Report: Sector Audit Summaries, Sector Evidence Details, Annexure: Sector Scores),* Neil Fraser and Associates (trading as Urban Inc.) for City of Johannesburg.

————. 2008p. *Linear Markets for the Inner City of Johannesburg: Master Business Plan,* Metropolitan Trading Company, October 2008.

————. 2008q. *Region G: Strategic Framework for Economic Development,* Urban-Econ Development Economists for City of Johannesburg, April.

————. 2008r. *Sector DED: Commitments Delivery Audit Ratings Matrix, Total Score for Period 2008/09.* Available: www.joburg-archive.co.za/2011/inner_city/charter/assessment_ded_delivery_matrix.pdf [Accessed 11 October 2014].

————. 2008s. *Statement by the Executive Mayor of Johannesburg, Clr Amos Masondo, at the Media Briefing on the Formalisation and Regularisation of Informal Settlements, Metropolitan Centre, Mayoral Parlour, Braamfontein.* Available: www.joburg.org.za/index.php?option=com_content&task=view&id=4142 [Accessed 24 October 2012].

————. 2009a. *Approval and Adoption for Prumulgation [sic] of the Informal Trading By-Laws, Report to Council, 4 June 2009,* Economic Development Department.

————. 2009b. *Citywide Township Renewal Strategy and Programme,* Riana du Plessis Urban Planning, Business Enterprises (University of Pretoria Department of Town and Regional Planning) and SATPLAN for City of Johannesburg.

————. 2009c. *Joburg Has a Plan for Migrants,* 7 October. Available: http://joburg.org.za/index.php?option=com_content&id=4395&itemid=210 [Accessed 2 October 2015].

————. 2009d. *Joburg Inner City Urban Design Implementation Plan,* VISI Africa Strategic Planners cc, Annemarie Loots, Khuthele Projects (Pty) Ltd., Insite Landscape Architects and MandalaGIS for Johannesburg Development Agency and Department of Development Planning and Facilitation.

———. 2009e. *Latest on the Inner City Charter: May 2009.* Available: www.joburg.org. za/index.php?option=com_content&task=view&id=3852 [Accessed 11 October 2014].

———. 2009f. *Latest on the Inner City Charter: September/October 2009.* Available: http://joburg. org.za/index.php?option=com_content&task=view&id=4477& Item [Accessed 23 January 2015].

———. 2009g. *Software to Beat Billing Blues,* 11 December. Available: www.joburg.org. za/index.php?option=com_content&view=article&id=4638 [Accessed 30 April 2015].

———. 2009h. *State of the City Address, by Executive Mayor of Johannesburg, Councillor Amos Masondo.* Available: www.joburg. org.za/index.php?option=com_content&task=view&id=3538&It [Accessed 29 April 2012].

———. 2009i. *Stretford Station Node Urban Design Framework Report: A Node Reconsidered,* ASM Architects & Urban Designers for Johannesburg Development Agency.

———. 2009j. *Summit Looks at Housing,* 26 November. Available: www.joburg.org. za/index.php?option=com_content&task=view&id=4579 [Accessed 21 October 2012].

———. 2010a. *The 2010 'State of the City' Address.* Available: www.joburg.org. za/index.php?option=com_content&task=view&id=4933&It [Accessed 29 April 2012].

———. 2010b. *2011–2016 Built Environment Performance Plan: Building Sustainable Human Places in the City of Johannesburg (Submission of the City of Johannesburg Metropolitan Municipality in Support of Its Motivation for Funding from the Urban Settlements Development Grant).*

———. 2010c. *A Changing City: The Impact of Urban Management (Region F),* Region F: Stakeholder Management and Liaison.

———. 2010d. *City Gets Unqualified Audit,* 27 January. Available: www. joburg.org.za/index.php?option=com_content&view=article&id=4780:c [Accessed 17 May 2015].

———. 2010e. *City Power Johannesburg (Pty) Ltd: Annual Report 2009/2010,* City Power.

———. 2010f. *Consolidated Annual Report of the City of Johannesburg for 2009/10: Performance Report.*

———. 2010g. *Group Annual Financial Statements for the Year Ended 30 June 2010.*

———. 2010h. *Integrated Development Plan 2010–2011.*

———. 2010i. *Jozi Gets Gold for Phakama,* 30 June. Available: www.joburg.org. za/index.php?option=com_content&view=article&id=5394 [Accessed 30 April 2015].

———. 2010j. *New Call Centre to Ease Operations,* 13 August. Available: www.joburg.org. za/index.php?option=com_content&view=article&id=5563 [Accessed 30 April 2015].

———. 2010k. *Orange Farm Integrated Development Framework and Business Plan,* Urban Dynamics/ ASM Consortium for Johannesburg Development Agency.

———. 2010l. *Phakama Roll out Successful,* 25 January. Available: www.joburg.org. za/index.php?option=com_content&view=article&id=4764 [Accessed 30 April 2015].

———. 2010m. *Phakama Rolls out to Midrand,* 8 March. Available: www.joburg.org. za/index.php?option=com_content&view=article&id=4909 [Accessed 30 April 2015].

———. 2010n. *Regional Spatial Development Framework: 2010/11 (Administrative Region G).*

———. 2010o. *Terms of Reference: The Johannesburg Informal Trading Forum Department of Economic Development.* Available: http:// joburg-archive.co.za/2010/pdfs/ informal_trading_forum.pdf [Accessed 10 March 2014].

———. 2011a. *The 2011 'State of the City' Address.* Available: http://joburg.org.za/index. php?option=com_content&view=a rticle&id=6324:the-...24 [Accessed 24 January 2015].

———. 2011b. *Acceptance Speech by the Executive Mayor of the City of Johannesburg, Councillor Mpho Parks Tau.* Available: http://joburg. org.za/index.php?option=com_con tent&view=article&id=6652:acc [Accessed 24 January 2015].

———. 2011c. *Annual Performance Report for the Period 01 July 2010 to 30 June 2011.* Available: www.joburg-archive.co.za/2011/ annual_report_1011/performance_ report11.pdf [Accessed 8 August 2015].

———. 2011d. *Building Sustainable Human Places in Johannesburg: End of Term Report 2006–2011,* Central Strategy Unit.

———. 2011e. *Change Is Coming to Orange Farm.* Available: www.joburg.org.za/index. php?option=com_content&view=a rticle&id=7034:change-is-coming- to-orange-farm&catid=198:urban- development&Itemid=198 [Accessed 27 October 2012].

———. 2011f. *Changes to Johannesburg Billing System Are Showing Results,* 13 May. Available: www.joburg.org. za/index.php?option=com_ content&view=article&id=6603 [Accessed 30 April 2015].

———. 2011g. *City Moves to Solve Billing Issues,* 21 February. Available: www.joburg.org. za/index.php?option=com_ content&view=article&id=6256 [Accessed 30 April 2015].

———. 2011h. *The City of Joburg Is Listening,* 22 February. Available: www.joburg.org. za/index.php?option=com_ content&view=article&id=6260:2 [Accessed 15 May 2015].

———. 2011i. *City of Johannesburg Metropolitan Municipality: Group Annual Financial Statements for the Year Ended 30 June 2011.*

———. 2011j. *City of Johannesburg: Final Results Presentation to Investors for Year Ended 2011 (Revenue Step Change Roadmap, Gerald Dumas, Chief Operations Officer).*

———. 2011k. *City Sets up Billing Hotline,* 22 February. Available: www.joburg.org. za/index.php?option=com_ content&view=article&id=6268 [Accessed 30 April 2015].

———. 2011l. *City Works to Resolve Billing Queries,* 15 April. Available: www.joburg.org. za/index.php?option=com_ content&view=article&id=6512:c [Accessed 17 May 2015].

———. 2011m. *CoJ Institutional Review: Executive Summary of Discussion Document on High Level Institutional Review,* Vortex Strategic Alignment for City of Johannesburg.

———. 2011n. *COJ Responds to Audit Report,* 30 June. Available: www.joburg.org. za/index.php?option=com_ content&view=article&id=6825 [Accessed 11 April 2015].

———. 2011o. *Customer Satisfaction Survey 2010,* Johannnesburg.

———. 2011p. *Customer Service, Billing and Credit Control: Statement by the Executive Mayor of the City of Johannesburg, Clr Amos Masondo, on the Occasion of the Media Briefing on Issues Relating to Customer Service, Billing and Credit Control in the City of Johannesburg, Held at the Metropolitan Centre, Mayoral*

*Parlour, Braamfontein –
Johannesburg,* 26 January.
Available: www.joburg.org.
za/index.php?option=com_
content&id=6140:customer-
service-billing-and-credit-
control&Itemid=114 [Accessed 5
June 2012].
———. 2011q. *Dealing with the
Billing Crisis,* 16 December.
Available: www.joburg.org.
za/index.php?option=com_
content&view=article&id=7579&
[Accessed 3 May 2015].
———. 2011r. *Fowler Steps in
as City Manager,* 3 October.
Available: www.joburg.org.
za/index.php?option=com_
content&view=article&id=7252
[Accessed 31 May 2015].
———. 2011s. *Joburg 2040: Growth
and Development Strategy – A
Promising Future,* Johannesburg,
Corporate Planning Unit.
———. 2011t. *Mayor Meets Police
in Soweto,* 6 July. Available:
www.joburg.org.za/index.
php?option=com_content&view
=article&id=6853&catid=88&Ite
mid=266 [Accessed 30 April 2012].
———. 2011u. *No Billing
Crisis – Mayor,* 26 January.
Available: www.joburg.org.
za/index.php?option=com_
content&view=article&id=6141
[Accessed 7 September 2015].
———. 2011v. *Sharing the Legacy:
Executive Mayor's End of Term
Report 2006–2011,* Central
Strategy Unit.
———. 2011w. *Tribute Paid
to Masondo,* 30 May.
Available: www.joburg.org.
za/index.php?option=com_
content&view=article&id=6668
[Accessed 29 April 2012].
———. 2012a. *The 2012
'State of the City' Address.*
Available: www.joburg.org.
za/index.php?option=com_
content&id=7865&Itemid=114
[Accessed 16 February 2014].

———. 2012b. *Billing Gets National
Attention,* 20 March. Available: www.
joburg.org.za/index.php?option=com_
content&view=article&id=7853&
[Accessed 12 May 2015].
———. 2012c. *City of Joburg Property
Company (SOC) Ltd.: Annual
Report 2011/12,* City of Joburg
Property Company.
———. 2012d. *City of Johannesburg
Metropolitan Municipality: Group
Annual Financial Statements for the
Year Ended 30 June 2012.*
———. 2012e. *Growth Management
Strategy: Growth Trends and
Development Indicators Fourth
Annual Assessment – Stakeholder
Presentation June 2012,*
Development Planning and
Facilitation Directorate.
———. 2012f. *Integrated Development
Plan 2012/16: Committing to a
Promising Future,* Group Strategy
(Policy Coordination and Relations
Department).
———. 2012g. *Joburg on Top
in Annual Report,* 26 January.
Available: www.joburg.org.
za/index.php?option=com_
content&view=article&id=7675:j
[Accessed 17 May 2015].
———. 2012h. *A. Report on the Status
of the Inner City (Region F), B. A
Proposed Initiative and Programme
to Address Current Challenges,
Development Planning Section* 79
Committee, 2012-10-10, Office of
the MMC.
———. 2013a. *2012/16 Integrated
Development Plan: 2013/14 Review,
Corridors of Freedom, 'Re-Stitching
Our City to Create a New Future'.*
———. 2013b. *2013/16 Integrated
Development Plan (IDP):
Implementing the Joburg 2040
Strategy.*
———. 2013c. *Integrated Annual
Report 2012/2013: Committing to a
Promising Future.*
———. 2013d. *Position Paper on
the Inner City Transformation
Roadmap Approach to Informal*

Trade and Markets: Report to Executive Management Team, 11 November, Development Planning Department and Johannesburg Development Agency.

———. 2013e. *Progress of the Inner City Informal Trading Task Team, Notes of Meeting Dated 12 November,* Office of the Chief Operations Officer.

———. 2013f. *State of the City Address by the Executive Mayor of the City of Johannesburg, Councillor Mpho Parks Tau, Linder Auditorium, University of the Witwatersrand.* Available: http://joburg.org.za/images/stories/2013/May/joburg%20state%20of%20the%20city%20address%20soca%202013.pdf [Accessed 9 April 2015].

———. 2013g. *Traders and Joburg Agree on a Joint Operations Committee,* 25 November. Available: http://joburg.org.za/index.php?option=com_content&view=article&id=8875:traders-and-joburg-agree-on-a-joint-operations-committee-&catid=217:press-releases-2013&Itemid=114 [Accessed 19 October 2014].

———. 2014a. *2012/2016 Integrated Development Plan: 2014/2015 Review.*

———. 2014b. *City Hails Unqualified Audit,* 30 January. Available: http://joburgopen.com/index.php?option=com_content&view=article&id=8961 [Accessed 19 May 2015].

———. 2014c. *COJ Approves Informal Trading Implementation Framework,* 22 May. Available: http://joburg.org.za/index.php?option=com_content&view=article&id=9059:220 [Accessed 11 October 2014].

———. 2014d. *Group Integrated Annual Report 2013–14: 'Corridors of Freedom – Re-Stitching Our City to Create a New Future'.*

———. 2014e. *State of the City Address 2014.* Available: http://joburg.org.za/index.php?option=com_content&view=article&id=8626%3Astate-of-the-city-address-speech&catid=88%3Anews [Accessed 15 April 2014].

———. 2015. *State of the City Address 2015, Delivered by the Executive Mayor, Councillor Mpho Parks Tau.* Available: http://joburg.org.za/images/stories/2015/May/soca%202015%20speech%2006.05.15.pdf [Accessed 6 May 2015].

———. 2016. *Presentation to Inner City Informal Trading Sector: Promulgation of Trading Areas,* Economic Development.

———. 2019. *City of Joburg Includes Informal Traders in Policy Formulation,* 25 March. Available: www.joburg.org.za/media_/Newsroom/Pages/2019%20Newsroom%20Articles/March%202019/City-include-informal-traders-in-policy-formulation-.aspx [Accessed 25 April 2016].

City Press. 2000. *Protest Will Fail to Derail ANC Victory but It Would Be Political Hari-Kiri for the ANC Leadership to Ignore the Long-Term Implications of These Protests,* 19 November, p. 5. Available: http://152.111.1.87/argief/berigte/citypress/2000/11/19/5/1.html [Accessed 1 May 2012].

———. 2002. *The City of Jozi Will --,* 29 December. Available: http://m24argo2.naspers.com/argief/berigte/citypress/2002/12/29/25/4.html [Accessed 15 May 2015].

———. 2010. *Joburg Hawkers Hand over Memorandum Detailing Abuse,* 10 November. Available: www.citypress.co.za/news/joburg-hawkers-hand-over-memorandum-detailing-abuse-20101110/ [Accessed 3 October 2015].

———. 2011. *Headline-Hogging ANC Councillors Dumped,* 29 May. Available: www.citypress.co.za/politics/headline-hogging-anc-councillors-dumped-20110528/ [Accessed 21 October 2012].

CityBuzz. 2014. *City Hosts Public Meetings on Informal Trading*, 29 July. Available: http://citybuzz. co.za/17311/city-hosts-public-meetings-on-informal-trading/ [Accessed 11 October 2014].

Clarno, A. 2013. Rescaling white space in post-apartheid Johannesburg. *Antipode*, 45(5), 1190–1212.

Coalition Against Water Privatisation, Anti-Privatisation Forum and Public Citizen. 2004. *'Nothing for Mahala': The Forced Installation of Prepaid Water Meters in Stretford, Extension 4, Orange Farm, Johannesburg, South Africa*, Durban, Centre for Civil Society, University of KwaZulu-Natal, Research Report No. 16.

Cohen, J. L. and Arato, A. 1994. The contemporary revival of civil society. *Civil Society and Political Theory*, Cambridge, MA, MIT Press, 29–82.

Collins, R. 2008. *Violence: A Micro-Sociological Theory*, Princeton, NJ, Princeton University Press.

Comaroff, J. and Comaroff, J. 2004. Criminal justice, cultural justice: the limits of liberalism and the pragmatics of difference in the new South Africa. *American Ethnologist*, 31(2), 188–204.

Community Agency for Social Enquiry. 1995a. *Our Daily Bread: Earning a Living on the Pavements of Johannesburg. Part I: The Census*, Johannesburg, Community Agency for Social Enquiry.

———. 1995b. *Our Daily Bread: Earning a Living on the Pavements of Johannesburg. Part III: Possible Future Scenarios*, Johannesburg, Community Agency for Social Enquiry.

Corbridge, S., Williams, G., Srivastava, M. and Véron, R. 2005. *Seeing the State: Governance and Governmentality in India*, Cambridge, Cambridge University Press.

Cowan, S. 2004. Informal traders' action undermine their goal. *The Star*, p. 13.

Cox, A. 2012. *Senior Journalist for The Star Newspaper and Founder and Lead of MetroWatch, a Weekly Local Government Watchdog Feature on Johannesburg's Service Delivery Failures*, Johannesburg, interview with author, 21 June.

Crankshaw, O. 1993. Squatting, apartheid and urbanisation on the southern Witwatersrand. *African Affairs*, 92(366), 31–51.

Crankshaw, O. and Hart, T. 1990. *The Human and Social Impacts of the Squatter Relocation to Orange Farm*, Pretoria, Human Sciences Research Council (National Institute for Personnel Research), Contract Report C/Pers No. 416 submitted to the Urban Foundation.

Crowder, G. 2006. Chantal Mouffe's agonistic democracy. *Australasian Political Studies Association Annual Conference*, 25–27 September, Newcastle.

Cunningham, F. 2002. *Theories of Democracy: A Critical Introduction*, London, Routledge.

Daily Maverick. 2009. *Service Delivery Problems Go Middle Class*, 14 December. Available: www.dailymaverick.co.za/article/2009-12-14-service-delivery-problems-go-middle-class/#. VlDAKSHovBY [Accessed 11 April 2015].

———. 2013. *Tshwane Metro Metering Contract Branded 'Blatantly Corrupt'*, 12 December. Available: www.dailymaverick. co.za/article/2013-12-12-tshwane-metro-metering-contract-branded-blatantly-corrupt/ [Accessed 12 December].

———. 2014. *Analysis: Bonfires of Discontent, in Horrifying Numbers*, 5 February. Available: www. dailymaverick.co.za/article/2014-02-05-analysis-bonfires-of-

discontent-in-horrifying-numbers/
[Accessed 12 March 2018].
Daily Sun. 2004. *CEO Bows out after
Suspension,* 17 June. Available:
http://m24argo2.naspers.com/
argief/berigte/dailysun/2004/06/17/
[Accessed 15 May 2015].
Dawson, M. 2010a. The cost of
belonging: exploring class and
citizenship in Soweto's water war.
Citizenship Studies, 14(4), 381–394.
———. 2010b. Resistance and
repression: policing protest in
post-apartheid South Africa. *In:*
Handmaker, J. and Berkhout,
R. (eds.) *Mobilising Social Justice
in South Africa: Perspectives from
Researchers and Practitioners,*
Pretoria, Hivos/ISS Civil Society
Building Programme with Pretoria
University Law Press, 101–136.
de Kadt, D. and Lieberman, E. S.
2015. *Do Citizens Reward Good
Service? Voter Responses to Basic
Service Provision in Southern Africa,*
Afrobarometer, Working Paper No.
161.
de Satgé, R. and Watson, V. 2018.
*Urban Planning in the Global South:
Conflicting Rationalities in Contested
Urban Space,* Cham, Springer.
Death, C. 2010. Troubles at the
top: South African protests and
the 2002 Johannesburg Summit.
African Affairs, 109(437), 555–574.
———. 2011. *Governing Sustainable
Development: Partnerships, Protests
and Power at the World Summit,*
Abingdon, Routledge.
DefenceWeb. 2011. *Minister of
Police Affirms Importance of Public
Order Policing Policy,* 4 October.
Available: www.defenceweb.
co.za/index.php?option=com_con
tent&view=article&id=1968
2:minister-of-police-affirms-
importance-of-public-order-
policing-policy&catid=3:Civil%20
Security&Itemid=113 [Accessed 30
April 2012].
DeHoog, R. H., Lowery, D. and
Lyons, W. E. 1990. Citizen
satisfaction with local government

services: a test of individual,
jurisdictional, and city specific
explanations. *Journal of Politics,*
52(3), 807–837.
della Porta, D. 2013. *Can Democracy
Be Saved? Participation, Deliberation
and Social Movements,* Cambridge,
Polity Press.
della Porta, D. and Mattoni, A.
(eds.). 2014. *Spreading Protest:
Social Movements in Times of Crisis,*
Colchester, ECPR Press.
della Porta, D. and Reiter, H. R.
(eds.). 1998. *Policing Protest: The
Control of Mass Demonstrations in
Western Democracies,* Minneapolis,
MN, University of Minnesota
Press.
Democratic Alliance. 2011. *The
Johannesburg Billings Crisis,* circa
February–May. Available: www.
dajhb.co.za/billingcrisis.html
[Accessed 30 April 2012].
———. 2012. *DA to Send Billing
Queries to Auditor General for
Further Investigation,* 9 September.
Available: http://dajhb.co.za/?p=640
[Accessed 10 April 2015].
———. 2017. *Jozi Billing Crisis –
Mashaba Takes Action,* 1 August.
Available: www.da.org.za/2017-08/
jozi-billing-crisis-mashaba-takes-
action.
Diamond, L. 2008. *Democracy
in Retreat.* Available: www.
realclearpolitics.com/
articles/2008/03/democracy_in_
retreat.html [Accessed 28 March
2012].
Diani, M. and McAdam, D. 2003.
*Social Movement Analysis: The
Network Perspective,* Oxford, Oxford
University Press.
Dinat, S. 2012. *Informal Trading
Development Programme Head within
City of Johannesburg's Economic
Development Unit between 2003 and
2006, following Various Roles in the
City Administration since the Late
1990s,* Johannesburg, interview
with author, 16 November.
Domhoff, G. W. 2005. *Power
Structure Research and the Hope*

for Democracy. Available: http://observatory-elites.org/wp-content/uploads/2012/06/Power-Structure-Research-.pdf [Accessed 7 August 2016].

Dryzek, J. S. 2005. Deliberative democracy in divided societies: alternatives to agonism and analgesia. *Political Theory*, *33*(2), 218–242.

du Toit, A. 2008. Living on the margins: the social dynamics of economic marginalisation. *Development Southern Africa*, 25(2), 135–150.

Dugard, J. 2010. Civic action and legal mobilisation: the Phiri water meters case. *In*: Handmaker, J. D. and Berkhout, R. (eds.) *Mobilizing Social Justice in South Africa: Perspectives from Researchers and Practitioners*, Pretoria, Hivos/ISS Civil Society Building Programme with Pretoria University Law Press, 71–95.

Duncan, J. 2010. Voice, political mobilisation and repression under Jacob Zuma (draft paper). *A Decade of Dissent: Reflections on Popular Resistance in South Africa, 2000–2010*, 12–14 November, Johannesburg.

———. 2014a. *Johannesburg Metropolitan Municipality: Notifications of Intention to Gather, Jane Duncan (Rhodes University School of Journalism and Media Studies), Online Database, Johannesburg Metropolitan Police Department (JMPD) Data 2011–2013*. Available: https://docs.google.com/spreadsheets/d/15A32swv-5UcvZ8VyhFyOI-OiWZPvGTtlX2PHnN8DmRA/edit#gid=1487789520 [Accessed 29 April 2014].

———. 2014b. The politics of counting protests. *Mail & Guardian Online*, 17 April. Available: http://mg.co.za/article/2014-04-16-the-politics-of-counting-protests [Accessed 7 May 2014].

———. 2016. *Protest Nation: The Right to Protest in South Africa*, Pietermaritzburg, University of KwaZulu-Natal Press.

Earle, L. 2011. *Literature Review on the Dynamics of Social Movements in Fragile and Conflict-Affected States (Issues Paper)*, Birmingham, Governance and Social Development Resource Centre.

Eisner, M. 2009. The uses of violence: an examination of some cross-cutting issues. *International Journal of Conflict and Violence*, 3(1), 40–59.

Elias, E. 2006. City folds its arms as metro police trample the rights of city hawkers. *The Star*, p. 11.

Ellis, S. and van Kessel, I. (eds.). 2009. *Movers and Shakers: Social Movements in Africa*, Leiden, Brill.

Emdon, E. 1998. Greater Johannesburg metropolitan area. *In*: Sutcliffe, M., McCarthy, J., Sewell, B. and Emdon, E. (eds.) *Further Research into Metropolitan Government Systems: Current Realities and Responses to the White Paper on Local Government*, Pretoria, Department of Constitutional Development, 70–99.

———. 2003. The limits of law: social rights and urban development. *In*: Tomlinson, R., Beauregard, R. A., Bremner, L. and Mangcu, X. (eds.) *Emerging Johannesburg: Perspectives on the Postapartheid City*, New York, Routledge, 215–230.

eNews Channel Africa. 2018. *Joburg's Billing Crisis Remains a Mess*, 14 August. Available: www.enca.com/news/watch-joburgs-billing-crisis-remains-mess [Accessed 4 April 2019].

Engineering News. 2004a. *Joburg on Track to Meet Revenue Targets*, 27 May. Available: www.engineeringnews.co.za/print-version/joburg-on-track-to-meet-revenue-targets-2004-05-27 [Accessed 15 May 2015].

———. 2004b. *Joburg on Track to Meet Revenue Targets*, 26 May. Available: www.engineeringnews. co.za/print-version/joburg-on-track-to-meet-revenue-targets-2004-05-27 [Accessed 15 May 2015].

Erman, E. 2009. What is wrong with agonistic pluralism? Reflections on conflict in democratic theory. *Philosophy and Social Criticism*, 35(9), 1039–1062.

Everatt, D. 2008. The undeserving poor: poverty and the politics of service delivery in the poorest nodes of South Africa. *Politikon*, 35(3), 293–319.

———. 2010. 'That Violence Was Just the Beginning …': Views on Foreigners and the May 2008 Xenophobic Violence as Expressed in Focus Groups Staged at the Time, Johannesburg, Gauteng City Region Observatory.

———. 2011. Xenophobia, state and society in South Africa, 2008–2010. *Politikon*, 38(1), 7–36.

Eyewitness News Online. 2010. *Jo'burg City Prioritises Billing Discrepancies*, 6 October. Available: http://ewn.co.za/2010/10/06/Joburg-city-prioritises-billing-discrepancies [Accessed 16 May 2015].

———. 2011a. *Another Billing Crisis Hits JHB*, 23 November. Available: http://ewn.co.za/2011/11/23/Another-billing-crisis-hits-JHB [Accessed 16 May 2015].

———. 2011b. *Billing Problems, Potholes Top of State of the City Address*, 9 March. Available: http://ewn.co.za/2011/03/09/Billing-problems-potholes-top-of-State-of-the-City-Address [Accessed 15 May 2015].

———. 2011c. *City Council Slams Advocacy Group over Billing Claims*, 22 February. Available: http://ewn.co.za/2011/02/22/City-council-slams-advocacy-group-over-billing-claims [Accessed 16 May 2015].

———. 2011d. *City of JHB Tries to Act on Billing Problems*, 18 February. Available: http://ewn. co.za/2011/02/18/City-of-JHB-tries-to-act-on-billing-problems [Accessed 17 May 2015].

———. 2011e. *Half of JHB Billing Problems Resolved*, 21 April. Available: http://ewn.co.za/2011/04/21/Half-of-JHB-billing-problems-resolved [Accessed 16 May 2015].

———. 2011f. *JHB Makes Strides in Billing Crisis – Tau*, 3 August. Available: http://ewn. co.za/2011/08/03/JHB-makes-strides-in-billing-crisis---Tau [Accessed 16 May 2015].

———. 2011g. *JHB Making 'Significant Progress' in Billing Saga*, 22 April. Available: http://ewn. co.za/2011/04/22/JHB-making-significant-progress-in-billing-saga [Accessed 16 May 2015].

———. 2011h. *JHB Making 'Significant Progress' in Billing Saga*, 22 April. Available: http://ewn. co.za/2011/04/22/JHB-making-significant-progress-in-billing-saga [Accessed 16 May 2015].

———. 2011i. *JHB Sets Billing Deadline*, 22 November. Available: http://ewn.co.za/2011/11/22/JHB-sets-billing-deadline [Accessed 5 December 2015].

———. 2011j. *Joburg Connect Staff Admit They Are on a Go-Slow*, 1 February. Available: http://ewn. co.za/2011/02/01/Joburg-connect-staff-admit-they-are-on-a-go-slow [Accessed 14 May 2015].

———. 2011k. *Minister Steps in as JHB Billing Crisis Spirals*, 24 January. Available: http://ewn. co.za/2011/01/24/Minister-steps-in-as-JHB-billing-crisis-spirals [Accessed 17 May 2015].

———. 2011l. *NCC to Take Action over Unresolved JHB Billing Queries*, 4 August. Available: http://ewn.co.za/2011/08/04/NCC-to-take-action-over-unresolved-JHB-billing-queries [Accessed 16 May 2015].

————. 2011m. *Thousands of Billing Queries Resolved in JHB*, 17 March. Available: http://ewn. co.za/2011/03/17/Thousands-of-billing-queries-resolved-in-JHB [Accessed 16 May 2015].

————. 2012a. *Govt Intervenes in Joburg Billing*, 19 March. Available: http://ewn.co.za/2012/03/19/ Government-intervenes-in-JHB-billing-crisis [Accessed 16 May 2015].

————. 2012b. *JHB Billing Crises to Be Resolved – Minister*, 20 March. Available: http://ewn. co.za/2012/03/20/JHB-billing-crises-to-be-resolved---Minister [Accessed 16 May 2015].

————. 2012c. *JHB Billing Crisis to Be Resolved Soon*, 10 September. Available: http://ewn. co.za/2012/09/11/Joburg-billing-crisis-to-be-resolved [Accessed 16 May 2015].

————. 2012d. *Presidency Happy with Joburg's Billing Plan*, 19 March. Available: http://ewn. co.za/2012/03/19/Presidency-happy-with-Joburgs-billing-plan [Accessed 16 May 2015].

Fedsure Life Assurance Ltd and Others vs Greater Johannesburg Transitional Metropolitan Council and Others. 1998a. *Explanatory Note, Case CCT7/98, 1998/10/14, Constitutional Court of South Africa.* Available: www.saflii.org/za/ cases/ZACC/1998/17media.pdf [Accessed 3 April 2015].

————. 1998b. *Judgment, Case 328/97 [1998] ZASCA 14, 23 March 1998, South Africa: Supreme Court of Appeal.* Available: www. saflii.org/za/cases/ZASCA/1998/14. html [Accessed 2 June 2015].

————. 1998c. *Judgment, Case CCT 7/98, 14 October 1998, Constitutional Court of South Africa.* Available: www.saflii.org/za/cases/ ZACC/1998/17.html [Accessed 2 June 2015].

Fiil-Flynn, M. 2013. *Amanzi Ngawethu! Water and the Political Economy of South Africa*, Technological and Socio-Economic Planning Project, Roskilde University.

Fiil-Flynn, M. and Soweto Electricity Crisis Committee. 2001. *The Electricity Crisis in Soweto*, Johannesburg, University of the Witwatersrand, Queen's University, International Labour Resource and Information Group, South African Municipal Workers Union, Canadian Union of Public Employees, and International Development Research Centre.

Fin24. 2011. *Joburg Billing Plan Launched*, 22 November. Available: www.fin24.com/Economy/Joburg-billing-plan-launched-20111122 [Accessed 16 May 2015].

————. 2012. *Joburg Gets Second Qualified Audit*, 26 January. Available: www.fin24.com/ Economy/Joburg-gets-second-qualified-audit-20120126 [Accessed 11 April 2015].

Flyvbjerg, B. 1998. *Rationality and Power: Democracy in Practice*, Chicago, IL, University of Chicago Press.

Forester, J. 1987. Planning in the face of conflict: negotiation and mediation strategies in local land use regulation. *Journal of the American Planning Association*, 53(3), 303–314.

————. 2009. *Dealing with Differences: Dramas of Mediating Public Disputes*, Oxford, Oxford University Press.

————. 2011. Editorial: planning's dirty little secret and its implications. *Planning Theory & Practice*, 12(3), 325–328.

Fortis, M. F. D. A. 2014. *Bringing Politics and Administration Together: For an Agonistic Policy Model*, doctoral thesis, University of Westminster.

Fraher, A. and Grint, K. 2018. Agonistic governance: the antinomies of decision-making in U.S. Navy SEALs. *Leadership*, 14(4), 395–414.

Freedom House. 2005. *Map of Freedom 2005*. Available: https://freedomhouse.org/sites/default/files/inline_images/2005.pdf [Accessed 4 November 2011].

———. 2018. *Freedom in the World 2018*. Available: https://freedomhouse.org/report/freedom-world/freedom-world-2018 [Accessed 26 June 2018].

Friedman, S. 2001. Rethinking urban service delivery. *In*: Ruble, B. A., Stren, R. E., Tulchin, J. S. and Varat, D. H. (eds.) *Urban Governance around the World*, Washington, DC, Woodrow Wilson International Centre for Scholars, 187–189.

Friedmann, J. 1987. The mediations of radical planning. *In*: Friedmann, J. (ed.) *Planning in the Public Domain: From Knowledge to Action*, Princeton, NJ, Princeton University Press, 389–412.

Fuentes, M. and Frank, A. G. 1989. Ten theses on social movements. *World Development*, 17(2), 179–191.

Fung, A. 2003. Survey article: recipes for public spheres – eight institutional design choices and their consequences. *Journal of Political Philosophy*, 11(3), 338–367.

Gaon, S. 2010. Democracy: its premise and its promise, its crisis and its critique. *In*: Inter-Disciplinary.Net, *Problems of Democracy: Probing the Boundaries*, 30 April–2 May, Prague.

Gauteng City-Region Observatory. 2015. *Quality of Life Survey Viewer, 2011 and 2013 Quality of Life Surveys: Reports Extracted for Indicator1 X1_27 and Indicator1 1_31, Satisfaction: Billing Munic Services, for 2011 and 2013 (2011 Municipal Boundary), Locations: Johannesburg, Ten Municipalities of Gauteng, and Gauteng*. Available: www.gcro.ac.za/qolviewer [Accessed 18 May 2015].

Gauteng Provincial Government. 2016a. *15 Year Review of Democratic Local Government in Gauteng: 2000–2016*, Johannesburg, Gauteng Provincial Government.

———. 2016b. *Annual Report 2015–16*, Economic Development.

George, X. 2012. *Regional Director of City of Johannesburg's Region 11 between 2003 and 2006, Including Orange Farm, Prior to That He Served as Executive Director of Economic Development of the COJ in 2006 and 2007 and Then as CEO of South African Local Government Association*, Pretoria, interview with author, 17 October.

GeoTerraImage. 2015. *Gauteng Provincial Land-Cover (10m): Johannesburg (Dataset Summary Report & Metadata)*, Pretoria, Geo Terra Image (Pty) Ltd.

Gerneke, G. 2012. *Director within the COJ's JMPD until 2015 Who Worked on Metropolitan Policing, Traffic and By-Law Enforcement Matters with over Thirty-Five Years' Experience in Johannesburg's City Administration*, Johannesburg, interview with author, 29 November.

Glaser, D. (ed.). 2010. *Mbeki and After: Reflections on the Legacy of Thabo Mbeki*, Johannesburg, Wits University Press.

Glover, R. W. 2012. Games without frontiers? Democratic engagement, agonistic pluralism and the question of exclusion. *Philosophy and Social Criticism*, 38(1), 81–104.

Goi, S. 2005. Agonism, deliberation, and the politics of abortion. *Polity*, 37(1), 54–81.

Goldsmith, A. 2012. *Information Officer within Greater Johannesburg Transitional Metropolitan Council's Inner-City Office in the Late 1990s, Then Company Secretary for the City of Johannesburg's Johannesburg Development Agency since 2001*, Johannesburg, interview with author, 12 October.

Gotz, G. 2012. *Specialist of Strategy and Policy within City of Johannesburg's Central Strategy Unit (Office of the Executive Mayor) between 2006 and 2009, after Working as Consultant and Academic for Ten Years on Local Government and Urban Development Issues in South African Cities*, Johannesburg, interview with author, 22 November.

Gotz, G. and Simone, A. 2001. The implications of informality on governmentality: the case of Johannesburg in the context of Sub-Saharan urbanisation. *Coping with Informality and Illegality in Human Settlements in Developing Cities, ESF/N-AERUS Annual Workshop*, 23–26 May, Leuven.

Graaff, K. and Ha, N. (eds.). 2015. *Street Vending in the Neoliberal City: A Global Perspective on the Practices and Policies of a Marginalized Economy*, New York, Berghahn Books.

Grabow, S. and Heskin, A. 1973. Foundations for a radical concept of planning. *Journal of the American Institute of Planners*, 39(2), 106–114.

Gramsci, A. 1919. *The Conquest of the State*. Available: www.marxists.org/archive/gramsci/1919/07/conquest-state.htm [Accessed 6 August 2016].

Grant, L. 2014. Taking to the streets: who is protesting and why? *Mail & Guardian Online*, 28 April. Available: http://mg.co.za/data/2014-04-28-taking-to-the-streets-who-is-protesting-and-why [Accessed 7 May 2014].

Greater Johannesburg Metropolitan Council. 1996. *Cities State of the Environment Report for Greater Johannesburg*. Available: http://ceroi.net/reports/johannesburg/csoe/Default.htm [Accessed 6 October 2012].

——. 1997a. *Street Trading Law Enforcement within the GJMC,*

Report to the GJMC: Executive Committee, 97-07-15, Item B14, and Minutes, Metropolitan Public Safety and Emergency Services (Metropolitan Economic Development).

——. 1997b. *Street Trading Management Status Quo and Immediate Needs: Urgency Report to the GJMC – Executive Committee, 97-08-19, Item 6*, Johannesburg, Sport, Art, Culture and Economic Development (Metropolitan Economic Development).

——. 1998a. *Inner City Development Strategy: Priorities for 1998, Report to Inner City Committee, 12 March*, Metropolitan Planning, Urbanisation and Environmental Management.

——. 1998b. *Status Report: Informal Street Trading, Urgency Report to the GJMC Executive Committee, 1998-06-23, Item 4*, Metropolitan Sports, Arts, Culture and Economic Development (Economic Development).

——. 1999a. *Declaration of Restricted Trading Areas in the Johannesburg Inner City, Report to the GJMC: Transformation Lekgotla, 99-07-26, Item 11*, Johannesburg, Office of the Chief Executive Officer (Inner City Office).

——. 1999b. *From the Streets into Markets: Inner City Street Trading Management Strategy (Business Plan Executive Summary)*, Johannesburg, Urban Market Development Joint Venture for the Greater Johannesburg Metropolitan Council.

——. 1999c. *From the Streets into Markets: Inner City Street Trading Management Strategy (Business Plan Report)*, Johannesburg, Urban Market Development Joint Venture for the Greater Johannesburg Metropolitan Council.

——. 1999d. *iGoli 2002: Making the City Work ... It Cannot Be Business as Usual*, Johannesburg, Metropolitan Corporate Services.

———. 1999e. *Provision of Bus Shelters for Commuters: Orange Farm, Report to Ordinary Executive Committee, Item (04), 1999/02/02,* Johannesburg, Section 60 Committee: Planning and Economic Development.

Greenberg, S. 2004. *The Landless People's Movement and the Failure of Postapartheid Land Reform: A Case Study for the Globalisation, Marginalisation and New Social Movements in Post-Apartheid South Africa Project,* Durban, University of KwaZulu-Natal (School of Development Studies) and Centre for Civil Society.

Grégoire, Y. and Fisher, R. J. 2008. Customer betrayal and retaliation: when your best customers become your worst enemies. *Journal of Academy of Marketing Science,* 36(2), 247–261.

Grootes, S. 2011. Joburg's billing crisis: The horror. The horror. *Daily Maverick,* 2 February. Available: www.dailymaverick.co.za/article/2011-02-02-joburgs-billing-crisis-the-horror-the-horror/#.VlDNiyHovBY [Accessed 8 June 2012].

Gualini, E. (ed.). 2015. *Planning and Conflict: Critical Perspectives on Contentious Urban Developments,* New York, Routledge.

Guillaume, P. and Houssay-Holzschuch, M. 2002. Territorial strategies of South African informal dwellers. *Urban Forum,* 13(2), 86–101.

Gunder, M. 2003. Passionate planning for the others' desire: an agonistic response to the dark side of planning. *Progress in Planning,* 60(3), 235–319.

———. 2010. Planning as the ideology of (neoliberal) space. *Planning Theory,* 9(4), 298–314.

Gürsözlü, F. 2009. Debate: agonism and deliberation – recognizing the difference. *Journal of Political Philosophy,* 17(3), 356–368.

Gutmann, A. 2007. Democracy. In: Goodin, R. E., Pettit, P. and Pogge, T. (eds.) *A Companion to Contemporary Political Philosophy,* Oxford, Blackwell, 521–531.

Habermas, J. 1991 [1962]. *The Structural Transformation of the Public Sphere: An Inquiry into a Category of Bourgeois Society ['Strukturwandel der Öffentlichkeit: Untersuchungen zu einer Kategorie der Bürgerlichen Gesellschaft' Translated by Burger, T. and Lawrence, F. in 1989],* Cambridge, MA, MIT Press.

Haferburg, C. and Huchzermeyer, M. (eds.). 2014. *Urban Governance in Post-Apartheid Cities: Modes of Engagement in South Africa's Metropoles,* Stuttgart, Borntraeger.

Hagopian, M. N. 1974. *The Phenomenon of Revolution,* New York, Harper & Row.

Harber, A. 2009. The meaning of 'service delivery'. *The Harbinger,* 4 August. Available: www.theharbinger.co.za/wordpress/2009/08/04/the-meaning-of-service-delivery/ [Accessed 2 February 2012].

Harrison, P. 2012. *Executive Director of City of Johannesburg's Development Planning and Urban Management Department between 2006 and 2009, Now Focused on Development Planning Issues as Academic and National Research Foundation's Chair for Spatial Analysis and City Planning, School of Architecture and Planning at University of the Witwatersrand,* Johannesburg, interview with author, 1 December.

———. 2013. Making planning theory real. *Planning Theory,* 13(1), 65–81.

Harrison, P., Charlton, S. and Zack, T. 2013. The dark side of city council's clean sweep: indiscriminate approach could deal hammer blow to key trading economy. *Saturday Star,* 16 November, p. 14.

Harrison, P., Todes, A., Gotz, G. and Wray, C. (eds.) .2014. *Changing Space, Changing City: Johannesburg after Apartheid*, Johannesburg, Wits University Press.

Harrison, P. and Zack, T. 2014. Between the ordinary and the extraordinary: socio-spatial transformations in the 'Old South' of Johannesburg. *South African Geographical Journal*, 96(2), 180–197.

Hay, C., Lister, M. and Marsh, D. (eds.). 2006. *The State: Theories and Issues*, London, Palgrave Macmillan.

Healey, P. 1996. The communicative turn in planning theory and its implications for spatial strategy formation. *Environment and Planning B: Planning and Design*, 23(2), 217–234.

———. 2009. In search of the 'strategic' in spatial strategy making. *Planning Theory & Practice*, 10(4), 439–457.

Heintz, J. and Valodia, I. 2008. *Informality in Africa: A Review*, Cambridge, MA and Manchester, WIEGO, Working Paper No. 3.

Heller, P. and Evans, P. 2011. Taking Tilly south: durable inequalities, democratic contestation, and citizenship in the southern metropolis. *In*: Hanagan, M. and Tilly, C. (eds.) *Contention and Trust in Cities and States*, Dordrecht, Springer, 305–322.

Hillier, J. 2002. Direct action and agonism in democratic planning practice. *In*: Allmendinger, P. and Tewdwr-Jones, M. (eds.) *Planning Futures: New Directions for Planning Theory*, London, Routledge, 110–135.

Hindson, D. 1987. Orderly urbanisation and influx control: from territorial apartheid to regional spatial ordering in South Africa. *In*: Tomlinson, R. and Addleson, M. (eds.) *Regional Restructuring under Apartheid:*

Urban and Regional Policies in Contemporary South Africa, Johannesburg, Ravan Press, 401–432.

Hood, C. 1991. A public management for all seasons. *Public Administration*, 69 (Spring), 3–19.

Hough, M. 2008. *Violent Protest at Local Government Level in South Africa: Revolutionary Potential*. Available: www.scientiamilitaria. journals.ac.za/pub/article/download/41/69 [Accessed 5 October 2011].

Houwen, T. 2010. Populist representation and agonistic politics. *In*: Inter-Disciplinary.Net, *Problems of Democracy: Probing the Boundaries*, 30 April–2 May, Prague.

Human Rights Watch. 1998. *'Prohibited Persons': Abuse of Undocumented Migrants, Asylum-Seekers, and Refugees in South Africa*. Available: www.refworld. org/docid/3ae6a8430.html [Accessed 5 April 2014].

Hunter, R. and Phakathi, S. 2010. *Workers' Perspectives on Service Delivery in City Revenue Departments: Participant Observation Study in Johannesburg and Ethekwini*, unpublished paper.

ioL News. 2001. *Jo'burg Aims to Recoup R3,6bn Service Arrears*, 19 January. Available: www.iol.co.za/news/politics/jo-burg-aims-to-recoup-r3-6bn-service-arrears-1.55258 [Accessed 15 May 2015].

———. 2002a. *Jailed Protesters Want Jo'burg Mayor Arrested*, 8 April. Available: www.iol.co.za/news/south-africa/jailed-protesters-want-jo-burg-mayor-arrested-1.84620#. VlgiACHouRM [Accessed 30 September 2015].

———. 2002b. *Jo'burg's Rates in Shambles*, 23 January. Available: www.iol.co.za/news/south-africa/jo-burg-s-rates-in-shambles-1.81398 [Accessed 31 May 2015].

———. 2002c. *Private Firm to Control JHB Revenue Stream*, 24 January. Available: www.iol.co.za/news/south-africa/private-firm-to-control-jhb-revenue-stream-1.81201#. VXs6mzcw9y8 [Accessed 15 May 2015].

———. 2002d. *Rent Rage Sees Hawkers Hit the Streets*, 25 September. Available: www.iol.co.za/news/south-africa/rent-rage-sees-hawkers-hit-the-streets-1.95179 [Accessed 20 October 2014].

———. 2006. *Joburg Cops out on the Prowl*, 22 September. Available: www.iol.co.za/news/south-africa/joburg-cops-out-on-the-prowl-1.294851?#. VL5LtzccSGw [Accessed 14 October 2014].

———. 2009. *JMPD Keeps Watch*, 28 December. Available: www.joburg.org.za/index2.php?option=com_content&task=emailform&id=4692&itemid=266 [Accessed 20 January 2015].

———. 2011a. *ANC, Gauteng Mayors to Discuss Billing*, 2 February. Available: www.iol.co.za/news/south-africa/gauteng/anc-gauteng-mayors-to-discuss-billing-1.1020604 [Accessed 5 April 2015].

———. 2011b. *DA Calls for Resignations over Billing*, 4 February. Available: www.news24.com/SouthAfrica/Politics/DA-calls-for-resignations-over-billing-20110204 [Accessed 30 April 2012].

———. 2011c. *Joburg's Promises on Fixing Billing System*, 23 November. Available: www.iol.co.za/the-star/joburg-s-promises-on-fixing-billing-system-1.1184319 [Accessed 15 May 2015].

———. 2011d. *Voters Gatvol of Potholes*, 13 May. Available: www.iol.co.za/news/politics/voters-gatvol-of-potholes-1.1068721 [Accessed 12 April 2015].

———. 2012a. *Orange Farm Residents Angry*, 8 November. Available: www.iol.co.za/the-star/orange-farm-residents-angry-1419448 [Accessed 20 December 2018].

———. 2012b. *Orange Farm Residents in Battle for Service*, 5 June Available: www.iol.co.za/news/crime-courts/orange-farm-residents-in-battle-for-service-1.1311865 [Accessed 30 May 2013].

———. 2012c. *Presidency Asks about Joburg Billing Problems*, 19 March. Available: www.iol.co.za/news/south-africa/gauteng/presidency-asks-about-joburg-billing-problems-1.1259854 [Accessed 21 November 2015].

———. 2012d. *Thousands Queue to Tell of Billing Disputes*, 20 August. Available: www.iol.co.za/news/south-africa/gauteng/thousands-queue-to-tell-of-billing-disputes-1.1365894 [Accessed 10 April 2015].

———. 2013a. *93 Held for Looting, Vandalism in Joburg South Protest*, 24 May. Available: www.iol.co.za/news/93-held-in-joburg-protest-1521647 [Accessed 25 June 2019].

———. 2013b. *Irate Orange Farm Residents Lose Patience*, 19 March. Available: www.iol.co.za/news/south-africa/gauteng/irate-orange-farm-residents-lose-patience-1488678 [Accessed 11 October 2014].

———. 2013c. *Residents Create Stink over Rubbish*, 21 February. Available: www.iol.co.za/news/south-africa/gauteng/residents-create-stink-over-rubbish-1474452 [Accessed 12 December 2018].

———. 2014. *Parkhurst Wins the Paid-Parking War*, 7 July. Available: www.iol.co.za/news/south-africa/gauteng/parkhurst-wins-the-paid-parking-w... [Accessed 4 April 2015].

———. 2020. *Joburg Needs R20bn to Fix the City's Pothole-Ridden Roads*, 6 February. Available: www.iol.co.za/news/ south-africa/joburg-needs-r20bn-to-fix-the-citys-pothole-ridden-roads-42227855 [Accessed 9 February 2020].

iTWeb. 2003. *SPI and IBM SA Provide World-Class IT Services for the City of Johannesburg's R500m Outsourcing Contract*, 4 March. Available: www.itweb.co.za/index. php?option=com_content&view= article&id=17812:s [Accessed 14 May 2015].

———. 2007. *Masana Technologies Is Well-Positioned to Deliver*, 14 August. Available: www.itweb. co.za/index.php?option=com_ content&view=article&id=7756 [Accessed 14 May 2015].

———. 2009a. *City's IT Services in Limbo*, 21 September. Available: www.itweb.co.za/index. php?option=com_content&view= article&id=26461:ci [Accessed 14 May 2015].

———. 2009b. *City's Tech Supplier Goes Bust*, 9 September. Available: www.itweb.co.za/ index.php?option=com_ content&view=article&id=26076 [Accessed 11 April 2015].

———. 2010. *DiData Hopes for City Deal*, 13 January. Available: www.itweb.co.za/index. php?option=com_content&view= article&id=29200:di [Accessed 14 May 2015].

———. 2011a. *Billing Protest 'Disappointing'*, 18 February. Available: www.itweb.co.za/index. php?option=com_content&view= article&id=41289:bi [Accessed 3 June 2015].

———. 2011b. *DA Slams Joburg over Disconnections*, 10 November. Available: www.itweb.co.za/index. php?option=com_content&view= article&id=49155:da [Accessed 16 May 2015].

———. 2011c. *Joburg in New Billing Mess*, 25 August. Available: www.itweb.co.za/content/ KzQenvjrVxDvZd2r.

———. 2011d. *Joburg Served*, 6 December. Available: www.itweb. co.za/index.php?option=com_con tent&view=article&id=49922:jo [Accessed 25 May 2015].

———. 2011e. *Stop Helping!* 16 February. Available: www.itweb. co.za/index.php?option=com_con tent&view=article&id=41180:sto [Accessed 12 April 2015].

———. 2011f. *There Is No Crisis – Masondo*, 26 January. Available: www.itweb.co.za/ index.php?option=com_ content&view=article&id=40485 [Accessed 4 November 2012].

———. 2012a. *City Sets up Billing Escalation Team*, 10 February. Available: www.itweb.co.za/index. php?option=com_content&view= article&id=51450:ci [Accessed 25 May 2015].

———. 2012b. *DA Takes Billing Issue to NCC*, 17 October. Available: www.itweb.co.za/index. php?option=com_content&view= article&id=59344:D [Accessed 25 May 2015].

———. 2013a. *DA Lashes Joburg over Qualified Audit*, 5 February. Available: www.itweb.co.za/ index.php?option=com_ content&view=article&id=61546 [Accessed 17 May 2015].

———. 2013b. *Project Phakama Bites Again*, 19 February. Available: www.itweb.co.za/ index.php?option=com_ content&view=article&id=61850 [Accessed 10 April 2015].

———. 2017. *Massive Tech Glitch Hits Joburg Billing System*, 25 May. Available: www.itweb.co.za/ content/kxA9POvN9Gqo4J81 [Accessed 4 April 2019].

iWeek. 2011. *Joburg's New Mayor Vows to Fix Billing Crisis*, 8 June. Available: www.iweek.co.za/

in-the-know/joburg-s-new-mayor-vows-to-fix-billing-crisis [Accessed 14 May 2015].

Jain, H. 2010. *Community Protests in South Africa: Trends, Analysis and Explanations*, Cape Town, University of Western Cape (Community Law Centre: Local Democracy, Peace and Human Security Project), Local Government Working Papers Series No. 1, August.

Jenkins, J. C. and Klandermans, B. 1995. The politics of social protest. *In*: Jenkins, J. C. and Klandermans, B. (eds.) *The Politics of Social Protest: Comparative Perspectives on States and Social Movements*, Minneapolis, MN, University of Minnesota Press, 3–13.

Jessop, B. 1990. Putting states in their place: once more on capitalist states and capitalist societies. *In*: Jessop, B. (ed.) *State Theory: Putting Capitalist States in Their Place*, University Park, PA, Pennsylvania State University Press, 338–369.

Johannesburg Advocacy Group. 2010. *Joburg Municipal Billing Crisis Campaign*, 14 November. Available: www.joburgadvocacy.org/2010/11/municipal-billing-crisis-in-city-of.html [Accessed 21 November 2015].

———. 2011. *Update on the Joburg Municipal Billing Crisis*, 21 January. Available: www.joburgadvocacy.org/2011/01/residents-of-johannesburg-have-had.html [Accessed 21 November 2015].

———. 2014. *JAG Website*. Available: www.joburgadvocacy.org/ [Accessed 5 April 2015].

Johannesburg City Council. 1994. *Informal Trading: Strategic Projects, Report to Ordinary Meeting of Council, 28 June, Item 44*, Health, Housing and Urbanisation Directorate.

Johannesburg Inner City Development Forum. 1997. *The Golden Heartbeat of Africa: A Dynamic City That Works – The Johannesburg Inner City Renewal Strategy*, Johannesburg, Johannesburg Inner City Development Forum.

Johannesburg Land Company. 2014. *Submissions Concerning Informal Trading, 27 August, Letter from R. Koevort to COJ's Department of Economic Development*. Available: www.cidforum.co.za/content/resources [Accessed 20 November 2014].

Johannesburg Roads Agency. 2015. *JRA Mobile Find & Fix App*, 13 March. Available: www.jra.org.za/index.php/find-and-fix-mobile-app [Accessed 1 May 2015].

Karamoko, J. 2011. *Community Protests in South Africa: Trends, Analysis and Explanations*, Cape Town, University of Western Cape, Community Law Centre, 2011 Report.

Kasfir, N. 1998. Civil society, the state and democracy in Africa. *Commonwealth and Comparative Politics*, 36(2), 123–149.

Keane, J. 2003. *Global Civil Society?* Cambridge, Cambridge University Press.

———. 2004. *Violence and Democracy*, Cambridge, Cambridge University Press.

Khosa, M. 2002. Infrastructure and service delivery in South Africa, 1994–99. *In*: Parnell, S., Pieterse, E., Swilling, M. and Wooldridge, D. (eds.) *Democratising Local Government: The South African Experiment*, Cape Town, University of Cape Town Press, 141–157.

Kirshner, J. 2014. Reconceptualising xenophobia, urban governance and inclusion: the case of Khutsong. *In*: Haferburg, C. and Huchzermeyer, M. (eds.) *Urban Governance in Post-Apartheid Cities: Modes of Engagement in South Africa's Metropoles*, Stuttgart, Borntraeger, 117–134.

Knops, A. 2007. Debate: agonism as deliberation – on Mouffe's theory of democracy. *Journal of Political Philosophy*, 15(1), 115–126.

———. 2012. Integrating agonism with deliberation: realising the benefits. *Filozofija i Društvo*, 23(4), 151–169.

Koonings, K. and Kruijt, D. (eds.). 2009a. *Fractured Cities: Social Exclusion, Urban Violence and Contested Spaces in Latin America*, London, Zed Books.

——— (eds.). 2009b. *Mega-Cities: The Politics of Urban Exclusion and Violence in the Global South*, London, Zed Books.

Koseff, J. 2012. *Director of Social Assistance within City of Johannesburg's Department of Community Development between 2009 and 2013*, Johannesburg, interview with author, 8 November.

Kuhlmann, S. and Bouckaert, G. (eds.). 2016. *Local Public Sector Reforms in Times of Crisis: National Trajectories and International Comparisons*, London, Palgrave Macmillan.

Kute, P. 2012a. *Assistant Director of City of Johannesburg's Petitions Unit in the COJ since 2008*, Johannesburg, interview with author, 21 June.

———. 2012b. *Petitions Registers for July to December 2010 and July 2010 to June 2011*, email to author, 29 June.

Laclau, E. and Mouffe, C. 1985. *Hegemony and Socialist Strategy: Towards a Radical Democratic Politics*, London, Verso.

Lancaster, L. 2016. *At the Heart of Discontent: Measuring Public Violence in South Africa*, Pretoria, Institute for Security Studies, ISS Paper 2002.

———. 2018. Unpacking discontent: where and why protest happens in South Africa. *SA Crime Quarterly*, 64 (June), 29–43.

Lawhon, M., Pierce, J. and Makina, A. 2018. Provincializing urban appropriation: agonistic transgression as a mode of actually existing appropriation in South African cities. *Singapore Journal of Tropical Geography*, 39(1), 117–131.

Laws, D. and Forester, J. 2015. *Conflict, Improvisation, Governance: Street Level Practices for Urban Democracy*, New York, Routledge.

Lederach, J. P. 2014. *The Little Book of Conflict Transformation*, New York, Good Books.

Libération Afrique. 2003. Arrests by Red Ants, 26 January. Available: www.liberationafrique.org/spip. php?article215 [Accessed 7 April 2014].

Liberty Institute. 2002a. *'Bullshit Award for Sustaining Poverty' Awarded to Vandana Shiva*, 29 August. Available: www. libertyindia.org/wssd/ [Accessed 13 December 2014].

———. 2002b. *Mass March to Summit: Street Hawkers Demand Freedom to Trade*, 28 August. Available: www.libertyindia.org/ wssd/ [Accessed 13 December 2014].

———. 2002c. *Traders, Farmers Unite at Summit Protest*, 29 August. Available: www.libertyindia.org/ wssd/ [Accessed 13 December 2014].

Lipietz, B. 2004. 'Muddling-through': urban regeneration in Johannesburg's Inner City. *N-Aerus Annual Conference*, 16–17 September, Barcelona.

———. 2008. Building a vision for the post-apartheid city: what role for participation in Johannesburg's city development strategy? *International Journal of Urban and Regional Research*, 32(1), 135–163.

Little, A. 2008. *Democratic Piety: Complexity, Conflict and Violence*, Edinburgh, Edinburgh University Press.

Locke, J. 2009 [1690]. *Two Treatises on Government: A Translation into*

Modern English by Lewis F. Abbot, Manchester, Industrial Systems Research.

Lodge, T. 2005. Provincial government and state authority in South Africa. *Journal of Southern African Studies*, 31(4), 737–753.

Look Local. 2011a. *Billing Chaos Worsens*, 19 January. Available: www.looklocal.co.za/looklocal/content/en/midrand/midrand-search-results [Accessed 5 May 2012].

———. 2011b. *Protesting Parties Clash outside Billing Office*, 18 February. Available: www.looklocal.co.za/looklocal/content/en/north-east-joburg/ [Accessed 5 May 2012].

Lowndes, V. & Paxton, M. 2018. Can agonism be institutionalised? Can institutions be agonised? Prospects for democratic design. *British Journal of Politics and International Relations*, 20(3), 693–710.

Lund, F. and Skinner, C. 2005. Creating a positive business environment for the informal economy: reflections from South Africa. *In*: Donor Committee for Enterprise Development, *Reforming the Business Environment: Current Thinking and Future Opportunities*, 29 November–1 December 2005, Cairo.

Lundberg, A. K., Richardson, T. and Hongslo, E. 2018. The consequences of avoiding conflict: lessons from conservation planning for Europe's last wild reindeer. *Journal of Environmental Planning and Management*, 62(2), 266–285.

Mabin, A. 1994. Forget democracy, build houses: negotiating the shape of the city tomorrow. *Democracy: Popular Precedents, Practice, Culture (History Workshop: Programme for Planning Research)*, 13–15 July, Johannesburg.

———. 2014. In the forest of transformation: Johannesburg's northern suburbs. *In*: Harrison, P.,

Gotz, G., Todes, A. and Wray, C. (eds.) *Changing Space, Changing City: Johannesburg after Apartheid*, Johannesburg, Wits University Press, 395–417.

Mail & Guardian. 1997. 'Foreigners' Not Welcome on Pavements, 21–27 November. Available: https://mg.co.za/article/1997-11-21-foreigners-not-welcome-on-pavements [Accessed 25 June 2019].

———. 2003. *Jozi's Getting Its Jive Back*, 2 June. Available: http://mg.co.za/article/2003-06-02-jozis-getting-its-jive-back [Accessed 15 May 2015].

———. 2004. *Billing Bungle Hits ANC*, 3 May. Available: http://mg.co.za/article/2004-08-06-billing-bungle-hits-anc [Accessed 3 May 2015].

———. 2005. *City Squeezes Soul from Trade*, 28 July, p. 6.

———. 2006. *Municipal Medicine*, 27 January. Available: http://mg.co.za/article/2006-01-27-municipal-medicine [Accessed 11 April 2015].

———. 2007. *A Hawkers' Hell*, 14 June, p. 34.

———. 2008. 'Third Force' Allegations Abound, 23 May. Available: http://mg.co.za/article/2008-05-23-third-force-allegations-abound [Accessed 2 October 2015].

———. 2009a. *A 'Phiric' Victory for the Poor*, 21 July. Available: http://mg.co.za/article/2009-07-21-a-phiric-victory-for-the-poor [Accessed 24 June 2014].

———. 2009b. *Water Rights Reduced to a Trickle*, 21 October. Available: http://mg.co.za/article/2009-10-21-water-rights-reduced-to-a-trickle [Accessed 24 June 2014].

———. 2010a. *Jo'burg Hawkers Complain of Police Harassment*, 10 November. Available: http://mg.co.za/article/2010-11-10-jhb-hawkers-complain-of-police-harassment [Accessed 3 October 2015].

———. 2010b. *Protest – but Don't Target Us*, 26 February. Available: http://mg.co.za/article/2010-02-26-protest-but-dont-target-us [Accessed 19 December 2018].

———. 2011a. *The Connections That Disconnected Jo'burg*, 4 February. Available: http://mg.co.za/article/2011-02-04-the-connections-that-disconnected-joburg [Accessed 4 May 2012].

———. 2011b. *Jo'burg Residents Protest over 'Billing Crisis'*, 18 February. Available: http://mg.co.za/article/2011-02-18-joburg-residents-protest-over-billing-crisis [Accessed 10 April 2015].

———. 2012. *Jo'burg Scrambles to Clear Billing Crisis Backlog*, 19 March. Available: https://mg.co.za/article/2012-03-19-joburg-scrambles-to-clear-billing-crisis-backlog [Accessed 10 May 2019].

———. 2013a. *Half-Hatched Law Lays Hawkers Low*, 3 May. Available: http://mg.co.za/print/2013-05-03-00-half-hatched-law-lays-hawkers-low [Accessed 23 November 2013].

———. 2013b. *Jo'burg's 'Clean Sweep': The City Responds*, 1 November. Available: http://mg.co.za/article/2013-11-01-00-joburgs-clean-sweep-the-city-reponds [Accessed 11 October 2014].

Mäntysalo, R. 2011. The development of planning theory in relation to democracy theory since WWII: towards agonism. *Maa-20.3510: Strategic Urban and Regional Planning P (4 cr) Course*, 2011, Espoo.

Mäntysalo, R., Balducci, A. and Kangasoja, J. 2011. Planning as agonistic communication in a trading zone: re-examining Lindblom's partisan mutual adjustment. *Planning Theory*, 10(3), 257–272.

Marinova, D. M. 2011. When government fails us: trust in post-socialist civil organizations. *Democratization*, 18(1), 160–183.

Marx, K. 1897. *The Eighteenth Brumaire of Louis Bonaparte*, New York, International Publishing Company.

Matjomane, M. D. 2013. *Strategies Used by Street Traders' Organisations to Influence Trading Policy and Management in the City of Johannesburg*, honours report, University of the Witwatersrand.

Matlala, B. and Bénit-Gbaffou, C. 2012. Against ourselves: local activists and the management of contradicting political loyalties – the case of Phiri, Johannesburg. *Geoforum*, 43(2), 207–218.

Matshego, A. 2012. *Protest Action Data (Spatial and Non-Spatial Information, Department of Human Settlements)*, email to author, 15 October.

Mattes, R. 2019. *Democracy in Africa: Demand, Supply and the 'Dissatisfied Democrat'*. Available: www.africaportal.org/documents/18863/ab_r7_policypaperno54_africans_views_of_democracy.pdf [Accessed 27 May 2019].

Mayer, M., Thörn, C. and Thörn, H. (eds.). 2016. *Urban Uprisings: Challenging Neoliberal Urbanism in Europe*, London, Palgrave Macmillan.

Mazibuko vs City of Johannesburg et al. 2009. *Applicants' Submissions, Case CCT39/09, 2009/07/23, Constitutional Court of South Africa*. Available: www.escr-net.org/sites/default/files/Applicant_Submission_-_Con_Court_o.pdf [Accessed 24 June 2014].

Mc Lennan, A. 2009. *The Promise, the Practice and the Politics: Improving Service Delivery in South Africa*. Available: www.capam.org/_documents/adjudicatedpapers.mcclennan.pdf [Accessed 27 September 2013].

McDonald, D. and John, P. (eds.). 2002. *Cost Recovery and the Crisis of Service Delivery in South Africa*, Cape Town, Human Sciences Research Council.

McKinley, D. 2003. *Water Is Life: The Anti-Privatisation Forum and the Struggle against Water Privatisation.* Available: www.sarpn.org/documents/do000584/ [Accessed 6 June 2014].

McManus, H. 2008. Enduring agonism: between individuality and plurality. *Polity*, 40(4), 509–525.

McMichael, C. 2015. Urban pacification and 'blitzes' in contemporary Johannesburg. *Antipode*, 47(5), 1261–1278.

Merrifield, A. 2013. *The Politics of the Encounter: Urban Theory and Protest under Planetary Urbanization*, Athens, GA, University of Georgia Press.

Mihai, M. 2014. Theorizing agonistic emotions. *Parallax*, 20(2), 31–48.

Mill, J. S. 1863. *On Liberty*, Boston, MA, Ticknor & Fields.

Mintzberg, H. and Waters, J. A. 1985. Of strategies, deliberate and emergent. *Strategic Management Journal*, 6(3), 257–272.

Misago, J. P., Landau, L. B. and Monson, T. 2009. *Towards Tolerance, Law, and Dignity: Addressing Violence against Foreign Nationals in South Africa*, Pretoria, International Organisation for Migration (Regional Office for Southern Africa), 01/2009.

Misra-Dexter, N. and February, J. (eds.). 2010. *Testing Democracy: Which Way Is South Africa Going?* Cape Town, African Books Collective.

Mohamed, S. E. E. 2010. *The Participation of Informal Settlement Communities in City-Level Policy-Making Processes in Johannesburg*, doctoral thesis, University of the Witwatersrand.

Mohlakwana, D. E. 2012. *Sensemaking, Complexity and ERP Systems Adoption: A Conceptual Study with Reference to Project Phakama in the City of Johannesburg*, master's dissertation, Stellenbosch University.

Monson, T., Takabvirwa, K., Anderson, J., Ngwato, T. P. and Freemantle, I. 2012. *Promoting Social Cohesion and Countering Violence against Foreigners and Other 'Outsiders': Lessons Learned – A Study of Social Cohesion Interventions in Fourteen South African Townships*, Research Report, Johannesburg, African Centre for Migration and Society, University of the Witwatersrand.

Moreno, P. S. 2011. *A Global Revolution is Under Way.* Available: www.opendemocracy.net/pedro-silverio-moreno/global-revolution-is-under-way [Accessed 12 October 2019].

Morrell, M. E. 2014. Empathy, agonism, deliberation, democracy. *European Consortium for Political Research, ECPR General Conference 2014, Agonism and Democratic Innovation Panel, 3–6 September,* Glasgow.

Morwe, K. 2010. *A Critical Analysis of the Representation of Service Delivery Protests in the Mail & Guardian and The Star Newspapers,* honours report, University of the Witwatersrand.

Motala, S. 2002. *Organizing in the Informal Economy: A Case Study of Street Trading in South Africa,* Geneva, International Labour Office, SEED Working Paper No. 36.

Mouffe, C. 1999. Deliberative democracy or agonistic pluralism. *Social Research*, 66(3), 745–758.

———. 2000. *The Democratic Paradox*, London, Verso.

———. 2013. *Agonistics: Thinking the World Politically*, London, Verso.

———. 2014. Democratic politics and conflict: an agonistic approach. *In*: Lakitsch, M. (ed.) *Political Power Reconsidered: State Power and Civic Activism between Legitimacy and Violence*, Berlin, LIT Verlag, 17–30.

Mtshelwane, Z. 1989. Making the best of a home-made home. *Work in Progress*, 62–63 (November–December), 22–24.

Multi-Level Government Initiative. 2012. MLGI protest barometer. *Local Government Bulletin*, 14(3), 4–7.

Municipal Demarcation Board. 2015. *Municipal Boundary Data: Gauteng, 2015*. Available: www.demarcation.org.za/index.php/downloads/boundary-data [Accessed 14 December 2015].

Municipal IQ. 2009. *Municipal IQ Briefing #136: More on Protests – 2009 Trends*, 21 July. Available: https://municipaliq.co.za/publications/briefings/mun_iq_brief_136_wdr.pdf [Accessed 21 July 2010].

———. 2010. *Municipal IQ Briefing #260: Delivery Protests – A New Record Set by 2010*, 1 December. Available: https://municipaliq.co.za/publications/briefings/brief_260_protests_nov_10.pdf [Accessed 2 December 2010].

———. 2012. *2012 Tally: A Violent and Diverse Year for Service Delivery Protests*, 16 January. Available: www.municipaliq.co.za/publications/press/201301170823583255.doc [Accessed 9 June 2013].

———. 2018. *2018 Service Delivery Protests All-Time Quarterly Record*, 11 July. Available: www.municipaliq.co.za/ [Accessed 12 September 2018].

Munthe-Kaas, P. 2015. Agonism and co-design of urban spaces. *Urban Research & Practice*, 8(2), 218–237.

Murray, M. 2008. *Taming the Disorderly City: The Spatial Landscape of Johannesburg after Apartheid*, New York, Cornell University Press.

———. 2011. *City of Extremes: The Spatial Politics of Johannesburg*, Durham, NC, Duke University Press.

Murtagh, B. and Ellis, G. 2011. Skills, conflict and spatial planning in Northern Ireland. *Planning Theory & Practice*, 12(3), 349–365.

Muthialu, N. 2012. *Specialist Project Manager and Public Participation Consultant to Johannesburg City Council's Urbanisation Department on Implementation of Informal Trading Projects between 1993 and 1999*, Johannesburg, interview with author, 4 December.

Naidoo, P. 2007. Struggles around the commodification of daily life in South Africa. *Review of African Political Economy*, 34(111), 57–66.

———. 2010. *The Making of 'The Poor' in Post-Apartheid South Africa: A Case Study of the City of Johannesburg and Orange Farm*, doctoral thesis, University of Kwa-Zulu Natal.

Narsoo, M. 2012. *Housing and Informal Settlement Upgrading Policy Consultant in South Africa from Deputy-Director General of Housing in National Government to Specialist and Researcher over Thirty Years*, Johannesburg, interview with author, 5 December.

New York Times. 1989. *Johannesburg Acts to Ease Segregation*, 28 September. Available: www.nytimes.com/1989/09/28/world/johannesburg-acts-to-ease-segregation.html [Accessed 30 April 2012].

———. 2009. *South Africa's Poor Renew a Tradition of Protest*, 7 September. Available: www.nytimes.com/2009/09/07/world/africa/07protests.html [Accessed 30 April 2012].

news24. 2001. *Jhb's Finances Looking Up*, 26 March. Available: www.news24.com/xArchive/Archive/Jhbs-finances-looking-up-20010326 [Accessed 31 May 2015].

———. 2002. *Hawkers Take Council to Court*, 7 February. Available:

www.news24.com/xArchive/
Archive/Hawkers-take-council-
to-court-20020207 [Accessed 12
December 2014].
———. 2003. *Mobbed Mayor: 87
Are Freed*, 5 March. Available:
www.news24.com/SouthAfrica/
News/Mobbed-mayor-87-are-
freed-20030305 [Accessed 30
September 2015].
———. 2009. *No Service
Delivery Protests by 2014*, 21
October. Available: www.
news24.com/SouthAfrica/
News/No-service-delivery-
protests-by-2014-20091021
[Accessed 30 April 2012].
———. 2010. *1,500 Protest in Orange
Farm*, 22 February. Available:
www.news24.com/SouthAfrica/
News/1-500-protest-in-Orange-
Farm-20100222 [Accessed 12
December 2018].
———. 2011. *BRT to Be Rerouted
Away from Oxford Rd*, 29
October. Available: www.
news24.com/SouthAfrica/News/
BRT-to-be-rerouted-away-from-
Oxford-Rd-20111029 [Accessed
19 May 2015].
Ngwane, T. 2010. Civil society
protests in South Africa: the
need for a vision of alternatives.
*Centre for Civil Society Seminar:
Understanding Protest Action*, 9
March, Durban.
———. 2011. *Ideology and Agency
in Protest Politics: Service Delivery
Struggles in Post-Apartheid South
Africa*, master's dissertation,
University of KwaZulu-Natal.
———. 2012. Some methodological
points for the construction
of a protest event database in
South Africa. *Centre for Civil
Society Seminar: Ideology, Agency
and Protest Politics*, 18 April,
Pietermaritzburg.
Ngwane, T., Sinwell, L. and Ness,
I. (eds.). 2017. *Urban Revolt:
State Power and the Rise of People's
Movements in the Global South*,
Johannesburg, Wits University
Press.
Nonhoff, M. 2012. Book review:
'Institutionalizing Agonistic
Democracy: Post-Foundationalism
and Political Liberalism' by Ed
Wingenbach, 2011. *Critical Policy
Studies*, 6(4), 480–487.
Nyar, A. and Wray, C. 2012.
Understanding protest action:
some data collection challenges
for South Africa. *Transformation:
Critical Perspectives on Southern
Africa*, 80, 22–43.
O'Connor, K. 2014. *Public
Administration in Contested Societies*,
London, Palgrave Macmillan.
Oldfield, S. and Stokke, K. 2004.
*Building Unity in Diversity: Social
Movement Activism in the Western
Cape Anti-Eviction Campaign
(Case Study)*. Available: http://
abahlali.org/files/Oldfield%20
&%20Stokke%20WCAEC%20
Research%20Report.pdf
[Accessed 20 September 2013].
Olver, C. 2017. Houses, security
and comfort. *How to Steal a City:
The Battle for Nelson Mandela
Bay*, Johannesburg, Jonathan Ball
Publishers, 95–111.
Ortiz, I., Burke, S., Berrada, M. and
Cortés, H. 2013. *World Protests
2006–2013*, New York, Initiative
for Policy Dialogue and Friedrich-
Ebert-Stiftung.
Paret, M. 2015. Violence and
democracy in South Africa's
community protests. *Review of
African Political Economy*, 42(143),
107–123.
Parnell, S. and Pieterse, E. 1999.
Developmental local government:
the second wave of post-apartheid
urban reconstruction. *Africanus*,
29(2), 61–85.
Peacock, K. 2012. *Acting Head of
Communications between 1996
and 1999 in Johannesburg's
Eastern Metropolitan Local
Council Responsible for Customer
Relations Management, Worked*

*in Various Positions in City of
Johannesburg between 2000 and
2011*, Johannesburg, interview with
author, 12 November.

Peberdy, S. and Crush, J. 1998.
*Trading Places: Cross-Border
Traders and the South African
Informal Sector*, Cape Town,
Institute for Democracy in South
Africa and Southern African
Migration Programme, No. 6.

Peberdy, S. and Talibe, T.
1997. *SA Traders up in Arms.*
Available: www.queensu.ca/samp/
sampresources/samppublications/
pressarticles/1997/Peberdy.htm
[Accessed 4 November 2014].

Pernegger, L. 2001. *From Pavements
to Profits: An Assessment of the
Future Direction of the Metropolitan
Trading Company and the Trade-
Offs between Profits and Corporate
Social Responsibility*, Executive
MBA dissertation, University
of Birmingham (Birmingham
Business School).

———. 2014. The agonistic state:
metropolitan government responses
to city strife post-1994. In:
Haferburg, C. and Huchzermeyer,
M. (eds.) *Urban Governance in
Post-Apartheid Cities: Modes of
Engagement in South Africa's
Metropoles*, Stuttgart, Borntraeger,
62–78.

———. 2016. *Stories of City Strife
in Johannesburg: Agonism in Local
Democracy and Service Delivery*,
doctoral thesis, University of the
Witwatersrand.

———. 2020. Effects of the
state's informal practices
on organisational capability
and social inclusion: three
cases of city governance in
Johannesburg. *Urban Studies*,
online first (April), https://doi.
org/10.1177/0042098020910111

Peu Group. 2015. *Business Partners.*
Available: www.peugroup.co.za/
business.htm [Accessed 17 June
2015].

Phadi, M. and Ceruti, C. 2011.
Multiple meanings of the middle
class in Soweto, South Africa.
*African Sociological Review/Revue
Africaine de Sociologie*, 15(1),
88–108.

Picard, L. A. 2005. *The State of the
State: Institutional Transformation,
Capacity and Political Change in
South Africa*, Johannesburg, Wits
University Press.

Pieterse, E. 2008. *City Futures:
Confronting the Crisis of Urban
Development*, Cape Town, Zed
Books.

———. 2014. Corridors of freedom.
*Urban Age: Governing Urban Futures
Conference*, 14–15 September, Delhi.

Pillay, U., Tomlinson, R. and du
Toit, J. (eds.). 2006. *Democracy
and Delivery: Urban Policy in
South Africa*, Cape Town, Human
Sciences Research Council.

Pinkney, R. 1993. *Democracy in
the Third World*, London, Open
University Press.

Pløger, J. 2004. Strife: urban
planning and agonism. *Planning
Theory*, 3(1), 71–92.

———. 2006. Urban planning
and urban life: problems and
challenges. *Planning Practice and
Research*, 21(2), 201–222.

PoliticsWeb. 2011a. *2011 Elections:
Johannesburg Results*, 21 May.
Available: www.politicsweb.co.za/
politicsweb/view/politicsweb/en/pa
[Accessed 10 April 2015].

———. 2011b. *Joburg Billing
Problems Exaggerated – Amos
Masondo*, 26 January. Available:
www.politicsweb.co.za/iservice/
joburg-billling-problems-
exaggerated--amos-masondo
[Accessed 1 May 2015].

Powell, D. 2012. Imperfect
transition: local government reform
in South Africa, 1994–2012. In:
Booyens, S. (ed.) *Local Elections in
South Africa: Parties, People, Politics*,
Bloemfontein, African Sun Media,
11–30.

Property Owners and Managers Association vs City of Johannesburg Metropolitan Municipality et al. 2011. *Court Order, Case 2011/46597, 15 December 2011, South Gauteng High Court*, Johannesburg, South Gauteng High Court.

Prothro, J. W. and Grigg, C. M. 1960. Fundamental principles of democracy: bases of agreement and disagreement. *The Journal of Politics*, 22(2), 276–294.

Province of Gauteng. 1995a. *Local Government Transition Act, 1993 (Act No. 209): Delimitation and Determination of Area of Jurisdiction of Greater Johannesburg Transitional Metropolitan Council with Metropolitan Substructures as Contemplated in Section 8(3), Read with Premier's Proclamation No. 24 of 1994 and Premier's Proclamation No. 35 of 1995*, Provincial Gazette Extraordinary 1 (No. 66, Notice 42).

———. 1995b. *Local Government Transition Act, 1993 (Act No. 209): Delimitation and Determination of Area of Jurisdiction of Lekoa-Vaal Metropolitan Council with Metropolitan Substructures as Contemplated in Section 8(3), Read with Premier's Proclamation No. 3 of 1995 and Premier's Proclamation No. 35 of 1995*, Provincial Gazette Extraordinary 1 (No. 66, Notice 44).

———. 1995c. *Local Government Transition Act, 1993 (Act No. 209): Establishment of a Transitional Metropolitan Council with Transitional Metropolitan Substructures in Respect of the Vaal Metropolitan Area*, Provincial Gazette Extraordinary 1 (No. 1).

———. 1999. *Restriction on Trading in Certain Areas*, Provincial Gazette (No. 72, Notice 5390).

———. 2004. *City of Johannesburg Metropolitan Municipality Street Trading By-Laws (Bill No. 179)*,

Provincial Gazette Extraordinary (No. 179, Notice 824).

———. 2009. *City of Johannesburg Metropolitan Municipality: 2010 FIFA World Cup South Africa By-Laws*, Provincial Gazette Extraordinary (No. 15, Notice 36).

———. 2012. *City of Johannesburg Metropolitan Municipality Informal Trading By-Laws*, Provincial Gazette (No. 66, Notice 328).

———. 2013. *MEC Kolisile Holds Talks with Informal Traders across Gauteng*, 4 July. Available: www. ecodev.gpg.gov.za/MediaDesk/ Pressreleases/Documents/ MEC%20Kolisile%20Holds%20 Talks%20With%20Informal%20 Traders%20Across%20Gauteng. pdf [Accessed 5 February 2015].

Province of Transvaal. 1990. *Prevention of Illegal Squatting Act, 1951 (Act 52 of 1951): Regulations Concerning the Control and Management of the Area known as Orange Farm*, Pretoria, Administrator.

———. 1993. *Black Local Authorities Act, 1992 (Act No. 102 of 1982): Defining of an Area outside a Local Authority as Contemplated in Section 2 (11) of the Black Local Authorities Act, 1982 (Act No. 102 of 1982)*, Official Gazette Extraordinary (No. 236, Notice 4924).

QGIS. 2020. *Open-Source Geographic (Formerly Quantum) Information System (QGIS Version 3.10.0)*. Available: https://qgis.org/en/site/ [Accessed 16 January 2020].

Quantec. 2014. *South African Community Profiles, Quantec Research EasyData, RSA Regional Data online, with Collection of Variables at the Person, Household and Ward Level, Statistics South Africa Data on Population Census 1996, 2001 and 2011 at Ward and Sub Place Levels (2011 Demarcation), Pre-Built tables*. Available: http://o-www.quantec. co.za.innopac.wits.ac.za/easydata [Accessed 9–14 July 2014].

————. 2018. *Quantec Research EasyData, Regional Service, RSA Standardised Regional, Demographics.* Available: https://o-www-easydata-co-za.innopac.wits.ac.za/dataset/RPOP/ [Accessed 14 September 2018].

Radebe, N. W. 2007. *The Impact of Municipal Skills Development Programmes on the Informal Trading Sector: Johannesburg (2001–2006),* master's dissertation, University of the Witwatersrand.

Radebe, T. 2012. *Region G's Manager of Urban Management and Service Delivery in City of Johannesburg's Office of the Region since 2008,* Johannesburg, interview with author, 17 October.

Randburg Sun. 2016. *Over 80 Percent Petitions Unresolved – PSC,* 8 July. Available: https://randburgsun.co.za/293759/over-80-percent-petitions-unresolved-psc/ [Accessed 12 September 2018].

Rasmussen, J. 2007. Struggling for the city: evictions in Inner City Johannesburg. *In*: Buur, L., Jensen, S. and Stepputat, F. (eds.) *The Security–Development Nexus: Expressions of Sovereignty and Securitization in Southern Africa,* Stockholm, Nordiska Afrikainstitutet and Human Sciences Research Council Press, 174–190.

Ratliff, T. N. and Hall, L. L. 2014. Practicing the art of dissent: toward a typology of protest activity in the United States. *Humanity and Society,* 38(3), 268–294.

Rea Vaya. 2008. *City Starts Consultations with Rosebank and Saxonwold Residents on Rea Vaya Construction,* 28 November. Available: www.reavaya.org.za/routes/137-media-releases-2008/november63/70-281108 [Accessed 19 May 2015].

Reddy, P. S. 2003. Metropolitan unicity development in South Africa: a case study of the greater Johannesburg area. *In*: International Association of Schools and Institutes of Administration, *Public Administration: Challenges of Inequality and Exclusion,* 14–18 September, Miami.

Republic of South Africa. 1986a. *Abolition of Influx Control Act (Act 68 of 1986),* Cape Town.

————. 1986b. *White Paper on Urbanisation,* Pretoria, Constitutional Development and Planning Department.

————. 1987. *Assignment of Certain Powers, Duties and Functions of the Minister of Constitutional Development and Planning to the Administrators of the Various Provinces,* Government Gazette (No. 259, Notice 10565).

————. 1990. *Annual Report: 1 September 1989 to 31 December 1990,* Pretoria, Development Planning and Provincial Affairs Department.

————. 1991. *Businesses Act,* Pretoria (No. 71 of 1991).

————. 1993a. *Approval of Official Place Names,* Government Gazette (No. 336, Notice 14877).

————. 1993b. *Businesses Amendment (Act 186 of 1993),* Cape Town, Justice and Constitutional Development.

————. 1994. *White Paper on Reconstruction and Development,* Government Gazette (No. 353, No. 16085).

————. 1996. *Growth, Employment and Redistribution: A Macroeconomic Strategy,* Pretoria, Department of Finance.

————. 1998. *White Paper on Local Government,* Pretoria, Provincial Affairs and Constitutional Development.

————. 2001. *Media Statement by the Minister of Water Affairs and Forestry, Mr. Ronnie Kasrils,* Pretoria, Department of Water Affairs and Forestry (Chief

Directorate: Communication Services), 14 February.

———. 2004. *Project 'Consolidate': A Hands-On Local Government Engagement Programme for 2004–2006*, Pretoria, Department of Provincial and Local Government.

———. 2008. *15 Year Review: A Review of Changes in the Macro-Organisation of the State: 1994–2008*, Pretoria, Public Service and Administration Department (Constitutional Assembly).

———. 2013. *Draft Licensing of Businesses Bill (Notice 231 of 2103)*, Pretoria, Department of Trade and Industry, 19 March.

Ricks, F. and Charlesworth, J. 2003. *Emergent Practice Planning*, New York, Springer.

Robinson, J. 1996. *The Power of Apartheid: State, Power, and Space in South African Cities*, Oxford, Butterworth-Heinemann.

———. 2006. *Ordinary Cities: Between Modernity and Development*, Abingdon, Routledge.

———. 2012. *Ordinary Cities: Between Modernity and Development*, London, Routledge.

Rogerson, C. 1990. Informal sector retailing in the South African city: the case of Johannesburg. *In*: Findlay, A. M., Paddison, R. and Dawson, J. (eds.) *Retailing Environments in Developing Countries*, London, Routledge, 118–140.

———. 2003. The absorptive capacity of the informal sector in the South African city. *In*: Smith, D. M. (ed.) *The Apartheid City and Beyond: Urbanization and Social Change in South Africa*, London, Routledge, 161–171.

———. 2008. Policy and planning for changing informal retailing in South Africa. *Africa Insight*, 37(4), 230–247.

———. 2016. Progressive rhetoric, ambiguous policy pathways: street trading in Inner City Johannesburg, South Africa. *Local Economy*, 31(1–2), 204–218.

Roskamm, N. 2015. On the other side of 'agonism': the 'enemy', the 'outside', and the role of antagonism. *Planning Theory*, 14(4), 384–403.

SABC News. 2015. *Police Monitoring Orange Farm after Protest*, 22 November. Available: www.sabc. co.za/news/a/7ef077804aabebbea97 ba9a65ed2c195/Police-monitoring-Orange-Farm-after-protest [Accessed 12 December 2018].

Sager, T. 2013. *Reviving Critical Planning Theory: Dealing with Pressure, Neo-Liberalism, and Responsibility in Communicative Planning*, New York, Routledge.

Sandercock, L. 1998. The difference that theory makes. *In*: Sandercock, L. (ed.) *Towards Cosmopolis: Planning for Multicultural Cities*, Chichester, John Wiley, 85–104.

———. 2000. When strangers become neighbours: managing cities of difference. *Planning Theory & Practice*, 1(1), 13–30.

Saturday Star. 2014. *Traders Fear a Repeat of Last Year's Upheaval if They Move*, 25 October, p. 4.

Savage, D., Gotz, G., Kihato, C. and Parnell, S. 2003. *Strategic Review of iGoli 2002*, Johannesburg, City of Johannesburg (Strategic Support, Office of the City Manager), June 2003.

Schaap, A. 2006. Agonism in divided societies. *Philosophy and Social Criticism*, 32(2), 255–277.

Schindlers Attorneys. 2011a. *Schindlers City of JHB Challenged*, 6 June. Available: www.schindlers. co.za/city-of-jhb-challenged/ [Accessed 16 May 2015].

———. 2011b. *Schindlers Court Moves to Halt Joburg Service Cut-Offs*, 6 December. Available: www. schindlers.co.za/court-moves-to-halt-joburg-service-cutoffs/ [Accessed 16 May 2015].

————. 2013a. *City of Johannesburg: Electricity & Water Terminations*, 18 September. Available: www.schindlers.co.za/city-of-johannesburg-electricity-water-terminations/ [Accessed 16 May 2015].

————. 2013b. *City of Johannesburg: Queries Closed without Resolution*, 18 September. Available: www.schindlers.co.za/city-of-johannesburg-queries-closed [Accessed 16 May 2015].

Schreiber, L. 2013. *Why's the Voice of Middle Class Protest Absent from SA?* Available: www.politicsweb.co.za/news-and-analysis/whys-the-voice-of-middle-class-protest-absent-from [Accessed 7 June 2015].

Scott, J. 1998. *Seeing like a State: How Certain Schemes to Improve the Human Condition Have Failed*, New Haven, CT, Yale University Press.

Sekele, T. I. 2000. *Change Processes in the Greater Johannesburg Metropolitan Council from 1995 to 1999*, master's dissertation, University of the Witwatersrand.

Selzer, A. K. and Heller, P. 2010. The spatial dynamics of middle-class formation in postapartheid South Africa: enclavization and fragmentation in Johannesburg. *Political Power and Social Theory*, 21, 147–184.

Shah, A. 2011. *Public Protests around the World*. Available: www.globalissues.org/article/45/public-protests-around-the-world [Accessed 1 May 2012].

Sher, D. 2013. *Johannesburg Street Trading Policy, 1986–2010*, honours research report, University of the Witwatersrand.

Sibaya, N. 2012. *Development Manager for Orange Farm Stretford Station Precinct Project within City of Johannesburg's Johannesburg Development Agency*, Johannesburg, interview with author, 18 October.

Silver, H., Scott, A. and Kazepov, Y. 2010. Participation in urban contention and deliberation. *International Journal of Urban and Regional Research*, 34(3), 453–477.

Simone, A. 2009. *On Informality and Considerations for Policy*, Cape Town, Isandla Institute.

Skinner, C. 1999. *Local Government in Transition: A Gendered Analysis of Trends in Urban Policy and Practice Regarding Street Trading in Five South African Cities*, Durban, University of Natal (School of Development Studies), CSDS Research Report No. 18.

————. 2008. *Street Trade in Africa: A Review*, School of Development Studies, University of KwaZulu-Natal, Working Paper No. 51.

Skogly, S. I. 2002. Is there a right not to be poor? *Human Rights Law Review*, 2(1), 59–80.

Smelser, N. J. 1962. *Theory of Collective Behavior*, New York, Free Press.

Smith, A. 1981 [1776]. An inquiry into the nature and causes of the wealth of nations. *In*: Campbell, R. H. and Skinner, A. S. (eds.) *The Glasgow Edition of the Works and Correspondence of Adam Smith*, Indianapolis, IN, LibertyClassics, 1–543.

Smith, L. 2004. The murky waters of the second wave of neoliberalism: corporatization as a service delivery model in Cape Town. *Geoforum*, 35(3), 375–393.

Smith, L. 2006. *Neither Public nor Private: Unpacking the Johannesburg Water Corporatization Model, Social Policy and Development Programme*, Geneva, United Nations Research Institute for Social Development, Paper No. 27.

Socio-Economic Rights Institute of South Africa. 2011. *Basic Sanitation in South Africa: A Guide to Legislation, Policy and Practice*, Johannesburg, Socio-Economic Rights Institute of South Africa.

———. 2013. *Informal Traders to Take City of Joburg and JMPD to Court over 'Operation Clean Sweep'*. Available: http://seri-sa.org/images/SERI_Letter_of_Demand_14_November_2013.pdf [Accessed 9 October 2014].

———. 2015. *'The End of the Street?' Informal Traders' Experiences of Rights and Regulations in Inner City Johannesburg*, Johannesburg.

South African Government News Agency. 2010. *Zuma Gets Tough with Govt Managers*, 26 April. Available: www.southafrica.info/about/government/485340.htm#.Vgz4oCHotl8 [Accessed 1 October 2015].

South African Human Rights Commission. 2014. *Report on the Right to Access Sufficient Water and Decent Sanitation in South Africa: 2014*, Johannesburg, South African Human Rights Commission.

South African Institute of Race Relations. 1988. *SAIRR Race Relations Survey 1987/88*, Johannesburg, South African Institute of Race Relations.

———. 1990. *SAIRR Race Relations Survey 1989/90*, Johannesburg, South African Institute of Race Relations.

South African Reserve Bank. 2019. *Selected Historical Rates*. Available: www.resbank.co.za/Research/Rates/Pages/SelectedHistoricalExchangeAndInterestRates.aspx [Accessed 23 September 2019].

Southall, R. 2001. Opposition in South Africa: issues and problems. *Democratization*, 8(1), 1–24.

Southern Metropolitan Local Council. 1995. *Preliminary Report: Administration of Orange Farm, Report to Executive Committee, Report to Council, Item (10) (a)*, 1995/12/05, Executive Committee.

———. 1996a. *Capital Budget: Orange Farm and Environs (Page 12, Item (d), Meeting Held on 15 May 1996), Matters Arising from the Minutes, 1996/05/22*, Executive Committee.

———. 1996b. *Masakhane Workshop Orange Farm, Report to Executive Committee, Item (07), 1996/09/11*, Chief Executive Officer: GJTMC.

———. 1996c. *Orange Farm Administration: Capital Projects 1995/96 Budget – Ratification of Fast-Tracking Approval, Urgency Report to Council, Item (07) (Ur(10)), 1996/06/27*, Executive Committee.

———. 1996d. *Orange Farm: Allocation of Sites Stretford 9 and 10 (Item (d), Page 34 (12 December 1995), Item (f), 1996/01/17, Matters Arising from Minutes)*, Executive Committee.

———. 1997a. *Contract STS 0040 The Contractors of Sewers in Orange Farm Extension 3: Section 3, Report to Section 60 – Tenders Committee, Item A8, 1997/06/09*, Chief Executive Officer.

———. 1997b. *Establishment of a Housing Bureau in Parts of Orange Farm, Report to Council, Item (02) (15), 1997/11/27, Section 59 Committee: Planning, Housing and Environmental Management*.

———. 1997c. *Recommendations of the Commission of Inquiry: Orange Farm, Report to Council, Item (04) (04), 1997/04/24*, Executive Committee.

———. 1997d. *Street Trading Markets: Management through Lease Agreements, Report to SMLC – Executive Committee, 1997-08-20, Local Economic Development*.

———. 1998a. *Housing Transfer Bureau: Orange Farm, Report to Council, Item (02) (15), 1997/11/27, Section 59 Committee: Planning, Housing and Environmental Management*.

———. 1998b. *Informal Trading Projects within the Outlying Areas and the Informal Settlements 97/98 (Meeting Held on 6 February 1998), Report to Council, Item (05) (08)*,

1998/03/26, Section 59: Economic Development Committee.

———. 1998c. *Progress Report on the Consolidation Housing Subsidy Programme in Orange Farm and Surrounding Area, Report to Council, Item (04) (06), 1998/03/26,* Section 59 Committee: Planning, Housing and Environmental Management.

———. 1999a. *Development of a Neighbourhood Shopping Centre on Erf 1217 Orange Farm Proper, Report to Council, Item (12), 1999/10/20,* Section 60 Committee: Urban Development.

———. 1999b. *New Consolidation Housing Subsidy Programme – Orange Farm: Authorisation of Signatories, Report to Council, Item (04) (05), 1999/09/30,* Executive Committee.

———. 2000a. *Orange Farm Funding for Unplanned Extensions of Orange Farm, Report to Council, Item (14), 2000/02/24,* Executive Committee.

———. 2000b. *Orange Farm Water Supply Progress Report, Report to Executive Committee, Item (32), 2000-04-09,* Technical Services Committee.

Staeheli, L. A. 2010. Political geography: democracy and the disorderly public. *Progress in Human Geography,* 34(1), 67–78.

Stevens, L. and Rule, S. 1999. Moving to an informal settlement: the Gauteng experience. *South African Geographical Journal,* 81(3), 107–118.

Stiftel, B. and Watson, V. (eds.). 2005. *Dialogues in Urban and Regional Planning,* London, Routledge.

Strijdom, L. 2012. *Senior Planner within City of Johannesburg's Department of Development Planning and Urban Management Responsible for Strategic Planning in the City's Southern Regions and Sandton (Regions D, E and G),* Johannesburg, interview with author, 18 October.

Sunday Independent. 2002. *Hawkers Put Urban Prosperity Plans to the Test,* 10 February, p. 2.

Tambakaki, P. 2009. Cosmopolitanism or agonism? Alternative visions of world order. *Critical Review of International Social and Political Philosophy,* 12(1), 101–116.

———. 2014. The tasks of agonism and agonism to the task: introducing 'Chantal Mouffe: Agonism and the Politics of Passion'. *Parallax,* 20(2), 1–13.

Tanter, R. and Midlarsky, M. 1967. A theory of revolution. *The Journal of Conflict Resolution,* 11(3), 264–280.

The Citizen. 2005. *Joburg to Stamp out Street Trading,* 8 August, p. 1.

———. 2008. *Police 'Harass Vendors',* 18 April, p. 9.

———. 2013a. *City 'Didn't Target' Informal Traders,* 6 November, p. 8.

———. 2013b. *Cosatu Slams Treatment of Informal Traders,* 14 November, p. 6.

———. 2013c. *Joburg Hawkers Allowed Back,* 5 December. Available: http://citizen. co.za/95369/joburg-hawkers-allowed-back/ [Accessed 11 October 2014].

———. 2014a. *City to Consult on 'Lasting' Hawker Solution,* 13 July. Available: http://citizen. co.za/209880/city-consult-lasting-hawker-solution/ [Accessed 11 October 2014].

———. 2014b. *Hawker Problem Set to Be Tackled,* 20 September, p. 9.

The New Age. 2011. *ANC Blames Sabotage for Crisis,* 4 February. Available: www.thenewage. co.za/9579-1007-53-ANC_blames_sabotage_for_crisis [Accessed 10 April 2015].

———. 2012. *Hawkers and city's relations strained,* 7 June, p. 7.

———. 2013. *City Plans to Reregister Informal Traders,* 4 November, p. 7.

The Sowetan. 1990. *Residents to Help in Decisions,* 13 July, p. 8.

———. 2002. *Informal Traders Hit by Removals*, 21 August, p. 4.

———. 2008. *Jozi to Contest Ruling on Water*, 15 May. Available: www.sowetanlive.co.za/sowetan/archive/2008/05/15/jozi-to-contest-ruling-on-water [Accessed 5 August 2014].

———. 2010. *Joburg Metro Outcry: Board Members Resign as CEO Is Reinstated*, 6 August, p. 19.

The Star. 2006a. *We're Committed to Dialogue with Informal Traders*, 15 September, p. 21.

———. 2006b. *Work Together, Not against Informal Traders*, 19 September, p. 9.

———. 2009. *Rates Boycott Campaign Planned over Poor Service Delivery*, 6 August, p. 9.

———. 2011. *By-Law Culprits off the Hook*, 8 August, p. 1.

———. 2012a. *City Admits Roadmap Ruse and Claims It Has a Real Plan*, 9 August. Available: www.iol.co.za/the-star/city-admits-roadmap-ruse-and-claims-it-has-a-real-plan-1.1359383 [Accessed 16 May 2015].

———. 2012b. *City Pandemonium as Cops Raid Illegal Hawkers*, 2 October. Available: www.iol.co.za/the-star/city-pandemonium-as-cops-raid-illegal-hawkers-1.1394006 [Accessed 27 February 2015].

———. 2012c. *Joburg Does Not Have a Billings Roadmap*, 20 July. Available: www.iol.co.za/the-star/joburg-does-not-have-a-billings-roadmap-1.1345462 [Accessed 16 May 2015].

———. 2012d. *No Answers as City Misses Billing Chaos Deadlines*, 13 July. Available: www.iol.co.za/the-star/no-answers-as-city-misses-billing-chaos-deadlines-1.1341112 [Accessed 16 May 2015].

———. 2012e. *Parkhurst Library Saved from Closure*, 14 February. Available: www.iol.co.za/the-star/parkhurst-library-saved-from-closure-1.1233522 [Accessed 28 February 2015].

———. 2013a. *Clean-Up Project Hits Traders in Pocket*, 14 October, p. 2.

———. 2013b. *ConCourt Rules City of Joburg Offside for Evicting Hawkers*, 6 December, p. 17.

———. 2013c. *Rampant Trading Permit Fraud Forced City to Act, Cosatu Slams Forced Removals in Absence of Alternative Plan*, 8 November, p. 6.

———. 2014a. *ConCourt Rules in Favour of Traders*, 7 April, p. 15.

———. 2014b. *Critical Services Get R719m but Mayor Spends R1.2bn*, 4 July, p. 2.

———. 2014c. *Street Traders and City Still at Loggerheads*, 25 August, p. 6.

———. 2014d. *Street Trading Battle Goes to Concourt*, 5 December, p. 9.

Tilly, C. 2007. *Democracy*, Cambridge, Cambridge University Press.

Tilly, C. and Tarrow, S. 2015. *Contentious Politics*, New York, Oxford University Press.

TimesLive. 2010a. *Johannesburg Councillor Defends Hummer H3*, 18 May. Available: www.timeslive.co.za/local/2010/05/18/johannesburg-councillor-defends-hummer-h3 [Accessed 21 October 2012].

———. 2010b. *JZ 'Shocked People Still Live Like This'*, 17 May. Available: www.timeslive.co.za/local/2010/05/17/jz-shocked-people-still-live-like-this [Accessed 21 October 2012].

———. 2011a. *Crisis? What Crisis? Asks Joburg Mayor*, 26 January. Available: www.timeslive.co.za/local/2011/01/26/crisis-what-crisis-asks-joburg-mayor [Accessed 2 May 2015].

———. 2011b. *Joburg Redeploys Billing Chief*, 10 March. Available: www.timeslive.co.za/local/2011/03/10/joburg-redeploys-billing-chief [Accessed 15 May 2015].

————. 2011c. *Top Secret Memo from: James Lorimer MP, to: DA Party Hierarchy*, 4 February. Available: www.timeslive. co.za/local/2011/02/04/top-secret-memo-from-james-lorimer-mp-to-da-party-hierarchy [Accessed 30 April 2012].

————. 2015. *Cop Ghost Squad to 'Clean up' City Streets*, 12 February. Available: www.timeslive.co.za/thetimes/2015/02/12/cop-ghost-squad-to-clean-up-city-streets [Accessed 26 February].

Tissington, K. 2009. *The Business of Survival: Informal Trading in Inner City Johannesburg*, Johannesburg, University of the Witwatersrand, Centre for Applied Legal Studies.

Tomaselli, R. E. 1985. On the peripheries of the defended space: hawkers in Johannesburg. *In*: Haines, R. and Buijs, G. (eds.) *The Struggle for Social and Economic Space: Urbanization in Twentieth Century South Africa*, Special Publication No. 3, Durban, University of Durban-Westville (Institute for Social and Economic Research), 131–190.

Tomlinson, R. 1999a. From exclusion to inclusion: rethinking Johannesburg's central city. *Environment and Planning A*, 31, 1655–1678.

————. 1999b. Ten years in the making. *Urban Forum*, 10(1), 1–39.

Tomlinson, R., Beauregard, R. A., Bremner, L. and Mangcu, X. (eds.). 2003. *Emerging Johannesburg: Perspectives on the Postapartheid City*, New York, Routledge.

Transvaal Provincial Administration (TPA). 1990. *TPA Annual Report: 1989–1990*, Johannesburg, Transvaal Provincial Administration.

————. 1992. *TPA Annual Report: 1991–92*, Pretoria, Development Planning and Provincial Affairs Department.

Truluck, T. 2012. *City Refuses to Accept Billing Queries*, 22 August. Available: http://groupspaces.com/Ward117/emails/272477 [Accessed 10 April 2015].

Turok, I. 1993. The Metropolitan Chamber: a view from the sideline. *Urban Forum*, 4(2), 69–81.

Urban Inc. 2011. *Urban Renewal Models in the Johannesburg Inner City Regeneration Process, 1997–2011 (Short-Term Research Consultancy Report)*, Pretoria and Johannesburg, National Research Foundation and South African Research Chair in Development Planning and Modeling.

van den Berg, L., van der Meer, A., van Winden, W. and Woets, P. 2006. The case of Johannesburg. *In*: van den Berg, L., van der Meer, A., van Winden, W. and Woets, P. (eds.) *E-Governance in European and South African Cities: The Cases of Barcelona, Cape Town, Eindhoven, Johannesburg, Manchester, Tampere, The Hague, and Venice*, Aldershot, Ashgate, 83–108.

Van Onselen, C. 1982. *Studies in the Social and Economic History of Witwatersrand, 1886–1914: New Nineveh*, Johannesburg, Ravan Press.

van Rooyen, C., De Wet, T., Marais, I. and Korth, M. (eds.). 2009. *Water Dialogues: Johannesburg Case Study*, Durban, Water Dialogues South Africa.

Van Ryneveld, P. 2006. The development of policy on the financing of municipalities. *In*: Pillay, U., Tomlinson, R. and du Toit, J. (eds.) *Democracy and Delivery: Urban Policy in South Africa*, Cape Town, Human Sciences Research Council, 156–184.

Vink, E. 2007. Multi-level democracy: deliberative or agonistic? The search for appropriate normative standards. *Journal of European Integration*, 29(3), 303–322.

Visser, G. 2001. Social justice, integrated development planning and post-apartheid urban reconstruction. *Urban Studies*, 38(10), 1673–1699.

von Holdt, K. 2013. The violence of order, orders of violence: between Fanon and Bourdieu. *Current Sociology*, 61(2), 112–131.

von Holdt, K., Langa, M., Molapo, S., Mogapi, N., Ngubeni, K., Dlamini, J. and Kirsten, A. 2011. *The Smoke That Calls: Insurgent Citizenship, Collective Violence and the Struggle for a Place in the New South Africa*, Johannesburg, Society, Work and Development Institute.

von Schnitzler, A. 2015. Infrastructure, apartheid techno-politics, and temporalities of transition. *WISER Seminar*, 13 April, Johannesburg.

———. 2016. *Democracy's Infrastructure: Techno-Politics and Protest after Apartheid*, Princeton NJ, Princeton University Press.

Wafer, A. 2005. *Urban Identity in Post-Apartheid Soweto: A Case Study of the Soweto Electricity Crisis Committee*, master's dissertation, University of the Witwatersrand.

Walby, S. 2013. Violence and society: introduction to an emerging field of sociology. *Current Sociology*, 61(2), 95–111.

Walters, C. 2012. *African National Congress Councillor and Member of Mayoral Committee of City of Johannesburg, Managing Various Portfolios from 1994 to 2016*, Johannesburg, interview with author, 31 August.

Walzer, M. 2004. Complex equality. In: Farrelly, C. P. (ed.) *Contemporary Political Theory: A Reader*, London, SAGE, 134–144.

Ward, J. C. and Ostrom, A. L. 2006. Complaining to the masses: the role of protest framing in customer-created complaint web sites. *Journal of Consumer Research*, 33(2), 220–230.

Watson, V. 2003. Conflicting rationalities: implications for planning theory and ethics. *Planning Theory & Practice*, 4(4), 395–407.

Weale, A. 2016. Between consensus and contestation. *Journal of Health Organization and Management*, 30(5), 786–795.

Weber, M. 1946 [1919]. Politics as a vocation. In: Weber, M., Gerth, H. H. and Turner, B. S. (eds.) *From Max Weber: Essays in Sociology*, New York, Oxford University Press, 77–128.

———. 1978. Types of social action and groups. In: Roth, G. and Wittich, C. (eds.) *Max Weber: Economy and Society – An Outline of Interpretive Sociology*, Berkeley, CA, University of California Press, 1375–1380.

Webster, D. 2015. *Ke Molao Wa Rona: Joburg Continues Its Anti-Poor Approach*. Available: www.dailymaverick.co.za/opinionista/2015-02-27-ke-molao-wa-rona-joburg-continues-its-anti-poor-approach/#.VPxxvTccSGw [Accessed 8 March 2015].

Wenman, M. 2003. 'Agonistic pluralism' and three archetypal forms of politics. *Contemporary Political Theory*, 2(2), 165–186.

Westphal, M. 2014. Applying principles of agonistic politics to institutional design: draft. *European Consortium for Political Research, ECPR General Conference 2014, Agonism and Democratic Innovation Panel*, 3–6 September, Glasgow.

———. 2018. Overcoming institutional deficit of agonistic democracy. *Res Publica*, 25(2), 187–210.

Wikström, P.-O. H. and Treiber, K. H. 2009. Violence as situational action. *International Journal of Conflict and Violence*, 3(1), 75–96.

Wilcox, N. 2013. *South Africa the 'Protest Capital of the World': Inadequate Online Media Coverage of Protestors' Perspectives*. Available: http://nicolewilcox.co.za/Creative_Production_Rationale_

Nicole_Wilcox.pdf [Accessed 15 March 2014].

Willemse, L. 2011. Opportunities and constraints facing informal street traders: evidence from four South African cities. *Town and Regional Planning*, 59, 7–15.

Wilson, F. and Ramphele, M. 1989. *Uprooting Poverty: The South African Challenge*, Cape Town, David Philip.

Wilson, M. 2019. *Activism by Sandton Ratepayers in the 1990s*. Available: www.theheritageportal.co.za/article/activism-sandton-ratepayers-1990s [Accessed 11 May 2019].

Wingenbach, E. C. 2011. *Institutionalizing Agonistic Democracy: Post-Foundationalism and Political Liberalism*, Surrey, Ashgate.

Winton, A. 2004. Urban violence: a guide to the literature. *Environment and Urbanization*, 16(2), 165–184.

Woo-Cumings, M. (ed.). 1999. *The Developmental State*, New York, Cornell University Press.

Wood, A. 2014. Transforming the post-apartheid city through bus rapid transit. *In*: Haferburg, C. and Huchzermeyer, M. (eds.) *Urban Governance in Post-Apartheid Cities: Modes of Engagement in South Africa's Metropoles*, Stuttgart, Borntraeger, 79–97.

Xenowatch. 2018. *Trends & Incidents*. Available: www.xenowatch.ac.za/trends-incidents/ [Accessed 20 December 2018].

Yamamoto, A. D. 2017. Why agonistic planning? Questioning Chantal Mouffe's thesis of the ontological primacy of the political. *Planning Theory*, 16(4), 384–403.

Zinn, H. 2002. *Disobedience and Democracy: Nine Fallacies on Law and Order*, Cambridge, MA, South End Press.

Index

This is a subject index arranged alphabetically in word-by-word order, so that 'agonism' is filed before 'agonistic conflict management'. *See* and *see also* references guide the reader to the preferred or alternative access terms used. Page locators for Maps are expressed in **bold *italic* font**. Non-English words and document/report titles are *italicised*.